Ireland
and the
American Emigration
1850 - 1900

F. D. J. O'Neill

Ireland
and the
American Emigration
1850 - 1900

Arnold Schrier

Dufour Editions

Published 1997 by Dufour Editions Inc., Chester Springs PA 19425-0007

ISBN 0 8023 1317 5

Library of Congress Cataloging-in-Publication data:

Schrier, Arnold

    Ireland and the American Emigration, 1850 - 1900 / Arnold Schrier.

        p.   cm.

    Originally published: Minneapolis : University of Minnesota Press, [1958].

    Includes bibliographical references and index.

    ISBN 0-8023-1317-5

    1. Irish Americans — History — 19th century. 2. Ireland — Emigration
and immigration — History — 19th century. 3. United States — Emigration
and immigration — History — 19th century. 4. Ireland — Social conditions.
I. Title.

E184.I6S37 1997

325.2 415073 — dc21

                                           97-3415

                                           CIP

To Sonny
who made it all worthwhile

About the Author

Arnold Schrier is Walter C. Langsam Professor Emeritus of History at the University of Cincinnati. During his thirty-eight-year teaching career Professor Schrier was involved in Russian and world history and has published books in both areas. Currently he is engaged in a collaborative project with Kerby Miller of the University of Missouri, Bruce Boling of the University of New Mexico, and David Doyle of University College-Dublin. They are preparing for publication a comprehensive and representative selection of letters written by Irish emigrants to North America from the seventeenth to the twentieth century. The selections are drawn from the combined holdings of Professors Schrier and Miller. These joint holdings constitute the largest collection of Irish emigrant letters in existence.

A Note From The Author

The publication of this paperback edition of *Ireland and the American Emigration* comes nearly forty years after its first appearance in hardcover in 1958. I am pleased that its contribution to Irish migration studies will be made available to a new generation of readers. Readers should know that the primary purpose of the book when first published was to open new lines of inquiry into the migration phenomenon. The book was not intended to be a comprehensive study that would examine the influence of emigration on all phases of Irish life. Hence the book did not deal in depth with the impact of mass emigration to America on the Irish Catholic Church or on Irish politics. These important and complex topics deserve to be fully studied in their own right and await the historian who would undertake the challenge.

ARNOLD SCHRIER

Cincinnati, Ohio
January 1997

Preface

In the recent past both Americans and Irishmen on either side of the Atlantic have written much about the contributions made by Irish immigrants to American society. This is only as it should be. Americans, being relative newcomers as a distinct breed of men among the peoples of the earth, have been naturally curious about the various elements out of which their national amalgam has been forged. Irishmen, aware that their countrymen have been one of the more important elements in the American amalgam, have developed a deep pride in the achievements of their kith and kin on the American continent. Consequently in the field of immigration-emigration studies in general, and in the study of Irish immigration in particular, the emphasis has been heavily concentrated on an analysis of the role played by immigrant groups in the United States, as well as on the problems engendered by the process of assimilation. To date little has been done to describe the reverse side of the coin, or more specifically the impact of emigration on the country of origin.

This study is an attempt partly to redress the balance. It has been pursued along two major lines of inquiry, the first being an analysis of the impact on Ireland of emigration to the United States in the period 1850-1900, and the second being an analysis of American influences which filtered back to Ireland via the emigrant stream. Ireland is especially well suited to this type of analysis because in relation to total population, Irish emigration in the nineteenth century was the greatest in all western Europe. Furthermore, over 85 percent of all overseas emigration from Ireland in the half-century following the disastrous famine was directed toward American shores. Ireland was therefore in a position to feel the impact of emigration to a degree experienced by few other countries in western Europe.

Before launching into an account of the nature of that impact it seemed advisable to describe briefly the causes and characteristics of Irish emigration during its heyday in the last half of the nineteenth century, since such a survey would provide the essential background against which the entire study must be viewed. The magnitude of Irish emigration cannot be understood except in terms of a unique complex of predisposing conditions in Ireland; the fact that the bulk of it was directed toward American shores can be understood only in terms of the lure which America represented. That lure was crystallized in an image of America conjured up in Irish minds from the millions of emigrant letters that flooded back across the Atlantic. A mid-nineteenth-century artist named J. Nicol succeeded in capturing the very essence of that image in his "Outward Bound" and "Homeward Bound" (on pages 38 and 39). In portraying the dramatic difference between the ragged Irishman gazing wistfully at a steamship advertisement on a Dublin quay, and that same Irishman some years later standing in affluent attire on a New York dock and contemplating with obvious satisfaction a return visit to Ireland, the artist conveyed with striking simplicity the nature of the lure that lay in the promise of American opportunity.

The impact and repercussions of emigration were felt in three major areas of Irish life. One was the reaction to the steady drain of population on the part of the newspaper press throughout the country, and to a lesser extent the reaction of the Irish Catholic Church. A second area affected by continuous emigration was the Irish economy. It was during this fifty-year period, for example, that Irish agriculture underwent a revolutionary change which, if not directly caused by emigration was surely greatly facilitated by it. Moreover American financial influences entered Ireland on an impressive scale through the enormous aggregate sums of individual emigrant remittances, while a much smaller though not less important sum was contributed for the support of various political organizations.

The third and perhaps the most fascinating result of the impact of emigration was the development of a cultural-folkloristic reaction which was unique to rural Ireland. The most remarkable phenomenon in this folkloristic reaction was the growth of the "American wake," a custom which in effect represented a transfer and adaptation of the Irish death ceremony – the wake – to the emigration process. The emigration theme was also reflected in a host of ballads, charms, and expressions which became current in the daily lives of rural Irishmen. Finally, some degree of American social influences entered Ireland via the returning emigrant, and the "returned Yank" became a familiar figure in nearly every area of Ireland.

There was no convenient collection of source materials for a study of this kind. Very few emigrant letters were available in the major research institutions in Ireland, and the number which have appeared in print has been extremely small. The greater proportion of those which are still extant are in the possession of private families. Consequently I made a series of appeals to the Irish public via press and radio during the winter, summer, and fall of 1955, and thanks largely to the generous cooperation of many individuals throughout the country, both in the Republic and in Northern Ireland, it was possible to assemble a substantial and representative collection of original emigrant letters.

Data on the cultural and folkloristic reaction to emigration, as well as information on the returned Yank, have been obtained primarily from answers to a questionnaire that I constructed. This questionnaire was serviced by the Irish Folklore Commission through its country-wide network of professional interviewers during the early months of 1955. Information was also gathered through personal interviews that I conducted during the summer months of that same year. I am deeply indebted to the Irish Folklore Commission for the invaluable assistance so freely and cheerfully given me. I wish to express my thanks and gratitude to the field and headquarters staff of that excellent organization, and especially to its head, Professor J. H. Delargy, and to its Archivist, Mr. Séan O'Sullivan.

My two years of research in Ireland and the United States were made possible by a Research Training Fellowship from the Social Science Research Council, and a University Fellowship from North-western University. I wish to thank in particular the staff of the

National Library of Ireland for the generous manner in which the resources of that fine institution were made available to me. My appreciation must also be recorded for the efforts made on my behalf by the Dublin field office of the United States Information Agency, by Mr. Francis MacManus of Radio Eireann, and by Mr. Edward MacSweeney of the Dublin *Evening Herald*. And thanks are also due to the staffs of the following institutions for their patient cooperation: the Library of the American Irish Historical Society, the Library of the Catholic University of America, the New York Public Library, the Library of Holy Cross College, the National Archives, and the Public Record Offices in Dublin, Belfast, and London.

To Professor Franklin D. Scott of Northwestern University I owe a debt more easily acknowledged than repaid. To his role as teacher and scholar he brought the warmth of a friend. As wise counselor and gentle critic he gave of his time, of his energy, and of his inexhaustible good humor to lead a rather apprehensive graduate student along the path of sound scholarship and good teaching.

Finally, to my wife must go the credit for having buoyed up the spirits of a spouse who at times must have been a sore trial to her patience. Her, too, must I thank for having performed yeoman service as typist, editor, and critic, and for having saved me from all the grosser inelegancies of English expression. For any others that remain I have but myself to blame.

ARNOLD SCHRIER

Cincinnati, Ohio
May 1957

Table of Contents

Part I • The Flowing Tide

I

Causes and Characteristics

Of all the dynamic developments of the nineteenth century, none perhaps was so remarkable as that vast, voluntary, outward flow of peoples from the Old World to the New. In the half-century from 1850 to 1900 almost 25,000,000 Europeans sailed westward – the greatest human migration in all recorded history. Ireland, so atypical of Europe in all else and with one of the smallest populations in western Europe, played an important part in this expansion by contributing to the flowing tide nearly one sixth of the overall total.

Large-scale Irish emigration began with the terrible famine years of 1846-48 when the potato, that "least common denominator of Irish life," fell prey to a blight for three successive years. As the countryside lay covered with a mass of decaying vegetation there began a flight from hunger that did not spend its force until 1854. In those eight years over one and three-quarter million people fled from Erin's shores. Although this figure cannot be attributed entirely to the famine,[1] that catastrophe nevertheless set in motion a system of emigration which by the end of the century had removed nearly four million people from Ireland and had reduced her population from over eight million in 1846 to just under four and one half million in 1901.[2] Irish emigration thereby achieved the unenviable distinction of being the only migratory movement in modern history to have embraced a considerable proportion of a country's population and to have led

3

directly to a definitive population decline.[3]

Like the other European migrations of the later nineteenth century, the Irish movement was an exodus of the young and the unmarried. Between 1850 and 1887 over 66 percent of the emigrants ranged in age from 15 to 35, and for the remainder of the century the proportion almost never fell below 80 percent. Apart from the early famine years, the number of married emigrants going to the United States rarely exceeded 16 percent.[4] Thus the very old and the very young were left behind, a saddening sight which moved more than one observer to lament that emigration in Ireland had led to the "survival of the unfittest."

Unlike the movements from the rest of Europe, however, Irish emigration was characterized by a high proportion of women, higher, for example, than the proportion of women among the English and Scottish emigrants. In part this was because Irish girls were in great demand as domestic servants in nineteenth-century American homes. In the half-century down to 1900 the number of male emigrants exceeded females by only 170,000. Spread over a period of fifty years and measured against a total emigration of nearly four million, this represents a strikingly small difference between males and females.[5]

For the most part it was the agricultural laborers and the sons and daughters of small and average farmers who left the fields for the more promising prospects of Irish and American cities.[6] The greater proportion of them came from the south and the west, from the provinces of Munster and Connaught. Six counties alone out of the thirty-two in Ireland accounted for almost 48 percent of the total emigration up to 1900. Four of these counties (Cork, Kerry, Tipperary, and Limerick) are in Munster and the other two (Galway and Mayo) are in Connaught. These were the regions, moreover, which experienced the highest intensity of emigration, as is shown by the map on page 37.[7] These areas were also predominantly Roman Catholic and many contemporaries of the period, observing that great numbers of the emigrants were of the Roman Catholic faith, feared that the country would shortly be overrun by the progeny of Protestants * and Presbyterians.

* The term "Protestant" in Ireland has a specific connotation and means church

Their fears were without substantial foundation. Protestants as well as Roman Catholics emigrated in nearly equal proportions and Ireland, nearly 78 percent Roman Catholic in 1861, was still over 74 percent Roman Catholic at the end of the century.[8]

It was America which became the principal overseas destination for the vast majority who left the shores of Erin. In the half-century following the famine more than 85 percent of the nearly four million emigrants listed the United States as their destination, with most of the remaining 15 percent dividing between Canada and Australia-New Zealand. The truly startling thing, however, was that of all the Irish who came to the United States in the eighty years prior to 1900, nearly one third thronged into the country in the eight short years from 1847 to 1854 – a grim tribute to the rigors of the famine. Yet in the United States itself the Irish in the 1850s comprised only 35.2 percent of all immigrants and were outnumbered by the Germans who accounted for 36.6 of the total. From the 1860s to the end of the century the proportion of Irish in relation to total immigration steadily declined until in the 1890s it amounted to only 10.6 percent, while that of the Germans remained consistently high, higher actually than that of any other group during this half-century.

Demographically, however, it was Ireland, with a far smaller population, that suffered most from the emigration. As early as 1860 the United States census commissioner observed that for every Irish immigrant in this country only five people remained in Ireland; for Germany the ratio was 1:33, for Norway 1:34, and for England 1:42. In the United States in that same year the Irish-born accounted for only 5.1 percent of the total population, the highest figure it ever attained, and for 38.9 percent of the total foreign-born population. As the general European immigrant stream swelled to a flood, the proportion of Irish-born in both categories steadily fell although in absolute numbers there was a noticeable increase. Thus by the end of the century there were over a million and a half Irish-born living in this country whereas in 1850 there had been less than a million, yet in 1850 they were 42.8 percent of the total foreign-born population and in 1900

Church of Ireland (that is, Anglican). It is never used to refer to all Protestants generally as is done in the United States. For the purposes of this work the term will be used in its specific Irish sense and will refer only to members of the Church of Ireland.

only 15.6 percent. The ever-larger immigrant waves from southern and eastern Europe had by then completely overshadowed the continuing Irish contribution.[9]

Within the United States the Irish concentrated along the North Atlantic seaboard and only gradually expanded westward, moving and working along the lengthening network of roads, canals, and railroads. By 1870 they were firmly anchored in the Massachusetts-New York-Pennsylvania area and stretched across the northern tier of states to central Iowa and eastern Missouri, as the map on page 40 clearly shows. In that same year the seven states of Massachusetts, Connecticut, New York, New Jersey, Pennsylvania, Ohio, and Illinois contained more than 72 percent of the total Irish-born population; thirty years later the figure had risen to 75 percent.

The explanation for the concentration of Irish in these states is to be found in their affinity for city life and the nature of their occupations. These states contained the largest cities and in spite of repeated warnings to avoid the cities and go west, the Irish crowded into Boston, New York, Philadelphia, and to a lesser extent into Chicago, Jersey City, Pittsburgh, and St. Louis. The magnet of the big city was its already established Irish community where newly arrived immigrants felt at home among their friends and relatives. There too they found churches of their own religion whose pulpits were filled by fellow Irishmen. Equally as important was their general lack of funds upon arrival. Many simply could not afford to pay the fare west, and work had to be obtained immediately. The easiest and most natural course was therefore to settle in the city.

The character of the life they left behind also led many Irish men and women to choose an urban over a rural life in America. This may at first seem strange since the Irish have always been a predominantly agricultural people. But it must be remembered that the great majority of the immigrants were drawn from the small farmer and agricultural laboring classes. These, unlike their German contemporaries, had neither the capital nor the training for large-scale prairie farming.[10] When the Irish small farmer became an immigrant, therefore, he was to all intents and purposes an unskilled laborer, as were his daughters and sisters. It was the cities with their mills, factories, docks, and countless odd jobs that could offer work to large bodies of unskilled laborers, and it was in city homes that the majority of Irish women could find employment as domestic servants. In 1870, for example, out of a total work force of nearly a million Irish-born, over 47 percent were working as general laborers, as servants, in cotton mills, and on the railroads; only 14 percent were classed as farmers and agricultural laborers. A generation later the proportions were not much changed.

The choice of the city, however, was not always predestined; sometimes it was deliberate. Cities have always held out the attractions of a richer, more colorful life as well as greater social mobility. There is evidence that often before leaving Ireland young men had already decided on cities in preference to the land not only because they had ample reason to be disillusioned with agriculture, but also because they thought cities would offer them greater opportunities for rising in life. In this respect the Irish were not unique; English agricultural laborers harbored the same aspirations.[11]

The endless movement from Irish farm to American city led many an anxious contemporary into a fruitless discussion as to the principal cause of the phenomenon. They wanted to know whether the "pull" of American opportunity was more important than the "push" of Irish distress, an argument that has not yet lost its interest. All agreed that in the famine years there could be no doubt that the failure of the potato crop was the most important initial impulse to the vast emigration of that period. But in explaining the continuing drain, long after the famine had passed, there was no such unanimity. In 1869 the emigration commissioners strongly implied that emigration was regulated by conditions at home, while a generation later the registrar-general of Ireland boldly declared that emigration "is mainly dependent on the state of agriculture." Within a year, however, the registrar-general had reversed himself, and under persistent questioning by the Financial Relations Commission he admitted that repellent conditions in Ireland were relatively less important than the attractions of America. As late as 1941 Oscar Handlin took the position that from 1835 to 1865 the stream of emigration was "little affected" by conditions in America, a view which at best is an oversimplified reading of the emigration curve.[12]

The latter position, that the "pull" is stronger than the "push," has had adherents all through the half-century and down even to the present day. In 1862, for example, one observant Irishman cautioned his countrymen not to "overlook the influence on the minds of an imaginative people, of bright hopes of a land to which distance lends enchantment." Fifty years later C. H. Oldham asserted that Irish emigration "rises and falls according as times are good or bad in the United States" and that it was "little affected . . . by changes of prosperity in Ireland itself." So recently as 1935 the current chief of the Central Statistics Office in Ireland insisted that since the famine, "emigration has been due more to attraction from abroad than repulsion from within."[13]

Actually the two positions are not irreconcilable for both must be taken into account before Irish emigration – or indeed any emigration – to America can be properly understood. An argument as to which in the long run has been more important is useless and uninstructive, for it appears that only in periods of crisis can any definite correlation be found between emigration and the "push" or "pull" factors. A glance at Figure 1 will help make this clear. The years of heaviest Irish emigration to the United States, apart from the famine years of the late 1840s, were in the periods 1863-66 and 1880-83. In both the latter instances each period was preceded by a series of severe crop failures in Ireland and in the earlier period the specter of another famine was a far grimmer reality than all the reported horrors of being dragooned into a bloody civil war in America. Even the *Freeman's Journal* commented that "the battlefield has not so much terrors for the Irish tenant farmers as has the struggle for life . . . at home."[14]

The lowest points in Irish emigration to the United States came in the years 1858-62 and 1876-78. In the former case the appearance of the Know-Nothing movement in the early 1850s had some effect in diverting Irish Catholics from American shores, but more important was the commercial crisis and panic of 1857 when Irishmen were warned of the "utter madness" of emigrating to a country where trade and finances were in a "paralyzed condition."[15] In the second instance the panic of 1873, followed by five depressing years of "idle mills and idle men, of strikes, lockouts and bankruptcies," did its work in constricting the tide of emigrants to a mere trickle, a circumstance that most newspapers were happy to report.[16] It may be noted that the depression years do not correspond exactly with the ebbs in the emigrant stream, but as has been conclusively shown, one of the features of all migration movements to this country has been the "lag" behind the peaks and troughs of American business cycles. The full force of unemployment and distress on emigration was not felt until it had continued for one or two years.[17]

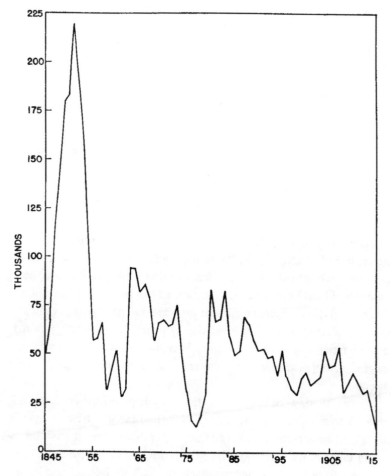

Figure 1. Yearly Irish Emigration to the United States, 1845-1915
(Based on Appendix Table 1)

The sharper peaks and deeper troughs in the emigration curve thus bear a direct relationship to the more unusual states of economic imbalance in each country, and one may rather easily deduce whether a particular peak or trough was caused by the "push" at home or the "pull" from abroad. In a field so difficult of generalization, this was one of the few that Marcus Hansen found applicable to all European emigration. He preferred, however, to view the problem in an American setting and noted that "the periods of greatest volume [of emigration] correspond with the eras of liveliest industrial activity in the United States."[18] In the Irish case they seem to correspond more closely with the periods of severest distress in Ireland.

In the long sweep of the emigration curve, however, no simple assignment of basic causes is possible. One cannot say that the principal cause of Irish emigration has been "push" or "pull," only that the two are inextricably intertwined in a myriad-threaded pattern of personal choices and desires whose total effect has been to produce a continuing stream of Irish emigrants. The persistence and the strength of that stream can be understood only in terms of a unique set of conditions which have made the Irish a people peculiarly disposed toward emigration. The direction of the stream toward the United States can be explained in terms of an "American pull" acting upon this predisposed pattern of pushing forces. Without that predisposition the "pull" alone would not have sufficed to draw the Irish from hearth and home. That emigration remains a current problem among the Irish indicates that the predisposing forces remain. The fact that the emigration is now channeled toward the United Kingdom shows that any strong magnet of opportunities, not just the American one, can control its direction.

What, then, were the factors which predisposed the Irish to emigrate? Foremost among them were the brutal facts of Irish economic life. It has been rightly observed that "no realistic view of Irish history can make much headway without relating social, political and even religious facts to the economic background." In Ireland this background was very largely dominated by the question of land. In a country where in 1849 five sixths of the population depended directly upon the soil, whereas at the end of the century two thirds did so, and where peasants married or murdered for land, not love, some knowledge of the land question is indispensable.[19]

In general, four groups or classes occupied the soil of Ireland and together formed a sort of social and economic pyramid. At the top were the landlords. Of this numerically small class, one fifth (that is, less than one percent of the total population) possessed 80 percent of the cultivated area in 1869. Below the landlords were the leaseholders who comprised 2.5 percent of the population, were mainly Protestant (that is, Church of Ireland), and held the land in perpetuity. Generally speaking leaseholders as a class did not engage in tillage and to a great extent were the occupiers of large grazing farms. Either under these leaseholders or directly under the landlords were usually one or more middlemen, that is, people who made their living by renting land themselves and then letting it out in smaller holdings on short leases or annual tenancies. Motivated solely by a desire for quick profits, middlemen were the most oppressive class of all and made as much money as they could at the expense of their subtenants. Under the landlords, leaseholders, and middlemen came the tenants who were the most numerous class of all and formed the broad base of the pyramid. Although some landlords and leaseholders did their own farming, it was largely on the crops raised on tenant farms that the people of Ireland lived.

There were three classes of tenants. The annual tenants, who numbered over half a million in 1870, formed 77 percent of the occupiers of farms. This was the typical "small farmer" class that settled mainly on lands valued at less than fifteen pounds per year, lands which comprised more than 50 percent of the total acreage under cultivation.[20] Next came the cotters who lived in poor cottages usually located on somebody else's land. They had very little land of their own and generally rented a patch of conacre (that is, land let annually on an eleven-month tenure to the highest bidder) to grow a crop of potatoes or to pasture their flocks. At the very bottom of the pyramid were the agricultural laborers. They had no land at all but often they too rented a patch of conacre. In a normal season the potato crop from one acre was enough to maintain a man, his wife, and six children for three quarters of the year, albeit in a shocking state of personal squalor.[21]

For the greater portion of the half-century the lot of all three tenant classes was one of misery and insecurity. The chief cause of this condition was found in the nature of the Irish land system, a dreary mosaic of rack rents (that is, exorbitantly high rents in relation to farm income), insecurity of tenure, and a frustrating law regarding improvements. Secure in the conviction that the demand and competition for land would never abate, landlords or their middlemen often charged exorbitant rents for the meager patches tilled by the small farmers. The peasant farmers, aware that if they could not meet the payments their landless neighbors would be ready and eager to step in and try, toiled on in desperation. There was no way to resist the extortionate demands of the landlords.

The law, moreover, discouraged farmers from attempting any improvements on the land. Legally all such improvements belonged to the landlords, not the farmers, so that when improved farms were sold the landlords were the ones who realized the profits from the enhanced value of the land, not the original improvers. Furthermore, if a farmer did effect an improvement, the landlord often took this as a sign of increasing wealth and raised the rent. The landlords themselves spent nothing on buildings or repairs since they recognized no obligations to their tenants. It was this last fact, it has been pointed out, that made the rents demanded really higher than the actual money amounts.[22] Worst of all, the tenants had no security of tenure and landlords had the right to evict on six months notice. With rents so high, large numbers of tenants often fell far behind in their payments and struggled for years under the shadow of debt and the threat of eviction.

Such then was the land system which prevailed among the vast body of Irish peasantry. It was not until 1885 that the first serious beginning was made on the long road that eventually led Ireland from a country of tenant farmers to a nation of owner farmers. For the greater part of the century, however, the old land system remained in force, a system, it has been said, by which "rack rents reduced ... [the peasants] to the margin of subsistence; the law in regard to improvements deprived them of hope; and insecurity of their tenure kept them in a state of terror."[23] Writing in 1880 to John Hay, then the assistant secretary of state, the United States consul in Cork commented that "the Irish ... peasant who becomes a good citizen in the United States is stagnated as a subject here. The result is a cataleptic embargo upon his existence which can only be permanently raised by immigration [sic!] ..."[24]

Were Ireland possessed of abundant minerals such as coal and iron, and of adequate investment capital, industrialization would have provided an outlet for the overburdened peasantry. But the lack of such resources coupled with Ireland's subordinate status in the United Kingdom worked to the detriment of any industrial development. As early as 1824, under the pressure of English manufacturers, Parliament withdrew the 10 percent protective tariff on manufactured goods imported into Ireland, a tariff that had been in effect at the time of the union with Britain in 1800. Deprived of any tariff protection local Irish industries were ultimately destroyed by the competition of large manufacturing firms in Britain.

For a while longer Irish farmers continued to enjoy a free market for Irish corn in Great Britain. But with the adoption of free trade by Britain just after the famine, the final blow was administered. While the repeal of the corn laws acted as a boon to British industry, it began the destruction of the Irish export trade in cereals as cheap foreign food flooded the British market. To be sure, the small peasant farmer or agricultural laborer in England and Scotland also suffered from the new policy of free trade, but he at least could hope to find employment in one of the rapidly growing industrial towns in his own country. No such hope was held out to his Irish counterpart.

This theme of lack of employment runs like a constant refrain through the latter half of nineteenth-century Irish history. When asked why all his brothers and sisters emigrated to the United States in the 1880s, the unhesitating reply from an octogenarian in County Cork was "because there was no great livin' for them in Ireland."[25] The same answer had a monotonous regularity in other counties as well. Not only men but women also faced bleak employment prospects, as is illustrated by the case of a County Mayo woman of ninety-nine who clearly remembered that her sister had emigrated in 1865 because there was no work for her at home.[26] The story could be repeated for almost all the thirty-two counties.

Even where employment was obtainable it was generally irregular and usually at a pitifully low rate of wages. On a trip through Ireland in 1851, Abbott Lawrence, then United States minister to Great Britain, noted that during the harvest season of that year agricultural laborers were paid four to five shillings a week, a circumstance which

13

led him to remark to Daniel Webster – not without a touch of prid – that "It is very natural that a laboring population should wish to remove to a country where they can hope to preserve some of the fruits of their toil."[27] Fourteen years later Charles Francis Adams noted only a slight improvement, while a little earlier the *Cork Examiner* reported that artisans and laborers in County Kerry could not obtain employment "at even inadequate wages."[28] Michael Kraus has alleged that in the eighteenth century it took desperation and courage to emigrate: "desperation to escape from a life without a future, courage to dare a terrifying ocean voyage . . ."[29] For the later nineteenth-century Irish peasant, life was still desperately without a future while the terrors of an ocean voyage had been considerably reduced.

This, then, was the economic background against which Irish emigration in this period must be viewed. While it was doubtless the most important element, it was not the only one in the pattern of predisposing conditions. The dynamics of rural Irish family life was also a contributory factor. Each farm was worked as a unit by a family of husband, wife, and children, and the farm was the support of all. As the children reached adulthood there was the growing realization that only one of them, usually the eldest son, would inherit the farm. Subdivision as a means of providing for the others had begun to die out by the mid-1840s. With the disappearance of the franchise formerly conferred by forty-shilling freeholds, proprietors no longer encouraged subdivision in order to increase their political influence, and with the decline in the price of agricultural produce which followed the conclusion of the Napoleonic Wars, subletting was no longer economically profitable. When this was then followed by the impact of the famine and the lesson it brought home on the dangers of excessive subdivision, the tide was finally turned and after 1852 the practice almost completely disappeared.

For the younger sons and daughters, therefore, the inheriting of the farm by their eldest brother meant only one thing: they "must travel." The eldest son then married, reared a large family of his own and the cycle was again repeated. Arensberg and Kimball have described this system as one "whose very nature predisposed it to disperse population" and since there was little or no industry to keep these younger sons and daughters in the country, emigration became a "logical corollary" of this dispersal.[30]

Emigration, however, became more than a corollary to the Irish; it became an accepted fact of life. So natural and normal did emigration seem to them that at the turn of the century the Frenchman L. Paul-Dubois considered it to be one of their customs. "Children," he declared, "are brought up with the idea of probably becoming emigrants . . ." Irishmen themselves were aware of this phenomenon and a contemporary of Paul-Dubois noted that "Emigration is a settled habit, and as a nation we are strongly wedded to our habits . . ." By the middle of the twentieth century the head of the Irish Central Statistics Office was still lamenting to his countrymen that "Migration seems to be one of our most ingrained national instincts." Some eighty years earlier the *Freeman's Journal* had already resigned itself to the "inevitability" of emigration, regardless of whether Ireland was prosperous or not, while a few years before an informed Irish witness was instructing a British parliamentary committee that going to America had become "the fashion" in the country — "fatally fashionable," one journal called it. In 1853, at the very beginning of this period, the *Newry Examiner* warned that emigration was no longer a casual circumstance but a settled system, and a generation later the *Cork Examiner* spoke of emigration as a "phenomenon beyond our control, like the weather." Almost a century afterward the leading authority on Irish emigration, William Forbes Adams, went so far as to contend that for thirty years prior to the famine of 1846-48 the spirit of emigration had been spreading steadily through the country until it became the "favorite remedy for hard times."[31]

If emigration became a custom among the Irish, it also became a tradition to go to America. The reasons are not far to seek. As Adams has shown, a considerable number of Irishmen already had established themselves in the United States long before the ravages of the famine descended upon the home country and opened the floodgates of the later emigration. Once the road to America had been laid down it became the principal highway out of Ireland and few would deviate from it. The existence of a prospering Irish community in the United States acted as a powerful magnet upon the overburdened Irish at home. When the famine struck, the destitute fled by the thousands to the land they knew best and further swelled the American-Irish community. From that time forward there was hardly a family remaining in Ireland which did not have a friend, relative, or near neighbor somewhere in America.

From that time too, few thought of emigrating who did not look first for help to their friends or relatives in America, and rarely were they disappointed. By 1854 the emigration commissioners were convinced that Irish emigration had assumed the character of an organized movement financed almost entirely by remittances from America.[32] The system of "one-bringing-another" had become firmly rooted and the Irishman who left home often went to join his kith and kin, the journey having been facilitated by a prepaid passage ticket. After securing work and saving some money, he in turn sent for another member of the family and again the cycle was repeated. In this manner brother followed sister, and sister brother, until entire families had been brought over. The Irish emigrant was likened to Goldsmith's Traveller who seemed at each remove to drag a lengthening chain: "But it is a chain which does not draw him back, but pulls forward those he has left behind."[33] At the end of the century the system was still in full operation.

Other influences were also at work in directing the Irish toward America. They shunned the British colonies not only because of a deep-seated hatred of England but for practical reasons as well. In 1849 the cost of a passage to Australia was four times that to the United States and the length of the trip was three times as great. A voyage from Liverpool to New York was about ten days shorter than a similar one to Quebec although the latter passage was slightly cheaper. Canada's population was so limited, however, that it could not offer work to the large numbers of unskilled Irish laborers. In 1847, moreover, the Canadian legislature increased the head tax on all immigrants. Most important of all, the United States, with a population of more than 23,000,000 and a seemingly unlimited territory, offered the prospect of certain employment to any number of emigrants. The consequence was that even among the fewer Irish landing in Canada, more than one fourth were passing southward across the border in the early 1850s.[34]

The pull of America was thus enhanced by the practical considerations of a short, cheap passage, the prospect of joining friends and relatives who would smooth the way, and the attractions of obtaining steady work at good wages. America became the "New Ireland" across the sea to the toiling peasants and the unemployed laborers. Many were more familiar with parts of the United States than with sections of their own country and looked forward to the day when they too could sail west. Their information was of the most intimate kind, for it was based almost entirely on the millions of letters which were so faithfully sent back by those who had gone before. It is to these letters that one must turn for an appreciation of the "lure" that was America.

II

The Lure of America

THE IMAGE OF AMERICA conjured up in Irish minds was the lure that beckoned young people westward across the Atlantic Ocean, an image made all the more attractive when contrasted with the unpromising picture of economic life in nineteenth-century Ireland. From countless bits and pieces of information was formed an alluring impression of America which came to predominate throughout the Irish countryside. Sometimes these tidbits of information were gleaned from travelers or "returned Yanks" or newspaper accounts, but for the vast majority of the population the greatest single source of knowledge was the myriad letters which flooded back from the emigrants in the New World. The American correspondent of the London *Daily News* left no doubts on this point. Writing from New York in 1864, he was convinced that

> What brings such crowds to New York by every packetship is the letters which are written by the Irish already here to their relations in Ireland, accompanied, as they are in a majority of cases, by remittances to enable them to pay their passage out. It is from this source, and this mainly, if not only, that the Cork or Galway peasant learns all he knows about the United States, and he is not in the least likely to trust to any other.[1]

Twelve years earlier a parish priest from County Armagh testified to the magnetic effect these letters had upon the people in his community, something he was well qualified to do since he read one third of all the American letters which came to his parish as a service for those who were illiterate.[2] Even the newspapers of the period, while generally opposed to emigration (as will be shown in the following chapter), could not help but mirror something of the attitude toward America which prevailed among the Irish. The "American fever" seemed to have permeated the entire country and no village, however small, was left unaffected. "It cannot be denied," observed the *Cork Examiner* in 1860, "that those feelings and motives [regarding America] have taken a deep root, and are very widely spread."[3]

What was this image which made America so alluring? Part of the answer is to be found in the fact that Irish emigration to the United States was so widespread and of such a magnitude that by 1851 it was declared that America was no longer regarded as a foreign country, but as if Ireland were "part and parcel" of it. A little more than a decade later it was stated "as a matter of the driest fact" that there was "no country upon earth in whose well-being the Irish people have the same interest, as in that of the United States," and that it would be "impossible to touch the greatness, unity, or security of the United States, without wounding the interests of the Irish race [which are] inseparably connected with those of America." America, confessed one journal in 1873, had long been "the mainstay and the hope" of the Irish people, a hope, explained another, founded on the belief that in America they would "cultivate a soil without rent, earn plenty of money without being servants, and belong to a nation of sovereigns."[4]

The prospect of belonging to a nation of sovereigns seemed to some journals to be particularly appealing to the emigrants, for, unlike Ireland, America offered its citizens participation in the state so that its people felt they had a "stake in the country." But as it was true of the Irish who emigrated before the famine, so was it true of those who left in the fifty years following that catastrophe, that the chance to join a "ready-made Republic" was not nearly so important as was the promise of high wages. High wages, affirmed William Forbes Adams, was America's one outstanding attraction for the Irish.[5]

On this point most journals were in agreement. Even during the American Civil War it seemed natural, thought the *Northern Whig*, that Irishmen should prefer a land where there were "high wages for fair work." The journal also thought American society particularly well suited to the Irish because, "like all newly-organised societies, it is rude and boisterous." High wages, therefore, was the "bribe" held out to young emigrants and not, as some Tory newspapers insisted, the bounties offered for federal enlistment. Witnesses before parliamentary committees were also agreed that so long as people could not reap the benefits of their labors at home and so long as wages in America remained higher than they were in Ireland, just so long would young Irish men and women continue to be drawn from hearth and home. After all, it was pointed out, the Irish emigrant was not going to a wilderness but to join friends in a new home where hard work would procure for him a decent maintenance and a high degree of comfort. By the end of the century a legendary Irish bull had it that "The only place in Ireland where a man can make a fortune is in America."[6]

Newspapers of the period often attributed to the Irish peasant a vision of America as a land flowing with milk and honey, where the streets were paved with gold, and where all a body had to do to scoop up a fortune was to stoop down. If we may judge from the letters themselves, however, such romantic illusions were belied by the realism and general truthfulness which characterized the writers of these direct reports. America, they made clear, was no idle paradise. It was a hard-driving business country where rewards came only to those capable of hard work, thrift, and industriousness. The Yankees were a "go-ahead" people and to keep up with them one had to be like them. Consequently Irishmen worked harder and longer in America than they were ever inspired to do at home, and the phrase "hard work" runs like a constant refrain through practically all of the letters. But there were compensations. Strenuous labor was well rewarded with good wages, and while some immigrants pointed out that the high cost of living often reduced their real value, the prospect of high wages and constant employment became by far the two greatest attractions.

While the great majority of these immigrant scribes stressed the economic opportunities available in America, some also spoke of the social equality found here. This was a land that contained no titled nobility, where class divisions were fluid, and where an ascent of the economic ladder was usually accompanied by an ascent of the social ladder as well. The two themes, hard work and social equality, were well summed up by the *Galway Vindicator*, which probably echoed the sentiments of a great many Irishmen when it declared that America was a land where "a man is a man if he's willing to toil."[7] Occasionally some writers reflected in their letters the tensions which developed between the Irish and the people who were pouring into the country from other European nations, as between the Irish and Scandinavians in the Midwest and the Irish and Italians in the eastern cities. But for the most part those who wrote home indicated that the Irish got along well in America and that generally people had little difficulty in living with their neighbors.

A great many immigrants encouraged friends and relatives to emigrate and in their letters often enclosed remittances to help pay the cost of passage. Some also proffered sound advice to the intending voyagers. America, they emphasized, was a country for young people, particularly unmarried ones, who were capable of long years of hard work. Aware of an Irish inclination for imbibing immoderately, they often stressed the importance of temperate habits and warned that drunkenness in America led only to disgrace and degradation, advice which was seconded by many newspapers. And like the newspapers, some writers also urged those who intended to emigrate to avoid the crowded eastern cities and travel to the interior or to the Far West. A few advised young people to stay at home and not emigrate at all if it were possible to live comfortably in Ireland, but these seem to have been either older, less successful immigrants, or those who wrote during periods of depression in America.

This, in general, was the "image of America" which was widely spread through Ireland by the inflow of millions of letters from the Irish in the United States. That these letters numbered as high as the millions may seem surprising since it has been frequently assumed that the vast body of Irish emigrants were largely illiterate. Such an assumption would appear to be in error. Although no systematic records were kept of literacy and illiteracy rates among Irish emigrants, Irish census statistics do provide figures for illiteracy among the total population as well as for the age group twelve to forty. Since more than 70 percent of all Irish emigrants were drawn from this age group, illiteracy rates for this group provide a reasonably accurate index to the illiteracy among the vast majority of Irish emigrants.

In 1851, almost five years after the famine, only one province, Connaught, had an illiteracy rate among the twelve to forty age group which was greater than 50 percent, while for Ireland as a whole illiteracy for this group was approximately 37 percent. A short decade later illiteracy for people under forty was below 50 percent even in Connaught, and throughout Ireland it was approximately 29 percent. Thus in 1851 six out of every ten persons in Ireland who were over twelve and under forty could read and write, while ten years later seven out of ten could do so. By the turn of the century only six out of every hundred people under forty in all Ireland could *not* read and write.[8] While not all people who left Ireland in the fifty years from 1851 to 1901 came from this age group, the vast majority did, and it seems clear that the greater proportion of them were literate.

How literate they were may be surmised from the number of letters they wrote home. In 1854 the postmaster general of the United States reported that over two million letters were sent to the United Kingdom; twenty years later the figure had risen to well over six million.[9] It is difficult to define precisely what proportion of these letters were ultimately destined for Ireland, but it would be fair to estimate that close to 50 percent were written by Irish emigrants and their descendants in the United States. Even 25 percent would represent a considerable figure. If one accepted only the lower estimate, it would indicate that of the more than 100,000 Irish who embarked for America in 1854, at least one out of two wrote a letter home that year. However, in view of the high rate of literacy and the strong bonds of filial loyalty which characterized Irish emigrants, particularly the women who made up nearly half the total number, and taking into account that more than twice as many people came to the United States in the 1850s from Ireland as did from Great Britain, 25 percent would seem too low. On the receiving end, even an estimate of 25 percent meant that approximately one out of every two families in Ireland received a letter from America in 1854. By 1874, as literacy increased among the emigrants, as population in Ireland dwindled, and as the total number of Irish-born in the United States approached two million, it is probable that there was hardly a family in Ireland which had not received at one time or another one or more letters from America.[10]

As might well be expected, the vast majority of these letters were intensely personal documents and dealt with the ordinary day-to-day problems of living. Yet those who wrote were seemingly always aware of their new surroundings; and among the endless questions and descriptions about family and friends, sickness and health, work and weather, they frequently included a phrase, a sentence, perhaps even a paragraph or more in reference to the new land in which they had settled. In many cases these references were almost incidental; in others they were more deliberately thought-out. At times there were those who described in great detail their work, their business, their farm, or their home and thereby unconsciously provided a picture of life in America which often stood in sharp contrast to its bleak counterpart in Ireland. Taken together, the incidental references and deliberate descriptions provided those at home with their principal source of information on the New Ireland beyond the sea, and from them was conjured up an image of America which became the lodestone of promise for hopeful young emigrants.

An intensive examination of the letters will reveal in more intimate detail the type of information sent home by Irish immigrants in America and will perhaps convey something of the flavor and personal force with which they expressed their individual convictions and observations. The style of the letters varied with the training and education of their writers, although nearly all were enhanced by a charm of expression inherent in the modes and manners peculiar to Irish speech. There is about many of them an air of unlettered eloquence and to their grammar and spelling belong "only the praises of bare originality." Beyond the standard opening sentence which seemed to characterize a great majority of the letters and gave to them a note of stilted formality, they were almost conversational in tone.[11]

On the part of some there was a tendency toward exaggeration and overstatement, but most appeared to be reasonably free of embellishment and hyperbole. Consciously or unconsciously the greater number of those who wrote home seemed to be guided by the sensible advice of the Reverend John O'Hanlon, author of the most popular Irish-emigrant guidebook of the period. O'Hanlon cautioned the immigrants when writing home to remember that the "Utopia of the imagination is not the United States of our experience," and that by substituting "fancy for judgment, romantic hopes are first formed to be afterwards destroyed."[12] Except in rare instances of deliberate misrepresentation, the immigrants appear to have had no wish to mislead their friends and family at home. Where overstatement did occur it was probably due much more to the first flush of enthusiasm attendant upon landing on American soil. This seems to have been the case with one young girl who landed in New York in 1850 and in her first letter home fairly gushed with praise:

> My dear Father I must only say that this is a good place and a good country for if one place does not suit a man he can go to another and can very easy please himself. . . . any man or woman without a family are fools that would not venture and come to this plentyful Country where no man or woman ever hungered or ever will and where you will not be seen naked . . .[13]

If the greater number of letters were somewhat less exuberant in tone, their writers were no less definite in urging the Irish to try their fortunes in America. In 1854 a farm laborer in Illinois wrote to his friend in County Kildare that he was doing well enough so that by the following spring he hoped to own his farm and advised his friend to "come to this country and I know you will do well — one thing is certain you can be your own master a good deal sooner." He even offered to lend his friend money for passage and instructed him that he "need not be anyway shy in putting down a big figer. I would as soon send you £20 as one." Twenty-five years later a doctor in Iowa observed to his nephew in Ulster that "every man is his own landlord in this country — 'Jack is as good as his Master.' " Some, as was the case with a railroad engineer in Cincinnati, were content to state simply that while they could never make a fortune in America, they could "earn an honest living."[14]

Others were more forceful and one young emigrant working as a ranch hand near Puget Sound — at a time when the state of Washington was still a territory — not only offered to pay his brother's passage, but made clear to him why he thought it worthwhile to emigrate as soon as possible: "I still think I am in as good a country as there is in the world today for a poor man. The majority of what men is in the country have risen from their own industry. Any man here that will work and save his earnings, and make use of his brains can grow rich."[15]

America, however, was preeminently a place for young single people and this was something which many immigrants continually stressed. Old people were cautioned to stay away from a country where the pace of life and work would be too much for them. Such was the advice given by a young worker in Philadelphia in 1854 to his uncle, a farmer in Ulster:

> I have got along very well since I came here and has saved some money. I never regretted coming out here, and any young person that could not get along well there would do well to come here, if they intended to conduct themselves decently. . . . but old people have no great chance here . . .[16]

From Iowa some fifteen years later an Irish farmer wrote to his brother in Dublin that "An unmarried man or girl can make out a living in any part of the country and have money too, provided he is not afraid of work," while a woman working as a domestic servant in Boston told her brother simply and directly in 1888 that "the younger the[y] come the better." For young girls there was the added attraction of perhaps finding husbands who would not be so interested in their dowries, as was the custom in Ireland. One such colleen, who had broken off her courtship and left for Philadelphia, later wrote to her former beau that "Over in Ireland people marry for riches, but here in America we marry for love and work for riches."[17]

The emphasis on youth, however, was not always a happy circumstance. Whatever else may have been its shortcomings, Irish society did not forget or discard the older members of the community. Families in Ireland were clannish and felt duty-bound to care for their old folk in their declining years. Not so in America. In 1905, forty-two years after he had landed in Philadelphia, during which time he had raised a family solely on the wages dearly earned as a day laborer, a sixty-three-year-old Irishman bitterly told his sisters in Belfast that he could send them only one pound because he had been unemployed for six months,

> not but there is a great deal of work going on here at present but the employers prefer younger men to do the work. Old

people are thought very little of in this country, especially
poor ones that have made no provision for old age. Not even
their own families have any regard for them when they
become played out from age and my own is no exception... [18]

If youth was stressed as a prerequisite for success, so was sobriety.
Intemperance, it was asserted, was not only an evil in itself but a disgrace to an Irishman's birthland and his fellow countrymen.
Americans, it was declared, detested drunkenness and the certain road
to failure was via the bottle. Anyone who could not cure himself of the
habit was better advised to stay home. A young lawyer who immigrat-
ed to Washington, D.C., in 1849 wrote to his uncle from that city four
years later and told him that a good many Irish who were then living
on the outskirts of the city were no models of ideal behavior:

I am sorry to have it to say that by their fighting and drunk-
eness they are disgracing their country in the eyes of
Americans. Generally speaking, Americans dont drink
[sic!], they are for the most part very temperate and disre-
gard – detest the drunkard. Now instead of saving their
wages, which are good, living orderly, keeping themselves
and children clad, well, and clean, they are continually fighting among themselves: the Kerry men, and Clare men, and
Limerick men: and for no other reason than this, because
they were born in these different counties. But they have
money to spend thus. So they have.[19]

Over thirty years later a laborer in Boston told his family in
County Cork that if his three brothers wished to emigrate he would try
to help them,

but I trust with the blessing of God none of them are fond of
drink if the[y] should be so it would be more advisable to
stop at home a Drunkered in America it would be better for
him to go to Mitchelstown poor house & stope theire all his
life.[20]

Much more pointed was the letter written to a friend by an emigrant in the Midwest which was printed in one of the provincial Irish
journals near his hometown under the stern caption "EMIGRANTS,
BE SOBER!" The greatest deterrent to success in America, he warned,
was "the old cursed habit we formed in Ireland of tippling..." Not all

shared the same convictions and one young girl who had just arrived in Ottumwa, Iowa, in 1884 to take up her duties as a domestic servant had complaints of her own which she made known to her friends in County Donegal: "Dear mr. and miss this countrey is not as good as it was, they are not aloud to sell no more liquor in the state of Iowa, they are aloud to make it but cannot sell it." Most, however, stressed the necessity for temperance. At the very end of the century, when asked for advice to give a nephew in Belfast who wished to emigrate, the reply came from the uncle, a laborer in Philadelphia, that the only advice to give was that the nephew be "strictly temperate bright & . . . [have] a knowledge of some trade."[21]

Youth and soberness were essential requirements for success in America, but even more fundamental was a capacity for hard work. Whether farm laborers or city workers, whether in the eastern metropolises or the western expanses, all were agreed that far more energy was expended on the Atlantic's western side than was done on its eastern shore. Unless one were prepared to put forth a great deal of strenuous labor, it would be wiser to remain in Ireland. "Believe me," the young lawyer in Washington told his uncle in 1853, "there is no idle bread to be had here. If you get a dollar a day, you have got to earn it *well*." Some thirty-five years later a Boston laborer informed his family that "the hard work of America is no joke, you must be able to hold the cutting." In a letter the year before he advised that one of his brothers get a job as a gardener before emigrating, for that would "give him musle and make him firm & hard which he or any other person must be for America." Still, while he admitted that he was working twice as hard as he ever did at home, he also conceded that he was a "continted willing hard worker." Housewives had no less hard a time of it, and one energetic woman wrote to her uncle from Denver in 1884 that in addition to raising a family of ten children she was also busy helping her husband with his business. "This is a regular driving country," she said with good reason. "A person with only small means has to keep on all the time . . ."[22]

Almost sagalike was the story of a small dairy farmer living fifty miles north of San Francisco. In 1868, after twenty years in America, he finally wrote to his relations in Ireland, eager to learn what became of them and equally desirous to tell them his proud tale — an odyssey of wandering and travail:

> Since my arrival in the U.S. I have been all over the Western
> & Southern States then traveled two thousand miles
> through Deserts & Wilderness. Landed in California the
> year A.D. 1865 and remained stationary ever since. I landed
> in this contry without anney thing and I hold my own ver-
> rey well....[States that he has a wife and six healthy chil-
> dren.] I feel proud of them. My means are small and I have
> work hard in this contry. But if God is willing I will have
> plenty to support human nature. . . .Forgive me for not writ-
> ing before this for it is Neglect, and you see that I am verrey
> poor hand to write and to spell. I have had verrey little prac-
> tice since I left home only hard work and I think that I done
> more hard labour than I could doe again.[23]

Toward the end of the century earning a living in America still
required the same intense effort as it did earlier, although to some in a
reminiscent mood the "old days" somehow seemed easier. "My dear,"
confided a steam railway engineer to his sister after nearly thirty years
in this country, "this America is not what it used to be, and there is
nothing to be got but by hard work."[24]

The energy expended on American soil, however, usually brought
ample rewards, and unlike Ireland, where wages were low and employment inconstant, in America there was held out the promise of high
wages and steady work. Just how good the wages were was illustrated
by the young lawyer in Washington who told his uncle in 1853 that
unquestionably,

> This is a good country for a labouring man. . . .At this time
> he can earn at least one dollar a day, equal to 4 shillings
> British. He is in good demand for this sum. He can board
> himself well – having meat three times a day, for ten dollars
> a month – two dollars and a half a week, or ten shillings
> British.[25]

An agricultural laborer in Ireland in 1850, if he were fortunate
enough in securing employment, received less than five shillings a
week for his labors, and rarely had meat more than two or three times
a year.

From Philadelphia in 1851 a young woman wrote to her brother in

Dublin that there was work for everyone and "No female that can handle a needle need be idle." In San Francisco that same year the prospects were even more alluring. In a letter published in the *Nation* it was claimed that laborers in that city could earn from one to two pounds per day. "If some of our hardy men of Tipperary were here," exclaimed the writer, "what a fortune would be open to them!" Over thirty years later wages for both men and women were still attractively high, as was made clear in a letter from a day laborer in Philadelphia:

> Single women can get along here better than men as they can get employment more readily than men. For instance liveing out girls or as the[y] are called at home servant girls gets from eight to twelve shillings per week and keep, that is from two to three dollars of American money and factory hands from twelve shillings to two pounds and sometimes more, but they are rare. Labouring mens wages averages from six to nine dollars per week that is from 24 shillings to thirty-six English money. But their work is not near so steady as womens.[26]

Despite the caution that employment for men was somewhat less constant than for women, the prospect of earning thirty-six shillings a week must have seemed tempting indeed to an Irish agricultural laborer whose weekly wages in 1880 averaged no more than nine shillings and in 1895 were still less than ten shillings. Little wonder that with the impetus added by agrarian distress in Ireland nearly three times as many people sailed for American shores in 1880 as did the year before.

Not only was America a place where a man through hard work had an opportunity to earn high wages, but with that money he was also entitled to the social prestige and physical comforts that usually accompanied an increase in earning capacity. His improvement was mirrored in the very clothes he wore, and this almost instantaneous change rarely failed to be a source of wonderment and pride to the new immigrants. Some of the letters reflected the delight at discovering that in America even the less affluent classes dressed well, so that it was sometimes difficult to distinguish rich from poor. Writing to his mother and brothers in County Cork after just arriving in Buffalo in

1850, one Irishman described what a simple change of clothing did for a fellow emigrant: "If you were to see Denis Reen when Daniel Danihy . . . dressed him with clothes suitable for this country you would think him to be boss or steward so that we have scarcely words to state to you how happy we felt at present."[27]

Twenty years later a young domestic servant wrote from the same city and wanted her former employer in Ireland to know that in America "thare is no end to fassions" and that her employer was to be sure to tell a certain lady member of the local gentry that "my sister has a nicer carrage than the one hur and i used to ride in." By 1894 the "end to fassions" was still not in sight, and a laborer who had arrived in Philadelphia thirty years before observed to his sisters that the factory girls in that city spent so much on clothes that "you can hardly distinguish a girl going to her work from a prosperous merchants wife or daughter."[28]

While high wages were doubtless the single most important attraction of America, they were not the only ones.[29] America offered other enticements which while less tangible were nevertheless appealing. It was a land of social equality where class divisions were fluid, where titles like earl or lord did not exist, and where one man felt himself equal to the next. In 1883 the ranch hand in Washington gave his family in County Limerick a practical illustration of American social democracy. "There are no Gentlemen here," he wrote. "If a farmer in Ireland made 3 or 4 thousand dollars in a year you couldnt walk the road with them. You would have to go inside the fence or they would ride over you."[30] Some twenty-five years earlier a Philadelphia laborer also reflected on the nature of class differences in Ireland and drew a comparison between his position at home and his newfound status in America:

> . . . people that cuts a great dash at home when they come here the[y] tink it strange for the humble Class of people to get as much respect as themselves for when they come here it wont do to say i had such and was such and such back at home but straingers here the[y] must gain respect by there conduct and not by there tongue. i know people here from the town of Newbridge that would not speak to me if the[y] met me on the public road and here i can laugh in there face when i see them.[31]

At the end of the century the appeal of equality must still have been as strongly inviting to those in Ireland who read the letters. Certainly the impression made on those who wrote them was evident enough. "This is all the home an irish man has and i know it," one emigrant wrote to his parents in 1899, two months after landing in San Francisco. His reason for thinking so was perfectly plain: "There is no lords or earls in this Country that you have too put your hand too your hat for." Perhaps the pithiest statement was penned in 1867 by a resident of St. Paul, Minnesota. In a letter published in a Cork journal he seemed to sum up the attractions of his newly adopted country when he declared, "America is a country for every man of energy and industry to rise to respectability and independence in."[32]

Unanimity, however, is not a typically Irish trait and not everyone was agreed that America was such a wonderful place to come to. There were those who cautioned their friends and relatives to remain at home if it were at all possible. America, after all, was not home and one could not expect to find the same warmth of associations found in the Old Country. Moreover, life was not easy or as easygoing as it was in Ireland. There were hardships and difficulties to be endured here just as there were at home and one must not think otherwise. Simply because a person was living in America was no reason to assume that his life was devoid of the normal burden of problems. One immigrant made this crystal clear. Fairly well-educated, he arrived in Washington, D.C., in 1851 and was forced to begin his career as a day laborer on public works. The following year he wrote to his brother in Dublin, and although he enclosed a remittance of twenty dollars, he also sent a sharp reminder that it was dearly earned:

> All you people in Ireland are deceived or at least deceive yourselves in your opinion of this Country. I am not going to enter into particulars. All that I will say is that persons coming here will find as much hardships and difficulty as ever they experienced home. There are some fare well, but that rare case. For myself I am now in a fair way bettering myself, but I will tell you what none of my people here knows, that I have suffered more than I thought I could endure, in a strange Country far from a friend, necessitated to go on public works from four o'clock of a summer morning until eight at night enduring the hardships of a burning sun, then by

sickness losing what I dearly earned for my short time in this country. I have experienced a great deal, which may serve me the remainder of my life.[33]

Laborers were not the only ones who had to endure privation and suffering. Farmers in the prairie states faced an even more formidable array of problems, and in 1859 an Irish farmer in Ottawa, Illinois, took pains to expound them for the edification of the editor and readers of the *Kilkenny Journal*. He gave details of the unscrupulous practices of American land speculators; how they induced unsuspecting immigrants to buy land which often turned out to be 160 acres of unfenced prairie, miles from any water; how prospective farmers had to borrow money at fantastically high interest rates — 30 to 50 percent — in order to make improvements; how terribly they suffered from the bitter cold; and how, after two or three unfavorable years, even the best of farmers were left "paralyzed." But people at home, he felt, did not want to know the truth and would probably not believe his "unexaggerated" account; for his pains he would doubtless be "denounced as a calumniator."[34] Almost forty years later a laborer in Philadelphia seemed to be speaking for a number of Irish immigrants when he wrote to his sister, the wife of an Ulster farmer, in the most candid terms:

You know how things is with you in ireland but what do you know how the[y] are with me – the[y] are not by a long way what you perhaps think the[y] are – because I am in america dont you for a moment doubt but I have my own difficultys to work through . . .[35]

There were other disadvantages about America than merely the economic. They were social and religious in nature and were directed against the Irishman because he was a foreigner and, in some cases, because he was a Roman Catholic. Religious bigotry against the Irish found its most violent expression in the Know-Nothing movement of the early 1850s. When a number of Irishmen were murdered and their property destroyed by a group of Know-Nothings in Louisville in 1855, one immigrant in business in Philadelphia wrote to his sister that things were becoming "fearful." He advised people to stay in Ireland because at least there, even if they were poor, they would be protected from "murderers like the Louisville affair." [36]

Racial tensions of a less explosive kind were also reflected in some of the letters. Brought into contact with the other national groups then pouring into America, all with different cultural backgrounds, speaking strange tongues, many of another religion, and sometimes competing for the same jobs, the Irish encountered a hostility which they quickly reciprocated in kind. In the Midwest they found Swedes, Norwegians, and Germans and toward the end of the century came the Italians to the eastern cities.

With the barriers of language and culture made more acute by the heat of economic competition, mutual mistrust and suspicion became the natural concomitant. In 1892 a railroad section foreman in Mapleton, Iowa, wrote his uncle in County Donegal that he had a new boss, a Norwegian, who in his first two months fired every Irish foreman except himself and a man from Tipperary: ". . . he hates the ground an Irishman walks on . . . and as you are well aware an Irishman is not badly stuck on him either." Five years later a brother, also employed by the railroad, wrote to the uncle from Battle Creek, Iowa, and made a promise to his nephew:

> Sometime I will write to him and tell him all about: snakes, squirrels, wolves, Indians, negros, Germans, Swedes & Norwegians and Yankees. The community I live in is composed of all these classes. They all hate an Irishman, but there is no love lost, an Irishman does not care much for them.[37]

In the cities along the eastern seaboard feelings were more intense because competition was more direct. By the end of the century the Irish, who had traditionally monopolized those jobs which involved heavy manual labor such as public works and construction, were being forced out by the newer immigrants from southern and eastern Europe. From Boston in 1890 a laborer wrote his mother and brothers that

> a man . . . B. very lookey to get work to do, for the contery is crowded from all Nations of corse the name of America at home sounds extra but when people get theire they find it a different wourld any person who can make a fair living at home are better stay theire.[38]

In a letter to his nephew fourteen years later a Philadelphia laborer explained why it was difficult for him to find work and in doing so seemed to be airing the fears of a good many Irish workmen:

... this country is getting to be a very uncertain place for the English speaking working man, as capitalists prefer the Italians & others, people from southeran parts of Europe such as Hungarians Polanders, etc, as they work cheaper & are more submissive than the English speaking working man.[39]

Some letters definitely advised people to remain at home at all costs, but the bulk of these seem to have been written during periods of economic depression in the United States. One of the severest depressions was inaugurated with the commercial panic of 1873 and lasted for five years. They were turbulent years of strikes, lockouts, and unemployment, and those who thought of emigrating were warned by their friends to stay away. In 1877 a streetcar conductor in Greenpoint, Long Island, wrote to his brother in Belfast and explained why he felt he had reason to be "thankfull to God":

While others is starving I and familey has anuff to eat and drink and ther thousens that canot tell that storey in truth. I am earning three pound of english money in the weeke and there is nothing left, times is [bad] and provisions is dear and them that has not stedy worke is starving and the Ames [alms?] house is ful in this state canot hold any more. . . . it is a sad storey this time in the year it was bad anuff in the winter last and in sumer is nothing beter.[40]

Three years later another Irishman wrote to the editor of the Clare *Independent* from Akron, Ohio, and warned the people of County Clare that the "panic times" had left a bill to be paid. He therefore recommended that they not be in a hurry to leave, "at least for another while, till the word 'tramp' and 'beggar' is heard seldomer here." [41]

The Civil War in America also occasioned a series of warnings to Irishmen to remain at home, but on this there was a division of opinion. Many newspapers contended that it was sheer folly to go to a country where a bloody civil war was in progress and where young emigrants were likely to be preyed upon by ruthless recruiting agents.[42] Worse still, if duped into the army they would be called upon to slaughter their fellow Irishmen in the Confederate ranks for a cause which was of no concern to them. To illustrate the problem, letters were printed from emigrants in America which described the horrors of living in a land rent by civil strife,[43] while private letters, particularly during the early months of the war, emphasized the prostrating effect the conflict was having upon the economy of the country. Writing on November 24, 1861, a carpenter in Boston advised his brother that if he emigrated he could only look forward to going off to war in Virginia and perhaps getting shot, because "the business of the Country is wholy prostrate nothing doing in any line of business or other industrial implowment, and all the people who have lived by their labour and only from hand to mouth . . . are gone to the War."[44]

But as the war dragged on and able-bodied men were drained off into the army, laborers became scarce and the prospects for employment improved considerably, as one immigrant newly arrived in Chicago made clear in 1863: "Times are pretty hard now in consequence of such a war everything is twice or three times dearer than it used to be but there is good pay for laborers and plenty of demand for working men & they can easily earn from one to two dollars per day." [45]

The following year another Irishman wrote to his parents from Boston that wages were still good, although the employment situation was not quite so attractive as it was in the booming metropolis of the Midwest: ". . .dont be laboring under an idea that men are very scarce here, its no such thing, there is plenty of them."[46] Nevertheless he admitted that work was available and no one need starve if he came to America.

Occasionally it was a series of disagreeable experiences encountered in a particular vocation which convinced some that life in America for an Irishman was worse than a living hell. This seems to have been the case with one unfortunate immigrant who spent twelve years working on the railroads in the antebellum South. In 1860 he wrote to the editor of the *Cork Examiner* from Sweet Springs, Virginia, and complained bitterly that

> . . . it would take more than a mere letter to tell you the despicable, humiliating, slavish life of an Irish labourer on a railroad in the States; I believe I can come very near it by saying that everything, good and bad, black and white, is against him; no love for him — no protection in life — can be shot down, run through, kicked, cuffed, spat on – and no redress, but a response of served the damn son of an Irish b— right, damn him.[47]

A few stressed the loneliness and homesickness from which they suffered, and one went so far as to declare that although he could do well in America, he could never rest contented until he returned to Ireland. Another confessed to his family that often, when cutting cord wood alone in the forest, he sat down and thought of everybody at home. "Indeed," he confided, "I do be thinking of ye when ye dont least suspect it."[48]

Some warned of the dangers of straying from their religion and if people insisted on coming to America, they were urged to avoid the vice-ridden cities of the East where only fraud and deception awaited them. One outraged Irishman, obviously familiar with the seamier sides of life in Boston and New York, cried out that it was "Better for many of our people they were never born than to have emigrated from the 'sainted isle of old' to become murderers, robbers, swindlers, and prostitutes here." Still, while there were perhaps more temptations in the large eastern cities, it was possible to go astray in the West also. From Cincinnati one emigrant counseled his countrymen that they had best remain in Ireland where they would be "mindful of their religion" instead of voyaging to America to become "tools in the hands of designing knaves and politicians." And a hired hand in Carson City, Nevada Territory, must have brought a smile or two to the face of the friend who read his letter in 1862. He never would advise anyone to come to America, he wrote, because "there is a great many that was studdy and religious at home that turns reckless hear and I am not far behind the reckless myself."[49]

Letters which urged extreme caution, however, or contained Cassandra-like warnings were the exception, not the rule. More often than not they emphasized the seemingly limitless opportunities in America which were open to people of initiative and enterprise. Nowhere, perhaps, was the scope of these opportunities more dramatically demonstrated than in those letters which recounted tales of personal success and good fortune. Some were from modest farmers and laborers; a smaller number came from successful businessmen and large landowners. What these writers shared in common was a notable improvement in their station in life over what they had or could reasonably have aspired to have in Ireland. Their letters radiated the sense of satisfaction they felt in having made the crucial change and

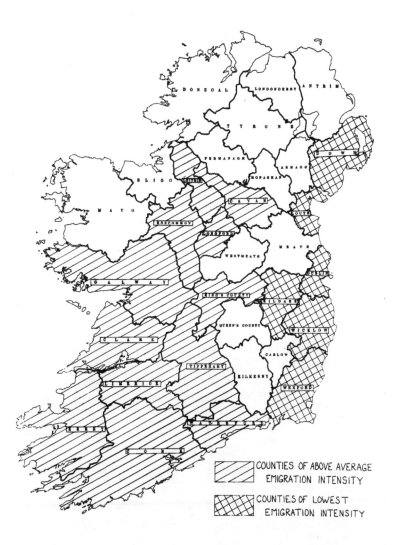

Irish Counties of High and Low Emigration Intensities
(Based on Emigration Statistics of Ireland for 1901, p.5)

Outward Bound
The Quay of Dublin
(Painted by J. Nicol. Drawn on stone by T. H. Maguire, Lithographic
Artist to the Queen. Printed by M. & N. Hanhart.)

Homeward Bound
The Quay of New York
(Painted by J. Nicol. Drawn on stone by T. H. Maguire, Lithographic
Artist to the Queen. Printed by M. & N. Hanhart.)

39

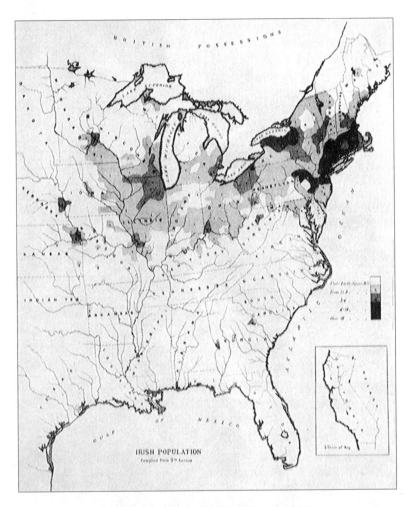

Irish-born in the United States, 1870
(From the Ninth United States Census, 1870)

conveyed the impression to those who remained and dared to hope that the same opportunities awaited future emigrants. In 1853 a farmer who settled near London, Ontario, had only one regret, that his brother in County Fermanagh did not follow him across the Atlantic:

> Dear Brother if you had onley plucked up courage an come to America a few years agoe and got a good farm in this part of the country before the land got dear you would have had no cause to rue it and I am sure you children would ever bless the day that the[y] came to Canady; I never was sorry for coming, but ever shall be that I spent so many of my dayes in Ireland . . . to make a long story short all my brothers and friends are well and have bettered their condishon by coming to America far beyont what it was possible for them to have done had the[y] stoped in Ireland . . .[50]

Nearly twenty years later a machinist in Westfield, New York, recounted a similar tale to his brother, a small farmer in County Down. For sixteen years, he wrote, he had been working in a machine shop at ten shillings a day. In addition he had a comfortable little home and four acres of land on which he pastured a cow and raised all the wheat, corn, potatoes, fruit, and vegetables he needed. Those four acres, moreover, were lands on which he paid "neither rent, cess nor title nor tax of any sort" because his service in the militia exempted him from all such duties. All his children were grown, had substantial farms of their own, and were doing well. "So you see," he told his brother, "I have no reason to regret coming to this country."[51]

Toward the end of the century a letter from a young seamstress in Winsted, Connecticut, mirrored the same spirit of optimism and satisfaction — which was probably not lost upon the younger sister who read it: "I am getting along splendid and likes my work it seems like a new life. I will soon have a trade and be more independint. . . . I am very glad I made the change. . . . You know it was always what I wanted so I have reached my highest ambition."[52]

Sometimes the more spectacular success stories found their way into the local newspapers, as was the case with one individual who wrote to his family from San Francisco in 1854. According to the journal in which the letter was printed, he had started out from Ireland to seek his fortune "relying alone upon his good conduct, industry, and a moderate share of education." After going first to Australia, which he found unsatisfactory, he went to San Francisco in 1850. In the short space of four years he had earned enough money to purchase over 4000 acres of rich land in the San Joaquin Valley, land which, at the time he wrote, was already worth "twenty times" what he paid for it. In addition he owned a large amount of stock in the city's water works and also held the position of engineer of the works at a salary of $500 a month. Moreover he held a contract which was to net him a profit of $50,000, and by the end of the year he hoped to have an invested income of $30,000 annually from the water works, as well as 50,000 acres of land "of the best quality." With good reason did he feel that he had come to "this fine country," as he put it, "in the nick of time." Finally he made an offer to his family which must have been well-nigh irresistible. "Should you and my brothers and sisters think proper to come out," he stated, "I will give to each 1000 acres, and help stock it for you also, without any condition or consideration for it whatever."[53]

Somewhat less spectacular but equally as impressive was the story of an Irishman who went into business for himself in New York City in 1855. That year, however, he suffered attacks of "billious fever" and smallpox from which he managed to recover. Business became dull and he decided to try his luck in California where he hoped to do better. Thirteen years later he wrote to his sister from Fort Ross, California, to tell her how well he had done — he had just purchased Fort Ross from a Russian fur company. The area comprised 7000 acres of well-timbered land and was seventy-five miles north of San Francisco. He had erected a saw mill and had begun manufacturing lumber for the San Francisco market, and he also intended to farm 1000 acres of oats. "Dear Catharine," he told his sister, "I must wind up this by stating I have been very successful in my business so far – and if my good luck should continue for a few years more, I will be considering myself quite *wealthy*." In the letter he enclosed a check for twenty pounds with a promise to send another "soon."[54]

Most emigrants did not attain such pinnacles of success in the New World, but there seems to be little doubt that the majority were able to improve their positions substantially. The Irish quickly absorbed the spirit of driving energy which characterized nineteenth-century America and, untroubled by any major barriers of language, they forged for themselves new and more prosperous lives. They wrote home to let family and friends know how they were getting on and in the process created a generally alluring picture for those in the Old Country of life and work in America. Some, through misfortune or personal failings, fell by the wayside and became a source of shame for the rest, although even the more successful ones did not gloss over the hardships which had to be endured. With energy, industry, and perseverance, however, most obstacles could be overcome, and the hope for a brighter future was the spur for a greater effort.

There was more to these letters than just their contents, however. The arrival of an "Amerikay letther," as it came to be called in Ireland, was a great event, and when one was received it was "borne in in triumph and opened with joy."[55] For not only was it expected to contain an often desperately needed remittance, but for many it was also the only source of news of beloved ones across the sea. When a family received a letter, news of its arrival usually spread quickly through the neighborhood; and especially in the earlier decades of heavy emigration — the 1850s and 1860s — the opening and reading of so important an epistle was attended by much ritual and ceremony. An old Donegal schoolteacher, who wrote his memoirs toward the end of the century, has left a graphic description of a typical reception accorded an American letter in the days of his youth:

> All members of the family and some friends gather round. Each one gives his opinion as to the best way of opening the letter without damaging the contents. "The Scholar" is sent for. He perhaps is not at home just then, or he may be from one cause or another rather long in coming, but as everyone could distinguish an "American Ticket" by the picture of the Eagle from another part of the document, anxiety overcomes patience, and a breach is made in the cover with a scissors or knife. Not a breath escapes while this operation is being performed. Soon fold after fold of the enclosed manuscript is opened. The last one is being turned up and alas! between hope and despair the "Ticket" appears. There is something in it whatever it is. This part of the letter, the pearl as may be called – is taken in charge by the old woman who opens her long cloth purse . . . and in the innermost . . . cavity the American Eagle finds a safe retreat.

[At long last the "Scholar" arrives, seats himself in the place of honor reserved for him, and takes up the letter.]

> In every family letter, there is always something, which strangers have no right to know. This is one. The value of the piece of paper is kept secret and the reader knowing this from experience pauses over the mention of it. The old woman herself though, knows it well, for the man of letters always takes a glance before reading aloud to see what is to be read and what is not. After doing this he notifies certain things to the old landlady and proceeds with his business.[56]

Sometimes, as in the Gaelic-speaking areas of western Ireland, the "Scholar" in addition to the reading had to translate the English and explain it almost word for word. He often was asked to repeat the reading a number of times. That night, still more neighbors flocked in to congratulate the fortunate parents. Generally the "Scholar" was present, and he read, reread, and translated the contents of the letter for the benefit of the new arrivals. Next day the letter traveled from house to house for those relatives or close friends to read who could not attend the night before, since the letter usually made mention of the welfare of many others in America from the same community. And for days afterward there were discussions on the news contained in the "Amerikay letther."

Although American letters were passed around among close friends and relatives and were items of profound significance and interest in the hamlets and villages of rural Ireland, they were rarely read out at fairs, social gatherings, or in church. Letters were intimate, personal documents and the people of rural Ireland were not inclined to make them public. Comparatively few, for example, were ever printed in the newspapers. Occasionally a woman going into the local village on a Saturday might carry an American letter in her bosom and upon meeting a friend pull it out and proceed to tell her how her Johnny or Biddy was getting on in "Amerikey." Sometimes one was passed around at a fair as a guarantee or as a form of security when a person wanted to borrow money, for money would often be lent on the strength of the letter's assurance that a remittance would be sent soon.[57] Perhaps if a small sum were sent along for the priest to help repair the local church, the letter might then be read out from the pulpit on Sunday. In the vast majority of cases, however, American letters were held to be private matters, and while many might learn of one's arrival, only those who had an interest in the writer or in the people he mentioned were privileged to read the letter or have it read to them.

Although the letters were restricted to immediate friends and relatives, the information they contained had much wider repercussions. The news of how an emigrant was doing passed quickly by word of mouth, and his descriptions of life, work, and wages in America traveled far and wide. The knowledge that those who had gone before generally did well encouraged those who remained to think that they too could do the same. The occasional cautions and warnings were minimized because the Irish, despairing of self-improvement at home, wanted to believe that it was attainable abroad. America for the Irish became a symbol of hope for a more abundant life in this world and to it they streamed in an unceasing tide, urged and emboldened by the American letters. What lured them westward was perhaps nowhere better summarized than by an anonymous poet in 1851 who called to his countrymen to "Come With Me O'er Ohio":

Desert a land of corse [that is, curse] and slave,
   Of pauper woe and tinsel splendour,
Poor Eire now is all a grave,
   And gone the few who dared defend her. . . .

We leave the slave's, the trickster's whine,
   The bigot's howl, the rage of faction,
To fell the oak, and plant the vine,
   And live in earnest, useful action.

Bring not grey Europe's silk or gems –
   A candid soul is ample dowry,
Where Freedom laughs at diadems,
   Beside the thunder-toned Missouri. . . .

Come! let us fly to Freedom's sky,
   Where Love alone hath power to bind us –
There honoured live, lamented die,
   And leave a spotless name behind us! [58]

Part II • Reactions and Results

III

The Futile Protest: Press and Pulpit

As the emigrant tide flowed irresistibly westward, lured on by hopes of a better life across the Atlantic, a shrill chorus of protest rose up from the newspapers in the country. Through the pages of the press rang the cry "Stay the emigration!" and it was the exceptional newspaper that did not add its voice to this wail against the ceaseless outpouring of humanity. From Cork to Derry, from Dublin to Galway, whether Catholic or Protestant, nationalist or tory, few papers failed to see in the steady drain the direst consequences for Ireland. The very terms used to describe the emigrants were a measure of the alarm generated. They were the "blood and bone," and far more often the "bone and sinew" of the country; they were the "fairest and bravest," the "youth and strength" of the land, the very "flower of the population," the "hope of the future." They were the "producers" and the "bold peasantry," the "lifeblood" of the country whose never-ending flight would lead to Ireland's total depopulation. The country would become one vast sheepwalk and pasture, its only inhabitants would be lowing herds and fleecy flocks, and Ireland would be left with a "cattle civilization."[1]

To stop this "bloodletting" remedies were earnestly proposed; the British government was vigorously damned, warned, entreated, and implored, all in turn; the clergy were beseeched to use their persuasive powers; and the emigrants themselves were either eloquently appealed to on patriotic grounds or else roundly denounced as "unpatriotic and

49

soulless creatures," or even traitors. In their fits of anger and alarm, few papers were sober enough to view the problem rationally. Seldom did they admit that emigration was relieving areas which were depressingly overpopulated in relation to developed resources. The population was dwindling and that was sufficient evidence that Ireland was being ruined.[2]

But their jeremiads went unheeded, and one paper grieved that "the curse of restlessness seems to be upon us." Neither the British government, the Catholic Church, nor the emigrants themselves were visibly moved by the fulminations in the press: the British government because it saw voluntary emigration as a solution for Ireland's ills; the Catholic Church because it was more concerned with rectifying the land system; and the emigrants because the forces compelling them to leave were stronger than any emotional appeals to patriotism.[3] Seldom have the newspapers of Ireland been so out of tune with the prevailing sentiment of the people. However, like all generalizations of this kind, this one too is subject to a number of qualifications, and these can best be brought to light through a more detailed elucidation of the nature of the protest and of the types of newspapers that voiced it.

To begin with, it must be pointed out that the great bisector of the Irish press was religion, not politics. Newspapers were primarily Roman Catholic or Protestant in their outlook and only secondarily nationalist, liberal, or tory. But religious divisions in nineteenth-century Ireland also represented economic and social distinctions. The large body of peasantry was predominantly Roman Catholic, while the landlord, professional, and governmental classes were heavily Protestant. Inevitably, therefore, the majority of Catholic papers identified their interests with those of the peasantry and small-farming classes, while most Protestant papers identified theirs with the upper social orders.[4] This does not mean that the former were considered as official spokesmen of the Irish Catholic Church, for as will be shown later, the Church per se had strangely little to say on the question of emigration.

Within these two major religious groupings were other distinguishing characteristics. Catholic newspapers, for example, were concentrated naturally enough in the south and west with about a half dozen or so in the east, the latter of which were clustered either in

Dublin (for example, *Nation, Freeman's Journal, Dublin Evening Post*) or in County Louth (for example, *Newry Examiner, Dundalk Democrat, Drogheda Argus*). There seemed to be no important Catholic papers in any of the Ulster counties. Protestant papers were concentrated mainly along the east coast and in the Ulster counties, but there were also a few in the south (for example, Cork *Constitution*, *Limerick Chronicle*, *Waterford Daily Mail*) and in the west (for example, *Mayo Constitution*, *Ballinrobe Chronicle*). This pattern of distribution helps explain the curious circumstance that newspapers such as the *Ballinrobe Chronicle* and *Limerick Chronicle*, which were located in areas of intense emigration, maintained a strange editorial silence on the emigration problem, while a paper like the *Dundalk Democrat*, located in a county of comparatively low emigration such as County Louth, frequently and vociferously expressed its views. If it be remembered that the former were Protestant papers catering to the upper social strata and the latter a Catholic paper of pronounced nationalist views, the silence of the former and the loquacity of the other are more easily understood. The accident of physical location was not nearly so important in conditioning the views of a newspaper as were its religious outlook, social identification, and political persuasion. It may be safely assumed that the attitude of the *Dundalk Democrat* toward emigration would have been the same regardless of where it was being published.

Politically, most Catholic papers were strongly nationalist and pro-home rule in sentiment, although some, to be sure, such as the *Limerick Reporter*, followed the Church's lead and refused to countenance secret and violent societies like the Fenians. A small minority among them were liberal in politics and antinationalist in outlook. In this category were the Cork *Southern Reporter* and the Dublin *Evening Post*, both of whose views were identified with the small aspiring group of Catholics among the professional classes. The majority of Protestant papers were politically conservative or tory and among these the greater number were also anti-Catholic and antinationalist. A few were liberal in their politics and not intolerantly anti-Catholic, but even within this small liberal Protestant group there was a sharp division on the issue of nationalism. The Belfast *Northern Whig*, for example, ensconced in the very citadel of Protestantism, was strongly opposed to home rule, while at the southern end of the island the *Waterford Daily Mail* took the opposite stand.

Outside the major religious bifurcation stood a small group of extremist, ultranationalist papers whose fiery views on emigration were conditioned primarily by the violence of their political convictions. These were the organs of the Fenians and their successors and included such papers as the *Irish People, United Ireland,* and the *Flag of Ireland.* All were published in Dublin and although their circulation was small, it will be useful to compare their attitudes with those of the more moderate journals.

For most newspapers there was a close parallel between the frequency and intensity of their antiemigration articles and the emigration curve. When emigration was greatest, comment was most frequent and vociferous; when emigration subsided, comment diminished in quantity and intensity. Thus the peak periods of emigration — 1848-53, 1863-66, 1880-83 — occasioned the greatest number of articles which were vigorously opposed to emigration, whereas the troughs in the emigration curve, 1878-79 and 1896-99, were matched by a comparatively mild silence on the problem. Within any given year, moreover, comment was normally heaviest when the emigration season was at its height, that is from March through May and from August through October, but especially during the spring months when the largest numbers of people left for America. In general the earlier decades of the 1850s and 1860s, when emigration was consistently higher, were also the decades when newspaper commentary was more numerous.

After about 1870, with the exception of the peak periods of emigration, articles on the subject diminished in frequency and appeared most often in those years during which the decennial census returns were published, that is, 1871, 1881, 1891, and 1901. The publication of the decennial censuses, charting as they did the progressive decline of the population, seemed to jolt many journals into a reawakened realization of the continuing magnitude of the emigration phenomenon. Total emigration statistics for a ten-year period were indeed impressive — or more probably alarming — and apparently startled even the most complacent of journals, papers which during the course of a single year might have noted some emigration but might not have thought it exceptionally high.

The great majority of newspaper articles on emigration were in the nature of editorials, often leading editorials, and varied in length from one-half to one and one-half columns of close print; comparatively little comment on emigration appeared in the form of news articles or letters to the editor. The tone and caliber of the editorials varied with the character of the journals in which they were printed. Some were moderate in language, shrewd in analysis, and sensible in advice. These were often found in the liberal press, both Protestant and Roman Catholic. In this category were such journals as the Belfast *Northern Whig* and the *Clare Journal*. The latter paper, for example, located in the county of highest emigration intensity, was nevertheless able to maintain its sense of balance and saw the problem of emigration in proper perspective:

> We do not wish it to be . . . understood that we deprecate a healthy emigration. To the youth and manhood of our land, we say, if you do not work, you are unworthy the name of man, and if you have nothing to do at home, pull yourself together, brace up your energies, hold your head erect, and go forth in quest of labour; go . . . if you will, to America. . . . We can willingly lend a hand to the encouragement of emigration from our overpopulated towns and cities, where youth grows up in purposeless existence, and manhood crawls about in slothful poverty for want of occupation. . . . It is in view of [the] lack of manufactures in Ireland that we can conscientiously bid the denizens of our lanes and alleys to emigrate to those lands where employment is afforded and labour well remunerated.

> It is when we become cognizant of the excessive drain of our agricultural population by emigration, that we are seized with alarm for the prosperity of our country, and feel called upon to cast about for the cause and the effect, as well as for devising the means for staying the outgoing flow. . . . We are behind the age in cultivation of the soil. We have the highest respect for the good, generous, and hospitable farmers of Ireland . . . but . . . we cannot withhold our honest condemnation of their carelessness in many instances. No doubt many of them have large families, and they think emigration a good thing, but they also occupy broad acres, and if, instead of sending their sons and daughters to America,

Australia, and Canada to "seek their fortunes," they kept them at home to plough and weed, and sow the many headlands run to waste, to pick the furze bushes up from the roots, to eradicate the stones from the fields, to level useless, broad, old ditches, and substitute palings . . . and a thousand and one things of this nature, they would do far better at home, we would have a land of prosperity, provided the landlords would, for their own interests, adequately recompense them for their labour and outlay.[5]

In the great preponderance of cases, however, editorials were neither particularly restrained in their language nor notably realistic in their analyses, and this was as true of the Catholic, nationalistic journals as it was of the Protestant, tory papers. Journals such as the *Cork Examiner* and the *Belfast News-Letter* were representative of these two major groups. While both were seriously concerned about the continuing emigration, each paper saw the question in diametrically opposite lights. To the *Cork Examiner* the problem was "perfectly clear":

As to the causes of the decrease in the population . . . it is perfectly clear that in a large measure, if not wholly, it may be attributed with certainty to the want of manufactures, the absence of that business enterprise which a paternal Government would do much to foster . . . and to the oppressive laws which reduced tenant farmers to a condition of continuous and hopeless struggle, and the labourers to a permanent and degrading destitution. . . . People do not fly at the rate of seventy thousand a year from a self-governed country of the size of Ireland and possessing the same natural advantages. If it be a fact, as it is beyond question, that Ireland is capable of supporting a far larger population in peace and comfort, is it such a "damnable heresy" . . . to suggest that to misgovernment, past or present, the blame for the depopulation which has been going on is to be attributed? We do not believe so, and we are confident that the Irish people do not believe so. And we are convinced that the beneficial influence of Irish self-government will in no direction be more conspicuous than in the cessation of the fearful drain on the population of the country, which has been doing its deadly work for the past half-century.[6]

The *Belfast News-Letter* was also convinced that emigration was a matter calling for the earnest consideration of all "true patriots," but its definition of the term "patriot" and its analysis of the population dilemma stood in marked contrast to that propounded by the *Cork Examiner*:

> It is no use denouncing the Union with England, and alleging that it is the cause of all our misfortunes. . . . The Nationalists might employ their time more profitably if, instead of bewailing the connection with Great Britain, which can never be severed, they endeavoured to find the real causes of the declining population, and endeavour to find a remedy. . . . there can be no doubt that the decrease is due to emigration. Large numbers of our people leave our shores every year, mostly for the United States. . . . Why do they emigrate? Simply to improve their position. . . . Agriculture is depressed. It cannot afford the constant employment and good wages which are obtainable in other industries. This depression is due to several causes, of which the principal is the pressure of foreign competition. But it is also attributable in some measure to antiquated methods of cultivation, and to a lack of energy and enterprise. Nationalists say that a Parliament in Dublin would remedy all this, but they do not show how it would do so. . . . What is wanted is some plan by which farming can be made more remunerative. . . . If the farmers will give proper attention to butter-making, the keeping of fowl, and other subsidiary industries, they may be able to make farming pay, and thus arrest to some extent the rural exodus. But in order to stop emigration more industries are needed. How are these to be established? If the Nationalists were to endeavour honestly to answer this question they might become more thoughtful and reasonable than they are. In the first place capital is needed, and capital will not flow into a country in which lawlessness is encouraged, and agitation is a trade. People will not spend thousands of pounds in creating new industries when they know that they may be ruined by a political or religious boycott. . . . There is too much reason to fear that the professional agitators and many of the priests would rather see their country impoverished and depopulated than that power should leave their hands.[7]

Despite the diversity of religious and political groupings among Irish newspapers, nearly all editorial comment on emigration revolved around several major issues, and these formed the principal threads of controversy throughout the entire half-century. First and foremost were sought the causes of the emigration. Rarely could causes be discussed, however, without a compulsion also to apportion blame. Thus the assessment of blame frequently became an important corollary to the question of cause. The second major consideration was whether the emigration was good or bad, both for the country as a whole and for the emigrants themselves. Although a good many papers were unequivocal in their condemnation on both counts, that view was by no means unanimous. Finally, the third great desideratum was the best remedy for staying, or perhaps even stopping, the continuing drain. On this point there was no dearth of nostrums proposed, some of which revealed a realistic recognition of Ireland's ills, while others simply betrayed an inspired imagination.

On the question of the causes of the emigration, Catholic newspapers with a pronounced pronationalist bias displayed a unanimity of opinion that is not surprising. Yet even here there were gradations. The more ardently nationalist among them could hardly discuss the matter at all without emotional outcries about England as the "greatest criminal of ancient or modern times," the "Union that debilitates us," or the "calm and cold-blooded cruelty" of the British. To such newspapers it was plain that English misrule and tyranny were solely responsible for emigration, and on occasion the judgment of John Stuart Mill was invoked in an attempt to humiliate the British government and lend dignity to the denunciations. Some even felt that it was a deliberate scheme on the part of the British to depopulate the country.[8]

Only slightly less irrational were those journals who transferred the burden of guilt to the shoulders of the Irish landlord class and identified the "yoke of oppressive land-lordism" as the principal evil. People were fleeing because the country was smitten by a "plague of bad land laws" and they wanted to escape from the "merciless influence of . . . exterminating landlords." To these papers it was an "iniquitous" land system and the "narrow-minded selfishness and stupidity" of Irish landlords that was driving the people from Ireland. Only a few were sensible enough to recognize that the lack of employment and the absence of industry were equally as important, if not more so, in accounting for the emigration. By the end of the century one of the latter was brave enough to declare that blaming emigration on land laws was a "heresy of humbug" since by then the land laws protected the tenant.[9]

However, as much as these Catholic, pronationalist newspapers may have differed in emphasis as to the causes of the emigration, there was little doubt in any of their editorial minds as to who was to blame for Ireland's deplorable state of affairs. It was the British government which was responsible for Ireland being a "dismal exception" to the general prosperity so prevalent in the rest of Europe. On this there was a common denominator of agreement.[10]

Among the small group of Catholic, antinationalist newspapers, neither the British connection nor the landlord class was singled out for such unrestrained condemnation. These journals viewed the problems largely through economic rather than political eyes. They saw in the paucity of manufactures and the concomitant lack of employment the great stimulus to emigration, although one of them did feel that insecurity of tenure for the tenant farmer was a more important cause. Unlike their pronationalist coreligionists, they felt no compulsion to apportion blame; their editorial pages were free from invective and vituperation.[11]

The great body of conservative, Protestant newspapers were antinationalist in outlook and viewed the problem in still another light. The more extreme among them were so swayed by their religious intolerance that they saw in the emigration only a flight from the "tyranny of priests" and the "endless exactions" of the Catholic Church. So long as the Irish remained under the "poisonous influence" of the Church, they would remain "inert and useless" and their only recourse was escape by emigration. The larger majority of Protestant papers, however, saw political agitation as the great bane of the country. It was "brawling demagogues" and "factious priests" which embittered landlord-tenant relations; it was political agitation which scared away investment capital, with the result that industries were not developed and the people were forced to emigrate in search of employment. A very few saw the land question as being at the bottom of the exodus. Of all the conservative, Protestant papers, only the *Belfast News-Letter* was willing to attribute emigration to British misrule, although by the turn of the century even this journal came round to the position that "lawlessness and agitation" were driving away capital and forcing people to emigrate in search of work.[12]

The very small number of liberal, Protestant papers professed to see in the "monstrous Land-Laws" a "feudal land system" which, by denying the tenant farmer any degree of security, was inducing him to sell his farm and flee the country. But they stoutly and loyally denied that he was being driven away by a tyrannical government, and by the turn of the century they came to condemn the "pernicious effect" and "devastating results" of nationalist agitation. The one lone dissenter was in the south of Ireland and it roundly denounced England's excessive taxation which, it declared, was draining the wealth of the country, reducing employment and stimulating emigration.[13]

When it came to a consideration of whether or not emigration was beneficial, either for Ireland or the emigrants, the degree of unanimity frequently transcended religious and political differences. Few indeed were the newspapers that did not see in the steady exodus the blackest results for their country. The more vituperative Catholic journals labeled emigration a "curse" and Ireland a nation "dying of inner decay." Population they identified with strength and the loss of one meant a decline in the other, while for the emigrant it meant hurrying forth to mix in the "racial chaos" of the New World. Anyone who dared suppose that Ireland might be benefiting from the emigration was guilty of a "most foul and . . . blasphemous assumption." As for the emigrants, not one in a thousand would be better off for the venture.[14]

The more reasonable Catholic papers were not so quick to deliver themselves of denunciations, but they were sincerely troubled and seriously questioned whether a nation could be prosperous and wealthy while its population steadily declined. They noted the grim irony of a movement which, by reducing the population, left more food for the fewer who remained and thus brought about a perverse kind of prosperity. For the most part they saw nothing but ruin for Ireland as a result of the constant drain on its laboring and farming population. Some thought it was also ruinous to the emigrants themselves who, as one feared, would become "sapless specimens of humanity wrecked in the awful wasting life of American cities."[15] The greater number conceded that the emigrants probably improved their lot in America. After all, advised one, it was "unreal to commiserate the lot of the poor emigrant who is flying from six shillings a week to four times that sum and more."[16]

The antinationalist Catholic journals, on the other hand, were universally agreed that the emigrants were bettering themselves by leaving a country where they could find no means of "honourable subsistence" to go to one where "the field of profitable industry is practically without a limit."[17] As for Ireland, only one of them thought emigration "ruinous" and a "melancholy index to the . . . deterioration of the country."[18] The more astute among them raised a point which none of their pronationalist coreligionists ever conceded. Not only did they feel that emigration had helped Ireland by diminishing competition for land and raising the value of labor, but they were also convinced that it was positively "necessary and desirable."[19] Plainly, if Ireland had not the means of employing its population, then that population was not an element of wealth.[20] Moreover, since an unemployed people was a discontented people, it was also a source of weakness, not strength. The question therefore was whether remunerative employment could be found for the people at home. The Catholic, pronationalist press cried "yes!" The antinationalists answered "no."

The great preponderance of the Protestant, conservative papers shared the views of their Catholic antinationalist contemporaries. Emigration, they felt, had benefited the country because it had reduced extreme competition among the tenant class. After all, to identify the prosperity of Ireland with the number of full or half-empty mouths in the country was nothing less than "sheer stupidity and folly." They denied that emigration diminished the capital of the country and professed to see a "marked improvement," not a deterioration in Ireland. One went so far as to declare that emigration was a "national remedy" for the "unhealthy state of our social system." So far as the emigrants were concerned, there was general agreement that for them it meant nothing but betterment. Furthermore, by settling in such large numbers in America, their own national qualities would help modify the "narrowness and rigidity of the Anglo-Saxon type" so dominant there.[21]

A few journals, however, stood out in sharp contrast to this prevailing Protestant sentiment. From the very beginning the *Belfast News-Letter* declared that it looked upon the emigration as an "unmitigated evil." "When will our rulers . . . learn," it cried, "that the glory of the Crown is the number of its loyal subjects?" — a reference, obviously, to the Ulster emigrants, not those from the south. The paper was joined by others who also felt the exodus to be a "national evil" and a sign of "national decay." One wryly remarked that the country could hardly be considered to be "buoyantly prosperous" while the people were fleeing at the rate of a quarter of a million a decade. Still, the emigrants, it was true, were improving themselves and if nothing else, there was the consolation that the numbers and influence of their fellow Protestants in America would always be a check against "Popish audacity" and the "inroads of infidelity" on the other side of the Atlantic.[22]

The liberal, Protestant papers saw in emigration only a synonym for self-exhaustion and a proof of disease. To be sure, for a period of twenty years, from 1871 to 1891, one of them thought the circumstances of the people at home much improved by the movement and saw nothing to be alarmed about, but a decade later the paper had come full circle and once again considered the phenomenon "unpleasant and disquieting." The emigrants may have gained by it, but in contradistinction to the view of the antinationalist Catholic papers, this paper held emigration to be no cure for the ills of Ireland.[23]

If emigration was indeed leading the country to ruin, what could be done to halt the onward march toward self-destruction? To this the pronationalist Catholic press unhesitatingly answered: self-government, land reform, and home industries. Many sincerely — and naively — believed that once granted home rule, all Ireland's ills, including emigration, would be cured. A domestic parliament would find employment for the people; with a simple change in government the Irish could support themselves "in abundance" and halt the "fearful drain." After all, it could not be expected that the English government would take any great pains about Irish problems. Home rule was therefore the only answer, and the day was longingly looked forward to when Ireland would be theirs to "make or mar." [24]

Others addressed themselves to the British government and insisted that just and reasonable land laws would make Irishmen "as loyal and prosperous under the British Crown, as under the Star-spangled Banner." It was the imperative duty of the government and the landlords to do something about the land system. Hand in hand with a reform of the land laws had to come large-scale reclamation of waste lands, and this too was earnestly urged upon their rulers. Equally as important was the necessity for developing natural resources and stimulating home industries. Firmly convinced that Ireland possessed abundant natural resources, some journals claimed that their development would not only stop emigration but provide employment for a population almost three times as large.[25]

Land alone, some recognized, was not enough to support the population; industries had to be established to provide employment and offer inducements to remain at home. A "practical patriotism" had to be inculcated in the people to boycott foreign goods and buy only Irish-made products so that these newborn home industries might be stimulated. Above all, the Irish were exhorted to rouse themselves from their "apathy and indolence" and warned that the "mere cry of 'Stay at home' and 'Stop emigration' won't boil the pot or bake the bread." If only the Irish would work as hard at home as they did in America, a few pleaded, they would be infinitely richer and happier in the old country. It was a "sad want of enterprise" that was keeping Ireland backward and forcing people to seek elsewhere for opportunities. The fact that Irishmen at home had neither the incentives nor the social pressures for such "enterprise" was conveniently overlooked.[26]

Some of the antinationalist Catholic journals also insisted that if Irish farmers worked "half as hard" at home as they had to abroad, Ireland would be a land of prosperity, but quickly added that this would be so only if landlords gave them adequate compensation and security of tenure. None were impressed with the argument that home rule was the panacea. Instead they advocated an improvement in agricultural techniques, the development of natural resources, the encouragement of home industry, and the reclamation of waste lands. With an envious eye on the comparative prosperity in the Ulster counties, one paper even urged upon landlords and merchants in the south and west the extensive cultivation of flax as a "patriotic investment." For these journals the solution lay primarily in economic not political action.[27]

Conservative Protestant papers, even more than Catholic ones, also implored the people to work as hard at home as they were compelled to do in America. One enlightened editor even urged all agricultural laborers to form a union which would prove they were "at least thinking of bettering themselves at home, instead of looking to emigration" as the only means of improving their lot.[28] Some saw a serious modification of the land system as a necessary measure, and one leading journal declared that emigration would stop only when "the American Constitution is the Constitution of Ireland, and the tenant is lord of the soil."[29] Practically all recognized the importance of establishing industries. The *Belfast News-Letter* rarely missed an opportunity to drive this point home, nor did its contemporaries. The *Irish Times*, for example, was convinced that "Until Ireland becomes a manufacturing country, it is as vain to stem the flow of emigration by other means as to stay with a rush the descent of the mountain torrent."[30] However, as much as they may have differed in emphasis as to the best economic remedies, on one point they all stood firm — their loyalty to the Crown. No conservative Protestant paper ever suggested that dissolving the Union was a feasible way out of the emigration dilemma.

On this question there were no dissenters even in the liberal Protestant camp. Here again it was simply a difference in emphasis as to economic means. While one saw the development of industries as the only effective answer to emigration, another stressed the land question and urged upon Parliament the consideration that "Without fixity of tenure as the nucleus of national and loyal associations, there will be little fixity of attachment to the throne or country; while the best of the people will still emigrate . . ." Both were agreed that political unrest and agitation would solve nothing.[31]

Diametrically opposed to this position stood a small clamorous group of ultranationalist papers to whom every evil in Ireland was directly traceable to the hated British government. In the continuing emigration they saw a "hellish design," a "deliberately conceived plan" by which English rule was "hunting labour and . . . wealth out of the country." Labor, as represented in the emigrants, was not only a source of wealth and emigration, therefore an enormous loss, but more importantly it was a weakening drain on the "army" of potential fighters for freedom. Consequently anyone who dared mention emigration as a rem-

edy for the peasants' ills was "England's ally and . . . Ireland's enemy."
It was on this account that Irish-Americans were severely upbraided for
sending back remittances and prepaid passages because the only contribution they were thereby making in the struggle against England was to
"seduce forty thousand a year of our sparse battalions." [32]

As is true of most fanatics, there seemed to be no consideration of
whether the emigrants were able to better themselves by leaving
Ireland. Instead it was proclaimed that all "true men" would not emigrate but "watch and wait and work for 'the long, long wished for
hour,' " for it was clear that only the "total destruction of English rule"
could "arrest the tragic process of emigration." Almost every nationalist in the hundred years prior to 1921, it has been observed, believed
that the principal goal of home rule was the development of native
industry and the improvement of agriculture, both of which it was supposed would reduce emigration, if not stop it altogether.[33]

The other great molder of public opinion in nineteenth-century
Ireland — in addition to the press — was the Roman Catholic clergy.
Evidence as to their attitude toward emigration is difficult to find,
however, and the meager material that is available reveals a comparative silence on the problem, which is rather curious, especially in view
of the generally outspoken opposition of the newspapers. The Irish
Catholic Church as such never declared itself on the question of emigration, and the result was that prelates and priests were left to speak
for themselves as individuals, a situation that was true even during the
emigrant flood of the famine years. Some were opposed to the emigration while others were not, but in general few actually tried to stand in
the way of the emigrants. The clergy as a whole probably regretted the
emigration every bit as much as any other group of sensitive Irishmen,
but for the most part they did not actively and openly oppose it. Being
close to the people, the priests were acutely aware of the peasants' problems, and the regret at seeing their flocks dwindle was tempered by a
sympathy with the laborers' lot and an understanding of the tenant
farmers' ambitions. Consequently many priests remained silent.[34]

Nevertheless there were some newspapers which insisted that
warnings from the pulpit on the dangers of emigration were constant,
frequent, and also futile. In 1853 the anti-Catholic *Belfast News-Letter*
positively declared that the priests had put a "ban" on emigration

because they dreaded a "diminution of their 'dues' " in Ireland and apostasy among the emigrants in America. The latter position had some support from the chief inspector of the government agricultural schools in Ireland who testified almost thirty years later that the Irish bishops and clergy opposed emigration not so much on the ground that it would lessen their incomes, as from the belief that Catholic emigrants in America would lose their faith and become "infidels."[35]

At about the same time a correspondent of the London *Times* reported from the west of Ireland that emigration was being solemnly denounced from the altar and that the priests were telling their flocks that "it is better to save their souls in Holy Ireland than to hazard them for this world's goods among American Heretics." He also reported that the warnings were largely ignored. James Hack Tuke, on the other hand, the philanthropist whose practical scheme of assisted emigration did so much to relieve congestion in the Connemara district in the early 1880s, gave it as his opinion that the priests in that area opposed only the emigration of households but favored it in the cases of individuals. Several years later an American traveler in Ireland reported that at least one parish priest he spoke to did not encourage emigration, but neither did he actively oppose it. Somewhat earlier a land agent in counties Clare and Limerick flatly denied ever having heard the clergy give any opinion on the subject.[36]

In any case, during the entire half-century the Irish Catholic Church per se came no closer to taking a stand on emigration than in a pastoral letter of 1859 which was signed by all the Irish bishops and archbishops and addressed to the Catholic clergy and people of Ireland. Even this failed to deal with the problem directly and dwelt instead on the injustice of the land laws and the cruelty of evicting landlords who, it seemed, preferred "cattle to Christians," especially of the Roman Catholic faith. The bishops looked forward to the day when there would be mutual respect between landlords and tenants and the latter would no longer be driven off the land to "perish in the swamps of America."[37]

Individual prelates were more direct. The following year the archbishop of Dublin in a pastoral address warned of the dangers of emigrating and urged the clergy in his diocese to caution the people in their parishes against "the exaggerated accounts of the advantages of emigration." The archbishop was also a realist, however, and added that if after careful consideration anyone felt that by remaining at home he would likely end his days in "crime and wretchedness," then he would do well to emigrate. Three years later, after a series of severe crop failures, the archbishop once again felt called upon to deal with the problem and asked the clergy of his diocese to pray for a good harvest so that a fresh impulse to the emigration might be averted.[38]

More outspoken was the archbishop of Tuam, John McHale, who in 1863 had no hesitation in writing open letters to Lord Palmerston and W. E. Gladstone, the latter then being chancellor of the exchequer. To both he complained bitterly of the cruel and capricious land laws whose systematic operation was driving the Irish to emigrate. He scolded Gladstone and the Irish landlords who pretended to be alarmed at the huge increase in Irish emigration and warned that the people would continue to fly the land so long as their just claims went "mercilessly unheeded." The only solution to the problem, he told Palmerston, was the restoration of a native legislature, a position he vigorously expounded again the following year in a Lenten pastoral to his diocese.[39]

Nearly a generation later a bishop from the west of Ireland protested in the strongest terms to the Richmond Commission that emigration would ruin the country, although he was willing to concede that for the emigrants it might be a blessing. His patriotic sentiments were echoed the following year by a priest from Cork who argued that his fellow prelates should be as anxious to preserve their dioceses as foreign bishops were to create theirs. Although he willingly recognized the contribution that the Irish had made to the growth of the Catholic Church abroad, particularly in America, his fervid Irish patriotism could not rest easy at the sight of the endless stream of Irish Catholic emigrants.[40]

Ironically in an article in the same journal some fifteen years later James Cardinal Gibbons, an American of Irish descent, suffused his writing with a strong note of American patriotism and praised the glories of America to the intending Irish emigrants.[41] Not all priests in America shared the cardinal's sentiments, and all during the half century warnings from them on the dangers of emigration were published in Irish papers. In 1855, for example, at the height of the Know-

Nothing movement, one priest in America proclaimed to his coreligionists in Ireland, "For every individual you keep, you snatch a soul from hell." At the turn of the century the bishop of Syracuse, New York, returned to his hometown in County Mayo and spoke to the assembled townsmen of the awful dangers of American city life — "the most terrible since the days of Babylon and ancient Rome." [42]

If there is any single index to the general attitude of the Irish Catholic clergy, it is probably found in a very small group of newspapers, the first of which began publication in 1853 and claimed to have the support of the Catholic clergy and laity throughout the United Kingdom.[43] Although the Irish Catholic Church never officially proclaimed them as its spokesmen, these papers nevertheless spoke in authoritative accents, and the archbishop of Tuam used them as his personal vehicle in the 1860s. They may therefore be considered as at least quasi-official spokesmen.

Their views did not differ markedly from those expressed by the archbishops of Dublin and Tuam. Emigration, they declared, was a movement of the unemployed seeking employment, but even more it was the result of a defective system of land laws which left the people to the tender mercies of "landlord heartlessness, oppression, and cupidity." It was a movement, moreover, that would continue so long as the country remained under the "upas-like influence of the present landlord laws," a bitter retort to Gladstone's famed "upas tree" allusion to Ireland. By the turn of the century emigration was bluntly called the "baleful result of British misgovernment." As to its effect on Ireland, it represented a terrible melting away of the rural and laboring population which could only be considered a "fearful and ruinous drain." For the emigrants it was worse still, a disastrous venture by which their religion in the United States would be plagued by the "lures of infidelity" and the "weeds of mammon-worship," and where they themselves would be corrupted and drawn into the "vortex of sin and depravity."[44]

To stop the emigration the British government was beseeched to rectify the land laws before it was "too late," and the introduction of industry was strongly recommended. But toward the end of the century it came to be felt that only home rule could stem the tide. Earlier it was even felt that nothing could effectively stop the emigration, and concern was fixed upon how best to minister to the religious needs of those who were leaving. The obvious answer was missionaries to accompany or follow the emigrants. On this point the Irish clergy needed no reminding from the *Belfast News-Letter* which taunted that priests did not accompany the emigrants because they knew full well that their power over their flocks lost its "talismanic efficacy" the moment they left their native soil.[45] As early as 1842 a seminary was established in Dublin for the specific purpose of training Irish priests as missionaries for America and other English-speaking countries in which Irish emigrants settled. The seminary, All Hallows, tried as best it could to meet the increasing demand for Irish priests and in the century following its founding sent out more than a thousand to the United States.[46]

Although the large body of Catholic clergy were generally opposed to emigration in principle, many not only recognized its necessity in specific instances but even sought means whereby assistance might be extended to those who had already emigrated or were about to do so. The help offered was not confined to the spiritual realm; it embraced practical matters as well. This practical desire to help found one of its most useful expressions in a number of emigrant guides or letters published in local newspapers. They furnished the intending emigrants with all sorts of information as to necessary preparations and precautions to be taken before embarking, as well as suggestions on what to do, where to go, and how to act in America. These particular guides and letters were written by Irish priests who had traveled or lived in the United States.

Among those who provided their information in the form of letters to newspapers were the Reverends Alexander J. Peyton and Daniel W. Cahill. Peyton, a parish priest in County Cork, was the earlier of the two and made a trip to the United States in 1851-52. He traveled extensively throughout the country and upon his return in 1852 published a long series of letters in the *Cork Examiner*. Although he took pains to point out the dangers of emigrating to America, the picture he painted was a generally favorable one and his letters became so popular that the following year he brought them out in pamphlet form. Peyton by no means wished to encourage emigration and urged that those who could live at home would "do well to remain quiet and contented." But this advice, he feared, was something very few would believe until they had "experience to the contrary."[47]

The Reverend Daniel W. Cahill was a well-known lecturer and prolific pamphleteer in Ireland long before he left for the United States in 1859. He remained in the country until his death some five years later and managed, in the first two years of his sojourn, to travel widely and send back a series of fortnightly letters containing his impressions and observations. All were faithfully published by the *Catholic Telegraph* and the entire series ran to fifty-seven letters. Cahill had a truly catholic curiosity, and although his letters were written ostensibly as advice for intending emigrants, they really formed an admiring commentary on American society on the brink of civil war.

Probably the best-known guide of the period was written by the Reverend John O'Hanlon, an Irish priest who lived in the United States for a considerable part of his adult life. The guide first made its appearance in Boston in 1851 and was originally intended for the famine Irish who were then crowding into that and other eastern cities. It was well written and went through many editions but was not published in Ireland until forty years later.[48] Although many copies were ordered from the United States prior to that date and some were sent home by emigrants already there, it was doubtless better known and more widely distributed among the Irish in America. However, the point to be remembered about its author, as well as the authors of the letters, is that here were priests who while personally not wishing to encourage emigration, nevertheless probably helped the movement along merely by providing information on America. For inevitably, even the barest recital of the vastness and the resources of America left an indelible impression of boundless opportunity which was hardly counterbalanced by the repeated cautions and warnings of the dangers of emigrant life in the United States.

Over the course of the entire half-century there were few who were not moved by the spectacle of the relentless flow westward of Irish men and women. The press, as the most articulate element in the steadily shrinking society, protested in the most vigorous terms. The clergy, though equally concerned, were less forceful in their protestations. Together they represented the most important molders of public opinion in Ireland, but the human clay they were attempting to fashion was possessed of a will stronger than their own. It was from self-interest the former objected; it was from self-interest the latter emigrated. The two were not synonymous and the protest that rang out from press and pulpit was a futile one.

IV

The Visible Result: Land and Labor

IN A COUNTRY LIKE IRELAND, where emigration has been a perpetual phenomenon for over a century, it was inevitable that the question should arise as to whether the nation was the gainer or the loser by it. The question not only arose, but was frequently the subject of vigorous and sometimes passionate debate. Too often, however, the issues were clouded with unedifying flights of rhetoric which were well calculated to gratify the emotions but contributed little to clarifying the question. It is only in recent years that rational inquiry has increasingly replaced impassioned oratory.

Foremost in any discussion of the impact of emigration on Ireland's economic structure must be the consideration of land. Many contemporaries and most newspapers of the later nineteenth century sincerely believed that with Ireland preeminently an agricultural country, the continued exodus from the rural areas could only have the most disastrous results for the land system. Not only were the small tenant farmers leaving en masse and thereby drastically reducing the number of small farms, it was also contended that the untilled land was being converted into pasture or worse still, being allowed to revert to waste. Emigration was draining the countryside of its agricultural laborers and leaving farmers little alternative but to convert their farms into grazing fields. Such developments were universally deplored, and it was unquestioningly assumed that a transition from tillage to pasture was necessarily detrimental to the best interests of

Ireland's agrarian economy. To what extent were these fears justified and to what degree was emigration responsible for the rapidly changing pattern of Irish agriculture? To answer these questions it is necessary to look more closely at the changes wrought in the system of Irish landholding and land use.

The most dramatic transformation in the total configuration of Irish landholding occurred during the decade of the 1840s, a period also of the heavy famine emigration. In 1841 over 80 percent of all farms in the country were concentrated in holdings of under fifteen acres; ten years later the proportion had dropped to less than 50 percent. During that decade also the number of holdings of fifteen acres and above rose from less than 20 percent to over 50 percent. In effect the character of this change represented an extensive elimination of the small garden farms held by the laboring classes (usually on conacre) and a sweeping reduction of the cotter tenantry. Over the course of the following fifty years farms of under fifteen acres declined by only 17 percent while those of over fifteen acres rose by a mere 7 percent.[1]

It is clear therefore that during the 1840s emigration and the alteration in the pattern of Irish landholding were closely related to one another. The nature of that relationship is not susceptible of any exact definition, and the best that can be said is that emigration was both cause and effect of the sharp decline in the number of small farms. The famine was the prime mover of that period, and many of the laborers and cotters who left did so because hunger, or the workhouse, faced them at home. Their departure meant the abandonment of the numerous small patches of ground upon which they had barely managed to eke out their subsistence. It was this abandonment which greatly facilitated the movement toward consolidation, a movement duplicated on a larger scale throughout rural Britain.

However, this was also a period of widespread forced clearances. Irish landlords, long distressed by the uneconomic practice of excessive subdivision indulged in by their tenants, and anxious also under the impact of the repeal of the corn laws to convert their lands to pasture as rapidly as possible, saw in the calamity of the famine an opportunity to consolidate their holdings. The large-scale clearances which they carried out further swelled the emigrant flood. The timing of these clearances was most unfortunate, for coinciding as they did with the terrors of the famine, they added measurably to the acute distress already prevailing throughout the country and imbedded in the hearts of the emigrants a hatred which rankled long after the Atlantic had been crossed. Thus the increases in larger holdings in the 1840s came about largely through the consolidation of the smaller ones, although in many cases the occupants of the larger farms were men who had been tenants of the smaller ones.[2]

The changes in landholding which took place in the fifty-year period following the famine were much less significant, and their relationship to emigration was less clear. The lack of correlation is most strikingly seen in comparisons with specific provinces and counties. Normally it would be expected that Munster, the province which suffered most heavily in population loss during the half-century, would also show the sharpest decline in holdings of under fifteen acres, while the reverse should be true for Ulster, the province with the smallest decline in population. The statistics reveal no such trend. The number of small holdings in Munster fell by only 16.6 percent while those in Ulster diminished by 25 percent. For the nation as a whole the decline was 17 percent. The same anomaly is found on a county level. Cork, the county which suffered the greatest drain on its population, experienced a decline of 17 percent in holdings of under fifteen acres while Wicklow, one of the counties with the least loss of people, suffered a drop of 19.5 percent. Plainly, once the initial impetus of the famine and the impulse to abandon land had passed, emigration had a less direct influence on the slowly changing pattern of Irish landholding.[3] The desire to own land reasserted itself in all its former vigor, and competition for its possession remained as keen as ever.

The transformation wrought in land use was no less important, and in some respects more striking, than that brought about in landholding. In addition, emigration appears to have been more closely related to the latter development than to the former, although too precise a correlation is difficult to establish. The facts are that from 1851 to the end of the century the total area under cultivation, excluding hay, shrank by 50 percent while the area devoted to meadow rose by more than 65 percent. Interpretations as to the significance of these figures have varied greatly. To C. H. Oldham and Thomas Kennedy they were indicative of a net economic loss and irrefutable evidence of national decay. To T. W. Grimshaw, registrar-general in the 1890s, and R. C. Geary, his more recent successor as chief of the Irish Central Statistics Office, they were proof of Ireland's increasing prosperity.[4]

The arguments offered by Grimshaw and Geary are interesting exercises in the uses of statistical techniques and merit further elaboration. Dr. Grimshaw devised a scale of simple ratios between rural population on the one hand and arable and pasture land on the other. By this device he was able to show that after 1841, as population decreased, the proportion of land per person steadily increased so that by 1891 the ratio of land per rural person was double what it had been fifty years earlier. This, he claimed, was progress since the country population of Ireland had "twice as much land per person to depend upon as it had in 1841."[5] Unfortunately he failed to consider whether all classes, those with small as well as large farms, benefited from the increasing ratio.

Dr. Geary's thesis is equally intriguing and somewhat more sophisticated. Having constructed a scale of stock valuation in relation to per capita rural population, he proceeded to show that after 1841, as population declined and cattle increased, there was also a remarkable rise in the per capita valuation of stock until by 1911 it was more than five times what it had been seventy years before. This was proof, he declared, that "more wealth remained for those who stayed at home."[6] Dr. Geary, however, like his predecessor, did not undertake to determine how evenly this wealth was distributed among the various classes which comprised the total rural population.

The important aspect to be considered here is the degree to which emigration may be held responsible for the great reduction in tillage and the equally marked increase in pasture and cattle. T. W. Freeman has noted that between 1841 and 1891 the rural population declined by one half and concluded that this decline was "very closely related" to the changing emphasis in farming. The generalization, though substantially valid, needs clarification. During the generation 1854-74 the greatest decrease in tillage by far occurred on holdings of one hundred acres and more. Since it was on holdings of this size that the largest numbers of agricultural laborers were employed, it was these holdings which suffered most seriously from the emigration of the agricultural population. The correlation is most clearly seen in the thirty-year period prior to 1881, when the relationship between decline in tillage and decline in rural population was extremely close. Where rural population decreased most, the area ploughed shrank the most; where rural population declined the least, the area ploughed shrank the least. In eighteen Poor Law unions,* for example, a decline of almost 35 percent in the rural population was accompanied by a reduction of nearly 60 percent in ploughed land. In twenty-four Poor Law unions where the fall in rural population was less than 15 percent, the decrease in ploughed land was less than 10 percent.[7]

After 1881 the interconnection became less pronounced, although at the turn of the century it was still declared that land was being laid down to grass because labor was scarce and dear. In twenty-four Poor Law unions where population declined by 27 percent during this later period, the area ploughed diminished by 44 percent, whereas in fourteen Poor Law unions where rural population fell by 23 percent the area ploughed decreased by only 5 percent. For the country as a whole it has been shown that when population was falling fast, tillage fell more than proportionately to population, and when population was falling more slowly, tillage fell less than proportionately to population.[8]

Rural emigration, however, was not the only factor which led to the decline in tillage; economic considerations also played a part. The revolution that took place in Irish agriculture in the fifty years following the famine was in effect a transition from the production of cereals to the production of animal products, or more correctly the raising of animals. By the turn of the century Ireland had become a great breeding ground for livestock, especially cattle. The movement was essentially a rational one and developed very largely under the impulse of price stimuli.[9] It was the continued increase in cattle prices, which resulted from Britain's growing reliance on Irish beef to feed her expanding industrial population, that led Irish farmers to abandon tillage for the more profitable and less arduous occupation of raising cattle. Over the course of the half-century, therefore, it would appear

---

* An artificial administrative unit created by the Poor Law commissioners. It varied in size from one to several counties and frequently transcended county boundaries.

that the rising price index for cattle was at least as important in accounting for the increase in pasture as was the continuous drain on the agricultural laboring population.

In this connection it is pertinent to observe that in the period prior to 1874 the greatest increases in cattle occurred on the smaller farms, not the largest ones. This fact tends to disprove the contention of a good many newspapers which continually complained that the rural exodus was caused by the large landholders who forced the tenants off their small holdings so that they could consolidate the land for pasturage. Although some emigration after the famine was undoubtedly caused by such consolidations, the statistics indicate that prior to 1874, at least, cattle were increasing at a much faster rate on small farms than on large ones, there being no increase at all on farms of over five hundred acres. Increases on holdings of five to thirty acres varied from 29 percent to 35 percent, while on those of fifty to five hundred acres it varied from 23 percent to 26 percent.[10] Apparently small farmers were even more responsive to the rising market price for cattle and abandoned tillage almost as quickly as the large ones. Whatever contribution consolidation may have made to the emigrant stream, it was far less important than that complex host of personal desires and decisions which operated on an individual level to produce a constant stream of voluntary emigrants.

The above figures also tend to support Dr. Geary's thesis of increasing rural wealth, for with larger increases in cattle on the smaller holdings it is evident that the position of the small tenants, as measured by a per capita valuation of stock, was improving at a proportionately faster rate than was true for the larger landholders. But after 1874 the situation altered drastically. From that date until 1912 only the very largest farmers witnessed significant increases in cattle while smaller ones saw practically none. Moreover, tillage on smaller farms in this period fell three to four times faster than it did on large ones. The cream of accumulating wealth floated to the top and only those at the apex of the economic pyramid enjoyed the pleasure of skimming it off. The gulf between the larger and smaller farms became an ever-widening one. While this illustrates the worsening position of the great body of small-tenant farmers and helps explain their readiness to support the Land League with its advocacy of extralegal methods, it also means that for these years Dr. Geary's thesis is untenable. The sudden rise in emigration in the early 1880s which resulted from the crop failures of those years is indicative of how precarious the level of living still was for a great body of the peasantry.

Second in importance to the land problem is the question of labor and whether it was substantially affected by emigration. In Ireland this meant primarily agricultural labor. Here again opinion differed widely regarding the beneficial as opposed to the detrimental effects of the exodus. Those on the negative side were many. As early as 1854 one Poor Law inspector in the west of Ireland reported that despite a considerable diminution in the number of workmen there was very little increase in the general rate of wages for agricultural laborers. From Cork, Kerry, Limerick, and Clare that same year came reports that although wages had risen, so had the price of food, and the wage increase, it was said, bore little relation to the advance in price of the necessaries of life. The *Newry Examiner*, on the other hand, was convinced that wages would rise so high as a result of the emigration that it would upset the scale of rents and lead to the ruin of small farms. More than a decade later the manager of several large estates in Ireland admitted to a parliamentary committee that emigration had raised wages but promptly informed them that in his opinion the rise was not sufficient to affect the "wholesome condition" of the laboring population because laborers still did not have constant and regular employment. At the very end of the century, C. H. Oldham, looking back over fifty years of continuous emigration, asserted that because of it "The farmer has, today, to pay more wages for a less efficient workman. . ."[11]

Adherents of the opposite view were just as numerous. John Locke, the Rathmines pamphleteer, was convinced in 1853 that emigration "blesses him that stays, and him that goes" because it improved those who left and raised the wages of those who remained. The lord lieutenant of Ireland writing the following year to Lord Aberdeen, then prime minister of England, assured him that emigration had had a "sensible and direct effect on wages, in itself a visible source of improvement," a view concurred in several years later by the emigration commissioners and the Poor Law commissioners. One clergyman felt certain that the effects of emigration were of the "greatest benefit" to the laboring classes and William Donnelly, then registrar-general, saw in it evidence of Ireland's increasing material prosperity. Indeed, asked one Irishman of his compatriots, if emigration has led to a rise in wages, "why should we affect to lament what has conferred a lasting and solid advantage on our countrymen?" Lord Dufferin, that self-appointed spokesman for Irish landlords, positively "rejoiced" that emigration had forced him to pay higher wages because he was "above all things, an Irishman," and anything which strengthened the independence of the tenant farmer or added to the comforts of the laborer's existence could not but please him. Some four years later the *Irish Times*, noting a 50 percent increase in wages during the 1860s and an absence of any similar increase in the price of basic necessities, concluded that emigration had improved the "average condition" of the population and deemed it an "egregious fallacy" to equate a reduction in numbers with a retrogression in national well-being.[12]

Statistics on Irish wages are unfortunately very deficient so that a correlation with emigration over a long period of years is not possible. There can be little doubt that wages rose significantly during the course of the half-century, but with incomplete statistics, especially for those years immediately succeeding the peak emigration periods, an attempt to relate them to emigration is exceedingly difficult. The only run of successive years is 1893-94-95, with 1895 being one of the minor peaks in emigration. In view of the fact that wages appear to have dropped in 1895 it seems probable that they were a contributory cause, not a result, of that year's high emigration. The other consecutive years for which figures are available are 1880-81. Although 1880 was a peak emigration year, the wages for 1881 marked no advance. This suggests that wages had little to do with the emigration of 1880, which was more likely the direct result of a series of severe crop losses, and it also suggests that in spite of the heavy emigration of 1880, wages the following year were little affected by it because of the prevailing distress in agriculture.

Regardless of the incomplete figures, however, there is evidence that between 1843-44 and 1860 the wages of agricultural laborers rose by more than 57 percent and this, it has been maintained, was mainly attributable to emigration. A. L. Bowley, the foremost student of the problem, concluded that over the course of the half-century emigration operated to the benefit of the laborers. Before 1870, he pointed out, work was unobtainable for a great part of the year. By the middle of the 1890s work was not only available, but wages were higher and food cheaper. The condition of the laborer had witnessed a considerable improvement and emigration, he felt, could take a large share of the credit.[13]

Emigration did more than contribute to a rise in wages. By reducing the number of laborers it had other effects as well, although not all were agreed that these were entirely beneficial. The commonest complaint was that there would not be enough laborers left to help with the planting and harvesting, and as early as 1851 there were reports of the difficulty of obtaining agricultural laborers. A generation later, according to one contemporary, it was "all but impossible" to get extra hands at harvest time in spite of increased wages. In the following decade a County Cork farmer testified that as a result of the labor shortage farmers employed no laborers at all and cultivated no more land than "their own help" (that is, family) enabled them to do, a circumstance, he stated, which forced them to keep the rest of their land in grass.[14]

Emigration also led to a depletion in the ranks of domestic servants, and this fact was noted by the Poor Law commissioners in 1854. Some years before, Nassau Senior recorded in his journal the personal inconveniences emigration was causing one individual who complained that he could not hold on to his servants. About thirty years later the London *Times* correspondent reported from Donegal that female domestic servants were becoming "scarcer every day" because as soon as they had saved up enough money for their passage they went out to America "in search of service and husbands." Somewhat less generous was the *Tuam Herald* which felt that no sooner did young girls attain working age than away they went to "slave and scrub and stifle in American cities."[15]

Offsetting the inconveniences occasioned by the diminishing number of laborers and domestic servants was the fact that for those who remained there resulted a degree of regularity in employment that had seldom been known. As early as 1850 the manager of the Provincial Bank of Ireland informed the lord lieutenant that if emigration had not raised wages, it had at least made labor more steady in some districts and more abundant in others and he only wished that that state of affairs were more general. His optimism was borne out a few years later by the emigration commissioners who noted that although wages were still at a minimum, more people were receiving them and unemployment was considerably reduced. They were seconded by the Poor Law commissioners, who reported that throughout Ireland there was a more continuous state of employment for male agricultural workers as well as for female domestic servants. More than a decade afterward, constancy of employment was again stressed as one of the two main advantages derived from emigration, the other being a rise in wages. By the end of the century A. L. Bowley thought the greater regularity of employment a more important result even than the increase in wages.[16]

The improvement in the general rate of wages coupled with a more continuous state of employment had still another effect: it tended to reduce pauperism, at least in the early 1850s. The Poor Law commissioners were aware of this in 1851 when they had no doubt that the "mainly operative cause of the depletion of the Workhouses . . . [was] the increased demand for labour, consequent on the drain produced by emigration." Several years later the Poor Law inspector for counties Kilkenny, Wexford, and Waterford definitely linked the decline in pauperism directly to emigration which, he declared, "reduced the number in the Workhouses, and insured work for those who remain." By 1857, however, the commissioners began to note that the effect of emigration in reducing pauperism was much less marked than in previous years and seven years later felt that the effect had become extremely slight. By then the series of acute crop losses in the early 1860s had so increased distress that even the heavy emigration of those years could not empty the workhouses any faster than they were being filled.[17]

Over the long sweep of the half-century, however, there does not appear to be any significant relationship between emigration and pauperism. A glance at Figure 2 (page 80) will help make this clear. During the famine period both emigration and pauperism rose precipitously, and in 1852 the percentage of the population in workhouses was 2.6. There then followed a sharp decline in the number of paupers which was paralleled by a similarly steep fall in emigration. For the next forty years the curves for pauperism and emigration were characterized by features that were common to both. The troughs in emigration in the

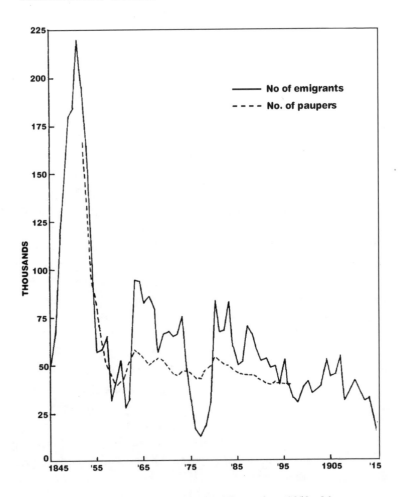

Figure 2. Irish Emigration and Pauperism, 1852 - 96
(Based on Appendix Tables 1 and 15)

1850s and 1870s were matched by corresponding, though less pronounced, troughs in pauperism. The peaks of the 1860s and 1880s were also coincident in each. At no time was there an inverse relationship of such a magnitude as to suggest that a significant rise in emigration led to a noteworthy decline in pauperism. This relationship existed to some extent in the immediate postfamine years, as the Poor Law commissioners indicated, but for the remainder of the period it appears that both curves were more directly reflections of Ireland's fluctuating economy than they were of each other.

Pauperism rose faster and fell quicker than did emigration, but only because unemployment was more immediately responsive to changing economic conditions. Despite the heavy emigration the number of paupers in 1895, though numerically less than in 1860, still represented a higher proportion of the total population than did the 1860 figure. At the turn of the century that ardent Celtophile, L. Paul-Dubois, argued that emigration had scarcely diminished pauperism at all and strongly implied that by removing the young and leaving the old, it might even have increased it.[18] The point, however, was more worthy of his Celtic sentiment than his Gallic scholarship, for it can be argued just as forcefully that had there been no emigration the workhouses would have been even fuller than they were, a matter upon which he chose not to speculate.

Another yardstick by which to measure the material welfare of those who remained may be found in the statistics on the number of inhabited houses in the country and the types of accommodation available for the people. For Ireland as a whole the number of inhabited houses fell from a peak of over 1,300,000 in 1851 to less than 900,000 in 1901, a drop of over 35 percent. In that same sixty-year period population diminished by more than 45 percent. On a provincial basis the correlation between house decline and population decline is also apparent, although not uniform. In the 1840s, when Connaught's population decreased the fastest with a rate of nearly 29 percent, the number of inhabited houses in that province fell by more than 30 percent. For the remainder of the century it was generally the case that the province which lost population quickest also saw the heaviest drop in inhabited houses. The one notable exception occurred during the decade 1871-81 when Ulster lost her population at a greater rate than any of the other three provinces although her decline in houses was only half that of Munster's. Nevertheless for Ulster it meant the heaviest house decline of the entire half-century and was more than twice her decline of the previous decade.[19]

These figures, however, are meaningless unless some analysis is made of the types of houses they represented and the proportion of families who occupied them. T. W. Grimshaw, registrar-general in the

1890s, defined four classes of inhabited houses and also four classes of house accommodation.[20] In terms of his classification he made clear that between 1841 and 1891 first-class houses increased by more than 75 percent as did second-class houses, while third-class houses diminished by over 40 percent and fourth-class ones by more than 90 percent. The last figure really represented the disappearance of the omnipresent mud cabins which were so largely occupied by the famine-stricken peasantry.

When it came to living accommodations, the registrar-general resorted to a bit of clever statistical deception, so eager was he to convince his readers that Ireland had benefited from emigration. In absolute numbers his table indicated that between 1841 and 1891 there were considerable decreases in third- and fourth-class accommodations and correspondingly significant increases in first- and second-class accommodations.[21] By measuring fourth-class accommodations in 1891 against what they had been in 1841 he was able to announce an impressive reduction to about one twelfth the earlier figure, while with third-class accommodations he "proved" a decline of over 37 percent. Similarly, he pointed out that first-class accommodations had doubled since 1841 and that second-class ones had nearly done so.

Dr. Grimshaw overstated his case. For his figures really to be meaningful he should have measured not the absolute reductions in each type accommodation, but the proportion of families occupying each type in any given period against the total number of families in that period. Analyzed on this basis it is evident that while the absolute number of fourth-class accommodations did indeed diminish by over 90 percent between 1841 and 1891, the proportion of families occupying such accommodations fell from 42 percent to about 6 percent, a smaller though substantial decline of 36 percent. The significance of the changes in third-class accommodations, on the other hand, were considerably less important than the registrar-general would have us believe. In absolute numbers he indicated that they fell by 37 percent. What he failed to mention was that the proportion of families living in such accommodations changed hardly at all: 39 percent of all families in Ireland in 1841 had third-class accommodations, 38 percent did in 1891.

Much more important were the increases that took place in first-

and second-class accommodations. Dr. Grimshaw calculated that in absolute terms the one had doubled and the other nearly had. From the population point of view, it appears that while 2 percent of all families had first-class accommodations in 1841, only about 7 percent had them in 1891. Thus only 5 percent more of the population enjoyed the doubled number of first-class accommodations at the later date. As for second-class accommodations, 16 percent of all families occupied them in 1841 and about 49 percent in 1891, an appreciable increase of 33 percent.

The true significance of these figures, therefore, lies not in the measure of absolute decrease or increase in house accommodations, but in the impressive fact that before the famine close to half the population lived in the one-roomed squalor of windowless mud huts, while fifty years later nearly half the people were enjoying the comparative comfort of second-class accommodations. This is evidence enough that there had been a decided improvement in living conditions for a considerable proportion of the population, notwithstanding – and more likely because of – the fact that the total number of families in the country had been reduced by 37 percent.

With somewhat greater regularity of employment, higher wages, and more comfortable living conditions, it would be natural to assume that these improvements would be reflected on a national scale. Yet so logical an assumption is not entirely borne out by the economic facts. In the field of Irish finance, for example, it has been pointed out that declining population was the central factor in accounting for an adverse situation. Whereas in the United Kingdom increasing population coupled with increasing prosperity helped contribute to the great increase in revenue, in Ireland the declining population served to counterbalance any economic advance. The result was not only a stationary level of revenue for Ireland, but also an increased rate of taxation for each person. In Great Britain taxation per head increased by less than two and one-half shillings between 1850 and 1860 despite the added expenditure of the Crimean War, and in 1870 sank to a point two shillings less than it was twenty years before. During that same period taxation per head in Ireland rose by eleven shillings and continued to increase for the remainder of the century.[22]

The changes which took place in the character and composition of the total Irish labor force have also been viewed as disadvantageous, if not distinctly harmful. For one thing the proportion of employed to dependent population varied little over the course of the half-century; 44.3 percent of the population was classed as employed and 55.7 percent as dependent in 1841; fifty years later the figures were 44.7 percent and 55.3 percent. Among the employed portion, moreover, the proportion of those engaged in productive industry (that is, agriculture, fishing, mining, building, and manufacture) steadily fell from 80.6 percent in 1841 to 64.8 percent in 1891, while those in nonproductive or nonindustrial occupations rose from 15.1 percent to 20.6 percent. In the productive occupations alone these percentages represented an absolute reduction of over a million and a half people, most of it concentrated in the field of agriculture. To C. H. Oldham this was nothing less than "startling" evidence of an "economic decadence" that had taken place in the quality of employment among the Irish people. As he viewed the problem it meant that the "direct wealth producers" in 1891 were maintaining an army more than twice as numerous as themselves, an army which was either totally unemployed or only "indirectly productive."[23]

It is doubtless true that in certain specific instances the labor drain caused by emigration had harmful effects. The *Limerick Reporter*, for example, contended that emigration had led to the ruin of the lace and woolen industries in that city because of the shortage of laborers it had caused. And the ubiquitous London *Times* reporter wrote from Galway that the lack of workers occasioned by emigration was seriously retarding the growth of a jute factory there, the second largest in Ireland. Aside from these isolated instances, however, Oldham's fears do not really seem justified. While it is true that the greatest reduction in the labor force occurred in the agricultural realm, it must be asked whether the large numbers so engaged in 1841 represented a profitable utilization of available manpower. Surely the evidence of excessive subdivision, subsistence living, and inconstant employment were strong testimony to the contrary. If there were less people in agriculture in 1891, agriculture was certainly on a sounder economic footing than it was fifty years before. The employment of as many people at the end of the century could have been accomplished only by a regression to subsistence farming which had proved so disastrous in the grim years of the famine. Faced with this alternative, one Irish economic historian was forced to the reluctant conclusion that perhaps it was better "to have four millions living as the people do now, than eight millions living on the verge of want."[24]

In perspective, there can be little doubt that the overall impact of emigration on the Irish economy was generally favorable. To some extent it relieved the pressure of unemployment and improved the condition of the laborers and tenantry by raising wages and leading to better living accommodations for a larger proportion of the population. It also facilitated the consolidation of small holdings and helped place agriculture on a more economic basis. In addition it made possible a transition in Irish agriculture which can justly be described as revolutionary. Whether in itself it appreciably retarded the development of Irish industry is doubtful since the fiscal and commercial policy of Great Britain operated as a far greater deterrent.[25]

In 1851 the London *Spectator* wondered whether North America might not become to Great Britain and Ireland what the American Far West, it assumed, was to Massachusetts and New York, that is, an equalizing safety valve; in this instance, a safety valve which would equalize profits and wages on both sides of the Atlantic. Were that to come to pass, it mused, there was a chance of social changes "in comparison with which . . . the greatest constitutional or dynastic revolutions may be deemed insignificant."[26] The changes actually wrought by emigration in Ireland's social economy may not quite have measured up to the enthusiastic expectations of the *Spectator*, but neither can it be said that they were insignificant.

V

The Invisible Result: Cant and Custom

Emigration has been so persistent a phenomenon in modern Irish history that its influence has penetrated areas of Irish life which are not susceptible of measurement by charts or columns of statistics. These were the repercussions which manifested themselves in the cant,* customs, legends, and ballads of the people of rural Ireland. In one form or another, emigration became a part of their daily consciousness. They talked about it, they sang about it, they even celebrated it. A proper analysis of the extent to which this cultural and folkloristic reaction pervaded Irish living would be worthy of a book in itself, and the best that can be done here is to indicate some of the more significant developments in this important albeit neglected field.

The ordinary crises faced by most human beings, such as birth, marriage, and death, are celebrated everywhere by some sort of ritual and the variations in these rituals often reveal something of the emotional mosaic which gives to each group its own stamp of uniqueness. The folkways and folk customs of the Irish, as is true with all people, are reflections of their pattern of living and express, in a stylized form, the joys, sorrows, hopes, and fears they have known and felt. This body

---

*The word "cant" as used by the Irish refers to general expressions which are peculiar to certain areas, much in the manner of colloquialisms or provincialisms, and carries no implication or connotation of hypocrisy, insincerity, or impiety. For the purposes of this book the term "cant" has been used in its Irish sense.

of folk tradition is an organic thing that grows and develops in response to those problems that are peculiar to each community. One of the most pressing problems of nineteenth-century Ireland was emigration, and it is therefore not surprising that so personally poignant a phenomenon should have found expression in the cant and custom of the Irish country people.[1]

Perhaps the most interesting custom that developed out of the century-old emigration to America was the "American wake," a custom which was unique to Ireland. Nothing comparable seemed to develop in England or Germany, two countries that also contributed heavily to American immigration in the latter half of the nineteenth century. The practice of "waking" (that is, watching) the dead had its origins in Irish antiquity. Essentially it meant watching by the corpse all through the night until burial time the next day. This night-long vigil was supposed to ward off evil spirits and prevent them from entering the body.

With the advent of Christianity the custom became less purely pagan and took on a degree of Christian religious ritual, such as the lighting of candles near the bed and the frequent sprinkling of holy water about the room. But the pagan element remained, and as a result the custom was frequently denounced from the altar. It was not the "waking" itself that the clergy so much objected to as the general revelry which always accompanied the occasion. This combination of mourning and merrymaking, which has been well described by William Carleton, the nineteenth-century Irish novelist, struck the priests as shockingly irreligious. They were determined to stamp it out and, after strenuous efforts, finally realized their goal in the early twentieth century when the custom became much less prevalent, although it has not disappeared completely.[2]

The wake, however, has not been without its defenders. It has been maintained, for example, that the Irish are an extremely gregarious people, and that more than at any other time they feel the need for companionship when death has visited them closely. The demise of a member of a family impels that family to seek consolation from its neighbors who, "ever quick in sympathy . . . crowd in to cheer up the spirits of the bereaved, to distract their thoughts from their sad loss."[3] Hence the peculiar mixture of sadness and gaiety which characterized an Irish wake, and later, an "American wake." For the "American wake," while not actually occasioned by a real death, nevertheless became a symbol for it. In the early years of emigration especially, when distances seemed greater because travel was so much slower, the prospect of an emigrant ever returning was remote indeed. In such circumstances the departure for America of a young son or daughter represented to the parents no less final a loss than if he or she had been carried off by disease or accident, instead of by a sailing ship. It is thus understandable that the ceremony used to commemorate death should have been carried over and adapted to mark the occasion of an exit from family and community life that for all practical purposes was just as irrevocable. In those days, it has been remarked, "people made very little difference between going to America and going to the grave."[4]

One observer thought it not without significance that so funereal a name should be given to these emigration ceremonies, for in his view the Irish emigrant was not the "personification of national adventure, but of something that . . . [had] the appearance of national doom." To the *Irish People* this "queer mixture of frolic and lamentation" was a "ghastly institution," and the paper despaired that the country was rapidly becoming "one vast 'American Wake.'" The *Tuam Herald*, on the other hand, was more compassionate and understood that for those who took part in such "pathetic proceedings" it meant they were meeting for the last time and that "the separation was for life." Nevertheless, the journal appealed to the young people to "have fewer American wakes and more Irish weddings," and not be deluded by the "vain glitter and glamour of America."[5]

Exactly when the American wake came into being is not certain, but there is evidence that it was known and practiced at least as early as 1830. As the emigration movement assumed increasingly larger dimensions, the custom became more widespread so that by the time the famine emigration had subsided, the American wake was known in one form or another throughout the entire country. It was especially strong in the areas of heaviest emigration, that is, in the south and west and also in Donegal; it was less well known in Ulster and the counties along the eastern shore. Although in most places it was known simply as an "American wake," the name for it differed in some areas. In Kilkenny and Tipperary, for example, it was sometimes grimly referred to as a "live wake"; in Wexford it was a "parting spree"; in Derry and Antrim it was a "convoy"; in parts of Galway it was known in Irish as "the farewell supper"; to the Gaelic speakers of Mayo it was the "feast of departure"; and to the people of Donegal it was an "American bottle night" or "bottle drink."[6]

However much the local name may have varied, the custom itself remained pretty much the same. Normally an American wake started at nightfall on the evening before an emigrant was due to depart and lasted through the night until the early hours of the morning. The precise times varied according to the seasons of the year, the distance from the local railroad station, and the departure time of the train. If held during the fall or winter months it began at about eight o'clock, but if held during the spring or summer it did not begin until ten o'clock. Similarly, if the local railroad station was relatively distant and the train was scheduled to depart rather early, the wake might finish at four or five in the morning, whereas if distances were shorter and departure time later, it might last until seven or eight o'clock.

It was the practice that the day before the wake, or perhaps during the preceding week, the young emigrant would make the rounds of all his friends and neighbors in the community to let them know that he was leaving and to wish them goodbye. These visits constituted a sort of informal invitation to attend the wake, and all who were visited made it a point to be there. Sometimes the emigrant did not have an opportunity to visit everyone he wanted, but word of his leaving spread quickly and all who desired to attend were welcome to do so. In most areas these casual invitations were not absolutely necessary. It was understood that all who felt close to the emigrant were expected to put in an appearance. A point of honor was involved, and failure to do so would only be reciprocated with a similar snub when a like occasion arose in the future.

In the early years of heaviest emigration, that is, the 1850s and 1860s, American wakes were wont to be extremely somber affairs, particularly in the poorer districts of western Ireland. In areas of Mayo and Galway where poverty was most acute, many households could not afford even to serve the customary tea, let alone food, whiskey, and porter. Sometimes a few neighbors or relatives brought a small quantity of poteen (that is, a clear beverage of high alcoholic content, brewed illicitly from potatoes), but more often in these cases there were no refreshments at all.

These earlier American wakes were characterized also by an absence of dancing and ballad singing. They were occasions for serious conversation only, and people spent the evening talking of America and of friends who had already gone there, tendered advice to the young emigrant, and often requested him to carry messages to friends or loved ones. A retired police inspector, a native of County Mayo, recalled that an atmosphere of gloom and dejection permeated the evening, that heavy sighs were often heard coming from the womenfolk, and that the men silently smoked their pipes to relieve the "tadium [sic] and depression of the rather heartsore occasion." It was a wake in every sense of the word, he reflected, "though not of a dead person, but of a living one, who next day would be sailing for the promised land."[7]

At times an old woman of the community who was noted for her ability to keen (that is, from the Gaelic "caoine," meaning to wail or lament) would be called in and set to keening over the "dead" one. This took the form of a long, sorrowful eulogy upon the virtues of the emigrant and the suffering being inflicted both on him and his parents. It was delivered in a shrill, piercing voice that resembled a continuous high-pitched wail. The effect was irresistible, and before long the old keener was joined by a chorus of wailing women and weeping men, including the emigrant himself. American wakes of so stark a nature have been described as "harrowing affairs" characterized by displays of "naked grief" and "elemental emotions."[8]

The greater majority of American wakes, however, were somewhat more convivial in tone. For days in advance the women of the house were busy baking, cleaning, and cooking in preparation for the event. If the family happened to be poor, the neighbors often contributed eggs, tea, bread, and jam. A half barrel of porter or stout was provided for the men. If the family could not afford this themselves, each man brought his own refreshment, or else a general collection was taken up and drink purchased for all. This latter method was known as "lifting a cess" and was particularly common in Donegal. In some cases the entire expense for an American wake was sent from America along with the sailing ticket.[9]

On the night of the wake there was a gay, almost festive air in the house. The kitchen, usually the most spacious room in every house (and also the warmest), was cleared of all central furniture. Seats were placed all around the walls and a musician with fiddle or melodeon was called in. In cases of poorer families someone was chosen to "lilt" the tunes (that is, carrying a tune with the use of the tongue, forming syllables but not singing words, as la-la-la). When everybody had at last arrived, the elder folk seated themselves around the open hearth, the young people took the floor, the music commenced, and the dancing began, usually jigs, reels, quadrilles, hornpipes, and Irish step-dancing. Occasionally a turf dance was performed (that is, tying a piece of turf to the leg and then swinging it in and out between the legs in rhythm with the music). Between bouts of dancing songs were sung, and these in turn were followed by liberal servings of tea and stronger refreshments.

But the veneer of merriment was at best a paper-thin cover for the strong undercurrent of sadness, especially in the case of the parents for whom it represented only a momentary distraction. Often their sorrow broke through. One woman could remember a father turning to his son at an American wake and saying, "Get up here son and face me in a step for likely it will be the last step ever we'll dance." "At that," she recalled, "there wasn't a dry eye in the house."[10] Frequently the songs sung were also sad. They were generally ballads which told of the difficulties of parting, the loneliness of parents, and the hardships of emigrant life. The rendering of such a ballad was usually the signal for a general outburst of weeping and lamentation. (The ballads will be discussed more fully later on.) Perhaps the most trying moment of all came with the breaking of the dawn, when the time arrived for the emigrant to part with his parents and relations. Harriet Martineau happened upon such a scene while traveling through western Ireland in 1852 and has left a graphic description of this final parting:

> The last embraces were terrible to see; but worse were the kissings and the claspings of the hands during the long minutes that remained. . . . When we saw the wringing of hands and heard the wailings, we became aware, for the first time perhaps, of the full dignity of that civilization which induces control over the expression of emotions. . . . Still, there it was, the pain and the passion: and the shrill united cry, when the [horse] car moved on, rings in our

ears, and long will ring when we hear of emigration.[11]

Less literary but more pithy was the statement of a woman who remembered her own American wake in the early 1890s and the effect that it had had upon her. "It would not have been so bad," she said, "only in the morning everyone said so-long to you and you would know by them that they never expected to see you again. It was as if you were going out to be buried."[12]

When the emigrant finally left the house of his parents, it was generally the custom that the younger people present accompanied him or her to the railway station, or if that were too distant, to a particular hill or crossroads. This was known as the "convoy" and was a feature common to all American wakes. The purpose behind the "convoy" was to make the emigrant's last hours on Irish soil as cheerful as possible, although in some areas it was also thought to be lucky for the emigrant. In a few places the "convoy" lent its name to the whole of the American wake, but this was not very common. Another variation appeared in parts of County Kerry where the emigrant was labeled "Yankee" even before he left. Here the practice was known as "convoying the Yankee."[13]

At the railroad station another scene of grief was enacted between the emigrant, his friends, and his parents, if the latter also came along on the "convoy." Again the characteristic Irish wail dominated the proceedings:

> A deafening wail resounds as the station-bell gives the signal of starting. I have seen gray-haired peasants so clutch and cling to the departing child at this last moment that only the utmost force of three or four friends could tear them asunder. The porters have to use some violence before the train moves off, the crowd so presses against door and window. When at length it moves away, amidst a scene of passionate grief, hundreds run along the fields beside the line to catch yet another glimpse of the friends they shall see no more.[14]

Among the Scots of Ulster there seemed to have been a greater exercise of restraint. But if the grief was not so manifest, it was nonetheless real, a trait the Milligans noted in the 1880s.[15]

It was to avoid the ordeal of the American wake, the "convoy," and the final parting that young emigrants sometimes decided to steal away. In one case a young emigrant, fearing that the strain would prove too great for her mother, stole away while the wake was already in progress. In another instance a young girl did so several nights before the wake was to be held. She was the last remaining daughter, all her elder sisters having previously emigrated, and she wanted to avoid the distress that would be produced upon her parents.[16]

American wakes were important occasions for the people of rural Ireland, and they ranked in importance only slightly lower than birth, marriage, and death. Very often local events would be dated from the night of a particular person's American wake. Moreover the term "American wake" became a general cant phrase which was used to denote this type of emigration ceremony for all emigrants, regardless of where they were going. Thus even if people were emigrating to Australia, New Zealand, South Africa, or Canada, the function was still described as an "American wake." The principal exceptions were for those people who emigrated to England or Scotland, and for them no wakes were held at all. There was not the same finality about crossing the Irish Sea as there was in crossing the Atlantic Ocean, and it was assumed that those who went to England or Scotland would soon return.[17]

Gradually, as modern means of transportation reduced the time and danger of an Atlantic voyage, the somberness of the American wake began to wane. By the turn of the century it no longer seemed so remote a possibility that the emigrant would one day return, if only for a visit. As a result, the American wake more and more began to assume the character of a long farewell party. With the advent of World War I and the sharp contraction it brought about in emigration to America, followed in the next decade by the imposition of immigration restrictions by the United States, the American wake almost completely disappeared. One is still occasionally held today, but for the most part it exists only as a vivid memory among the old men and women of rural Ireland.[18]

If the American wake was the most colorful and best-known custom, it was not the only one to have arisen in response to emigration. For the Irish are by nature not only demonstrative and emotional, as is reflected in the American wake, they are a highly superstitious people as well. Fairies, banshees, and leprechauns are not lightly dismissed, as Conrad Arensberg has well shown.[19] On the contrary, they are treated with the greatest respect, for in the eyes of rural Irishmen it is courting disaster to underestimate their powers for good or evil. The Irish are also firm believers in the power of charms and in the earlier decades of emigration, when sailing ships were the only means of transportation, one such charm used in County Tyrone was "frog bread." This was prepared by killing, roasting, and pulverizing a frog, and then mixing the ashes with the oaten meal from which the emigrant's bread was made (that is, the bread the emigrant would be using as part of his provisions on his voyage to America). The "frog bread," it was believed, would keep the emigrant immune from fever.[20]

Another charm which was used had to do with drowning and its prevention. Popular belief had it that a child born with a caul (that is, an inner membrane enclosing the fetus before birth, a portion of which sometimes enveloped the head of a child at birth) was always safe from drowning. The caul was removed and preserved and if carried by anyone during a sea voyage was supposed to protect him against drowning.

Consequently when an emigrant was preparing to leave for America he would make inquiries through the neighborhood in the hope that he might be able to borrow a caul for his journey. After his safe arrival in America he would post it back to the owners to be used for someone else.[21]

In order to ensure the safe return and continuing love of an emigrant, love charms were sometimes used in certain districts of Ulster. If a young man happened to be the emigrant, some pubic hair from the girl he was leaving behind would be sewn surreptitiously into his clothing. On the other hand if the girl were the emigrant, a young sister or brother with whom she slept would be bribed or induced to procure some of her pubic hair, and this would then be worn by her lover on his genitals. Another type of love charm was used only by girls. Shortly before their lovers were about to emigrate, a small piece of linen was allowed to absorb some of her menstrual fluid and this was then secretly sewn into the garment of the emigrant. From that moment on, it was believed, his love would remain constant.[22]

More widespread than the use of charms was the coinage of a host of phrases and expressions regarding America which has enriched the vocabulary of the Irish down to the present day. Some of these expressons originated in Ireland in response to the emigration process or as a reaction to the American letters. Others either were introduced by "returned Yanks" or were coined to describe their behavior. Among those which originated in Ireland were two that were common in areas of County Clare and related to those who had large families. About such people it was said that "They would have to have a lot of American wakes, as the childer' would have to go to the States in turn," or that "They would make a priest of the second eldest boy, marry the oldest girl to a Peeler [that is, police constable] and send the whole shoot off to the States."[23] In some districts of County Kerry there was a kind of pride about the fact that the best of the young people emigrated, and it was often said that every boat leaving Ireland with a cargo of emigrants carried a potential world champion on board.[24]

Apart from the news they related, American letters were also looked forward to for the money they might contain. In some areas of western Ireland any person of means was said to be "as rich as two Yankee letters." In County Donegal, if something was obtained with very little effort, it was "like money from America" — the Irish version of manna from heaven. The note of optimism which characterized a large number of letters gave rise to an expression that was used in many areas. When asked how one was getting on, the response would often be "Oh fine, like the American letter." Although there is a suggestion of sarcasm here, it was usually said with no such intent. If anything, the expression was meant to mock the use of the word "fine," which was considered to be a typical Americanism; the normal Irish reply would have been "well" or "very well." America's reputed prosperity was not minimized, as is evident from the expressions used to describe those in Ireland who were well-to-do. About such people it was said, "Sure, they have America at home," or that they were "as well off as a Yankee." The integrity of American money also found its way into Irish speech, and it was sometimes said that a person was "as honest as the Yankee Dollar."[25]

The Yank who returned brought with him not only an accent but also a manner of speaking which the Irish tagged as full of

"Americanisms." In speaking to one another the Irish often indulged in good-natured mimicry of this "Yankee talk," punctuating their speech with "Well, I guess, as the Yank says"; "well, I calculate, as the Yank says"; "well, I reckon, as the Yank says."[26] These and others found their way into everyday conversation, but when used they were always qualified with the phrase, "as the Yank says." To have used such expressions without the qualifying ending would have been considered an affectation and would have been the immediate cause of derision and ridicule.

The theme of emigration also became the subject of innumerable ballads of the day. These were often crudely printed on broadsheets and hawked through the country for a penny a sheet. Sometimes itinerant ballad makers tried selling their own compositions, much in the fashion of peddlers. From a literary point of view the great majority of the ballads were poor poetry indeed, nor could they be considered as genuine folk songs since many were originated by professional ballad makers. But despite their failings in prosody and their inability to measure up as authentic folk compositions, they nevertheless reflected the feelings and attitudes of the Irish toward emigration. Their great numbers and popularity, especially at American wakes, is evidence of the extent to which emigration permeated the public consciousness.

The general mood of these emigration ballads was characterized by a pervasive note of sadness. Rarely did they have a happy story to tell. More often they told of the great sorrow felt by those who were left behind, especially parents. They exuded the nostalgia of the emigrant and his resolve one day to return to Ireland. Seldom did they speak of the success of an emigrant or of his eventual return. To him was usually attributed a life of loneliness, of homesickness, and a longing to return to his loved ones. America was praised for its freedom and for the work that was readily available:

A beautiful country, no matter what's said
For those who are able to earn their bread, [27]

but the life of the emigrant was not a happy one; he was, after all, in the land of the stranger.

There would appear to be something of a contradiction between the melancholia of the emigrant's fate as represented in these ballads, and the general note of happiness and satisfaction conveyed by the majority of letters the emigrants actually sent home. But the contradiction will be seen as only apparent, not real, if it is remembered that the ballads reflected primarily the reaction of those who remained. Upon them the effect was invariably melancholic, to say the least, and the portrayal of a discontented life in America was really the projection of their own melancholy. Emigration for them left unhappy memories and without the actual experience of new adventures in a new country to erase them, that mood remained the dominant one despite the letters. Moreover the numbers of returned emigrants were too few and came too late in life to effect a substantial change.

A closer examination of some of the ballads will more adequately convey their general tenor. On the causes of emigration they had a common theme. It was poor crops and lack of work that drove young people to exile, as is illustrated in the following stanza from "Farewell Old Erin":

> Farewell ye green hills and verdant valleys,
> Where I with my sweetheart did often rove,
> Where I vowed her I'd never leave here,
> Whilst walking sweetly through each silent grove.
> But times are changing and crops are failing,
> And causing thousands to go away,
> In deep emotion to cross the ocean,
> To seek their fortunes in America(y).[28]

Others spoke of the insufficiency of land and the "slavery" of the land system, best expressed perhaps in "The Emigrant's Farewell to Donegall":

> Farewell dear Erin, fare thee well, that once
> was call'd the Isle of Saints,
> For here no longer I can dwell, I'm going
> to cross the stormy sea.
> For to live here I can't endure, there's
> nothing but slavery,
> My heart's oppress'd, I can find no rest, I
> will try the land of liberty.

This Donegal emigrant then goes on to explain the reason for his "oppress'd" heart:

> My father holds 5 acres of land, it was not
> enough to support us all,
> Which banished me from my native land, to
> old Ireland dear I bid farewell.
> My holdings here I can't endure since here
> no longer I can stay.
> I take my lot and leave this spot and try the
> land of liberty.[29]

Only a few stressed eviction as the cause of leaving, as seen in this verse from "The Irishman's Farewell":

> On Irish soil my father dwelt since the time
> of Brian Boru,
> He paid his rent and lived content,
> convenient to Carrockonsure.
> The landlord's agent into our cabin went,
> and moved my poor father and me,
> But we must leave our home far away to
> roam in the fields of America.[30]

Each verse in this ballad was followed by a chorus which lamented:

> So farewell, I can no longer dwell at home acushla
> asthore machree [that is, beloved of my heart],
> Oh sad is my fate I must emigrate to the shores of
> America.

The pain of parting was best described in a stanza from a ballad which had a number of different versions and was variously known as "The Irish Emigrant" or "The Emigrant's Song":

> Tears from their eyes they are falling like rain,
> Horses are trotting, going off for the train,
> Their hearts they are breaking for leaving the shore,
> Their friends and green Erin they ne'er may see more.[31]

Perhaps the most poignant section of this or any other ballad was a little prayer offered up for Irish mothers and fathers. In a few simple lines it expressed the universal tragedy of the seeming inevitableness of Irish emigration:

> God keep all the mothers who rear up a child,
> And also the father who labours and toils.
> Trying to support them he works night and day,
> And when they are reared up, they then go away.[32]

Although it was the exceptional ballad that ever spoke of ultimate success in America, many held out the hope that in America employment was at least available and that thrift, industry, and hard work would bring their own rewards. Yet, while the lure of America was recognized and appreciated, it seemed more fitting that the sorrow of leaving should not be overshadowed by the joyful promise of a more abundant life. Thus in "The Shores of Americay" one emigrant sang:

> It's not for the love of gold I go, and it's not
>   for the love of fame,
> But fortune might smile on me, and I might
>   win a name.
> But yet it is for gold I go, o'er the deep and
>   raging foam,
> To build a home for my own true love on
>   the shores of Americay.[33]

But his very next lines, in keeping with the mood of sadness, were full of remorse and self-pity:

> And if I die in a foreign land, from my home
>   and friends far away,
> No kind mother's tears will flow o'er my
>   grave on the shores of Americay.

This same combination of hope and self-pity was suggested in the closing lines of an original poem called "Gregnahorna's Braes," which was composed in the 1850s by an emigrating schoolteacher from County Donegal. After describing the natural beauties and physical splendors of his native district, he cried out:

A long farewell, my comrade boys, I hope
　　you'll for me pray
To reach that free-born country, four
　　thousand miles away.[34]

Many ballads were set in a romantic frame and pictured the young
lover who was leaving for America with the promise on his lips that he
would return to take his sweetheart with him. Such a one was "The
Emigrant's Farewell," part of which declared:

My love I'm bound for a foreign nation,
If the Lord be pleased to bring me o'er,
To seek promotion and look for labour,
Since all things failed on the Shamrock Shore;
But if you have patience – if fortune favors,
To crown my labours, believe what I say,
I will come, my love, with gold in store,
And bring you over to America.[35]

But the hope of prospering in America was sometimes tinged with
realism, and the emigrant was reminded that conditions there were not
always so roseate. A farmer in County Galway remembered a few lines
of one ballad which cautioned the young emigrant:

If you want to earn money you must be fully
　　inclined,
For there's poor people in America like
　　those left behind.[36]

A more humorous warning in Gaelic had it that (in translation):

Ireland is often despised and faulted,
But that should not be so.
Potatoes are growing plentifully there,
And a woman (wife) milking the cow.
Not so is it in Boston,
Or in any such state [sic].
If a man earns a dollar there,
His wife will be out drinking it.[37]

While not many told of the success or return of the emigrant, nearly all spoke of his loneliness and his longing to return and die in
Ireland, or else rang with the vow that he would never forget his coun-

100

try or his family. Perhaps the best-known ballad of the never-shall-forget type was one composed by Lady Dufferin in the 1860s and entitled "The Irish Emigrant." Here a husband, standing over the grave of his wife and baby, bids them farewell and promises:

> I'm bidding you a long farewell, my Mary,
>   kind and true,
> But I'll not forget you, darling, in the land I'm
>   going to.
> They say there's bread and work for all, and
>   the sun shines always there,
> But I'll not forget Old Ireland were it fifty
>   times as fair.[38]

A less mournful note was struck in an original ballad composed by a young emigrant from County Roscommon in the 1890s whose one wish was to earn enough money to return to his home in Briarfield:

> And when I reach America
> I'll labour day and night
> My purse to fill with golden coins
> All beautiful and bright.
> And then for dear old Ireland
> My passage I will take
> To end my course in Briarfield
> By the lovely Shad Lough lake.[39]

Probably the most famous return of all — and, significantly, also the most tragic — was that of "Noreen Bawn," a ballad still popular today. The tale recounted is that of a widow's daughter whose passage to America was paid by a relative already there. She sailed off to America

> To that place where the Missouri
> With the Mississippi flow

and after many weary years she finally returned to her waiting widowed mother – gorgeously dressed, but with the telltale signs of fatal disease upon her cheeks. She died and at her grave her mother wept:

'Twas the shame of emigration
Laid you low, my Noreen Bawn.[40]

The few exceptions to the overall note of sadness and sorrow, interestingly enough, were also the ballads which were the least known and least popular. One noteworthy example was "The Irishmen now going to America," a jolly, rollicking story of an Irish canal worker in the United States who won a wife with a dowry of two thousand dollars and a well-stocked farm of two hundred acres. With such evidence of his own good fortune he cried out to his fellow Irishmen to follow his example and emigrate:

So all you young labouring heroes get ready
    and do come away,
And sail to the sweet land of freedom where
    no poor rates or taxes to pay!
It's there that the dollars are plenty,
    employment without fail,
You'll have beef and mutton for dinner instead
    of your coarse Indian meal.[41]

Such unrestrained joy and optimism, however, did not truthfully reflect the sentiment of the Irish on the subject of emigration. Hence its popularity was foredoomed to failure. The Irish at home sang about emigration, but they did not laugh about it. They accepted it as a necessity, almost an inevitable one, and were inclined to find in it neither joy nor happiness. But they sincerely wished for the emigrant's success, even if their ballads reflected an awareness of the difficulties that lay ahead and betrayed strong doubts that he or she would ever return. If one were looking for the truest and most realistic expression of their feelings toward emigration and the emigrant, they were probably best summed up in a single verse from "The Emigrant's Song":

God speed these exiles wherever they may be,
Who are seeking their future in the land of the free;
May they prove their worth wheresoever they roam,
True to their country, their God, and their home.[42]

Part III • The Return Tide

VI

Alms and Agitation

IMPORTANT as the direct effects and repercussions of the emigration in Ireland were, an equally significant though more indirect consequence of the movement was that which may be described as the American return tide. The nature of this return tide manifested itself in a variety of forms, but for our purposes it can be summed up in two key words: men and money. From the very inception of heavy Irish emigration in the 1840s there began to flow back to Ireland a golden stream of dollars, which was as remarkable for its magnitude as was the trickle of returning Yanks for its minuteness.

It is the golden stream which concerns us here, a stream composed of two distinct and parallel branches but having a common origin: the reservoir of hard-earned money among the Irish emigrants in America. One branch, and by far the larger, was made up of the myriad individual remittances that flowed home as alms for the alleviation of family distress; the other branch, much smaller, came as political contributions to foster the agitation for national sovereignty. In the long run the latter might possibly have been more important in terms of the objectives achieved, but the immediate results of the former were probably of greater significance. A great deal has been said and written about the support of Irish-Americans for Irish causes; much less has been said of the uses of emigrant remittances, probably because of the paucity of information. An attempt will be made here to redress the balance, and while some mention will also be made of the contributions for political causes to indicate their extent and importance, the bulk of this chapter will deal with personal remittances and their uses.

Like so many other things in modern Irish history, remittances also must be dated from the famine and the impulse which it gave to large-scale emigration. Although Irish emigrants had been sending home money before the advent of that catastrophe, the practice did not become general until the enormous migrations of the 1840s had been set in motion. So large did the aggregate sums become that early in 1849 Earl Grey, then secretary for war and the colonies, requested the emigration commissioners to ascertain as best they could the extent of the funds sent by emigrants in North America during the preceding year.

Thus 1848 came to mark the first year for which information on remittances began to be collected systematically. Within two weeks the efficient commissioners forwarded their report to Earl Grey and pointed out that while it was impossible to form more than a "conjectural estimate," their information indicated that a sum of at least £460,180 had been remitted from North America, a figure that did not include transactions done through the important financial house of Baring Brothers, which was considerable, or money sent via private letters. Earl Grey was duly impressed and could only scribble in amazement that the figure was "very remarkable."[1]

Even more remarkable was the fact that not only did the bulk of the money come through Liverpool, where seven firms handled £420,939 of the total reported, but that none of these funds which flowed through Liverpool came from Canada; they all came from the United States. Even if the remaining £40,000 all came from Canada, which is highly unlikely, the fact remains that well over 90 percent of the total reported remittances for 1848 came from the United States. By 1868 over 99 percent of all funds were coming from the United States.[2]

For the next quarter of a century the emigration commissioners diligently gathered their statistics, imperfect as those figures were and notwithstanding innumerable difficulties. By 1860, however, they were complaining that returns could not be obtained from the Port of London, and by 1872 some of the principal Liverpool houses which had been supplying them with information declined to continue the practice. They therefore ceased their efforts, and for the next fifteen years the Board of Trade inherited the thankless task. With the continued refusal of many mercantile houses to supply information, the statistics were exceedingly unreliable, and by 1887 the Board of Trade also abandoned the project.[3]

Despite their incompleteness, the statistics for these forty years tell an impressive story. The total amount of remittances reported for the entire period came to more than £34,000,000, or an average of over £850,000 a year.[4] An appreciation of the immensity of these figures can be gained when it is realized that in the twenty-one-year period from 1852 to 1872 emigrants' remittances exceeded by nearly £1,750,000 the total government expenditure for poor relief in Ireland.[5] Various attempts have been made to ascertain the grand total, including those remittances transmitted by private means. The emigration commissioners in 1863 ventured an educated guess of half again as much as the amount for which they had returns, but later authorities have felt this figure too high. In 1875 John O'Rourke, the first historian of the famine, thought one fourth again as much a more reasonable estimate, as did Peter Condon two generations later. On the basis of this lower estimate the aggregate sum of remittances from all sources came to not less than an average of £1,000,000 annually. Translated into dollars at the then prevailing rate of exchange, it amounted to an annual average return of at least $5,000,000 or a grand total of over $260,000,000 in the period from 1848 to 1900.[6]

It is difficult to determine with any degree of accuracy what proportion of this money came from Irish emigrants and how much from English emigrants. That the bulk of it was remitted by the Irish there can be no doubt. In 1852 the *Dublin Evening Post* jeered that the English had not sent back a single pound sterling, but the judgment was much too harsh. John Locke of Rathmines was more generous when the following year he estimated that about one twelfth of the total came from English emigrants. More than a decade later the *Freeman's Journal*, which could hardly be accused of pro-British sympathies, allowed them nearly 25 percent of the total.[7]

Neither the harshness of the first nor the generosity of the last estimate seem close to the truth. John Locke's approximation of one twelfth would appear to be the more realistic and reasonable, particularly for the earlier decades of the 1850s and 1860s. In the thirteen years from 1847 to 1860, over 1,600,000 Irish poured into the United States, or more than twice as many people as came from Great Britain in the forty years between 1821 and 1860. The heaviest reported remittances for this period were during the seven years from 1850 to 1856 when nearly £1,200,000 a year were sent to the United Kingdom. In the decade of the 1860s, when British immigrants in the United States exceeded Irish immigrants by more than 30 percent, or over 170,000 persons, total reported remittances to the United Kingdom fell to an annual average of less than £500,000, or considerably less than one half what they had been during the preceding decade of heavy Irish immigration.

It seems clear, therefore, that the correlation between reported remittances and Irish immigration was extremely close. When the number of Irish in this country was at its peak, remittances to the United Kingdom were at their peak; when Irish immigration ebbed and was exceeded by the British, remittances shrank drastically. The same pattern was also discernible for the later decades, and when Irish immigration increased rapidly, remittances to the United Kingdom rose quickly; when it fell sharply, remittances decreased greatly. Locke's estimate would thus appear to be applicable for the entire half-century, and since there is no reason to suppose that the proportions among money sent via private channels were any different, it may be assumed that over 90 percent of all remittances from North America were sent by the Irish to their loved ones at home.

The remittances came back in many forms — bank drafts, money orders, cash, passage tickets — and through a variety of channels, such as banks, mercantile houses, shipping firms, exchange agencies, private letters, and returning emigrants. This hodgepodge led one journal as early as 1853 to regret that some sort of definite instruction was not given all intending emigrants as to the best and safest manner of remitting money. The journal itself strongly favored money orders drawn on Irish banks as the most reliable method. A few enterprising Irishmen in America saw in emigrants' remittances a golden business opportunity, and in 1854 Patrick Donahoe, editor of the Boston *Pilot*, which was the most widely read of all Irish-American newspapers, founded one of the first and most successful of the many exchange agencies which sprang into being. By 1880 Donahoe's agency was remitting over $180,000 annually from the Irish servant girls of Boston. To protect the Irish emigrants in New York from exploitation, the Irish Emigrant Industrial Savings Bank was founded in 1851, and over the next thirty-six years some $30,000,000 was remitted through this institution to Ireland.[8]

Sometimes money was sent back through a society, as was the case with the Irish Emigrant Society of New York, which in two years (1860-61) remitted over £145,000 via the Bank of Ireland. D. W. Cahill, an Irish priest with a catholic curiosity, reported from New York in 1861 that there were six principal houses in that city appointed for money orders to Ireland, as well as one associated company. Together the seven offices in 1860 handled nearly £600,000 in remittances, more than the total amount reported by the emigration commissioners for that year.[9]

By 1862 the need for an international postal money-order system was clearly evident and the United States consul in Dublin strongly urged William H. Seward, then secretary of state, that such a system, proposed to the consul in the first instance by W. Neilson Hancock, be established between the United States and the United Kingdom. This would be a great boon to the poor classes who received the small sums, he pointed out, for under the existing system they were deprived of much of them as a result of brokers' charges. But the problems of civil war in the United States were more urgent matters for Seward, and it was not until 1871 that an international postal money-order convention was signed with the United Kingdom, the first of a series into which the United States entered with many foreign countries.[10]

The postal money-order system was an instant success. Limited to amounts of less than $50 per money order, it was eminently suited for emigrant remittances and in the first nine months of its operation nearly $750,000 was sent back to Ireland and England in this manner.[11] Within two years Neilson Hancock was convinced that the remittance business of many commercial firms in Liverpool had been entirely supplanted by the new postal money orders and that they already protected more than half the remittances. Hancock, however, was somewhat hasty in his optimism, for the force of tradition among the Irish in remitting money through long-established channels remained deeply rooted. Nevertheless, while money orders did not completely replace the older channels by which money was sent back home, as time wore on and familiarity with them spread they began to account for an increasingly larger proportion of the total remittance business. The growing reluctance of mercantile houses in providing the emigration commissioners with information thus becomes understandable, for they did not wish to make known their sharp decline in business. By the 1890s over $5,000,000 a year was being remitted to the United Kingdom via United States postal money orders.[12]

The striking feature about these remittances is that individual sums were seldom large, rarely more than five pounds at a time, and came from a group composed largely of laborers and domestic servants. Moreover, it was Irish girls who contributed the lioness' share. D. W. Cahill stated in 1861 that eight out of every ten who sent money home were girls, a fact borne out several years later by John Francis Maguire, that peripatetic Irish member of Parliament. Maguire pointed out, however, that in small towns and rural districts, where "temptations" were less, the men were as constant in their remittances as the women.[13]

As a rule, those who were newly arrived sent home larger sums than those who had been in America for some time. The reason, as one witness saw it in 1852, was that after the first three or four years the Irish immigrants began to acquire the "expensive habits of the people of the States" and the result was a decline in remittances. In addition it seemed that emigrants from the poorest families were the most faithful in sending money home. Those from more comfortable families were neither as constant nor as generous, probably because the need in those families was not as great. In some cases, furthermore, money came regularly only as long as the emigrant remained single, or as long as the parents remained alive. Upon marriage of the emigrant in the United States or death of the old folks at home, remittances diminished in amount and frequency and often ceased altogether. As the responsibilities of an emigrant in the United States increased and his obligations in Ireland decreased, he sent home less and less money.[14]

Christmas and Easter were generally the two great festivals when the bulk of all money was sent, and the receipt of the "Christmas letter" became a tradition throughout the countryside. Maguire observed that during the months of December and March banks and offices in the large American cities were full of "bustling, eager . . . clamorous applicants" and that the clerks were hard-pressed to satisfy the demands of the impatient senders.[15] Except in very special circumstances, money was seldom asked for by those at home so that the amount varied more in relation to prosperity in the United States than to any pressure from Ireland. The one outstanding exception occurred in the early 1880s when, after three successive years of acute agrarian distress in Ireland, the Irish in America responded to the call for help by increasing remittances from over £1,000,000 in 1879 to more than £1,700,000 the following year, and attained a peak of over £2,200,000 in 1884, or more than $11,000,000.

Not all this money came back in cash; much of it came in the form of prepaid passage tickets. As early as 1848 nearly 39 percent of all reported remittances were prepaid passages. Twenty years later the proportion was 38 percent and by 1872 it had risen to 44 percent, which the emigration commissioners calculated was sufficient to have taken out three quarters of the total emigration from the United Kingdom that year. From the time when systematic records on remittances began to be kept, it was clear that total reported remittances were more than enough to defray the entire expense of annual Irish emigration. By 1862 it was more than double the amount necessary to pay the whole expense of Irish emigration. In fact, for the first twenty years of remittance records the amount which flowed back to Ireland was sufficient to cover the cost of total emigration from all the British Isles to North America, and this was exclusive of the sums sent by private means.[16]

In actual practice, however, only about 40 percent of all remittances were used to pay for emigration, and this was principally the 40 percent represented by prepaid passage tickets. In this sense the use of the general term "remittance" is misleading, for in the minds of the people at home there were two very distinct kinds of money. One was called "American money" and the other was called "passage money," or sometimes simply "passage." By grouping both types under the heading of remittance, a term the Irish themselves never used, many authorities (including the emigration commissioners) have erroneously assumed that because the total amount remitted often exceeded the cost of total emigration, the greater part of the money was indeed used in that fashion. However, widespread interviewing by the Irish Folklore Commission and personal interviews conducted by this writer have established that this was not the case. The money used for emigration usually came to Ireland in the form of prepaid passage tickets or was sometimes specifically designated by the sender to be used for someone's passage. Frequently it was sent in response to a request by someone in Ireland who wished to emigrate.

Passage money was never looked upon truly as "American money" because it never contributed in any way to the welfare of those at home. Except in very extreme cases of want and poverty, the people at home felt themselves under a moral obligation to use it only for passage. More often than not it was expected that the person who went to America on this passage money would either pay it back to the sender after he had found employment, or else send home an equal amount to bring out another member of the family. "American money," on the other hand, was seldom asked for, save in cases of dire need or sudden calamity, because people did not like to send "begging letters" and would avoid it if possible.

This use of the prepaid passage ticket in effect represented the operation of that system of "one-bringing-another" of which the Irish came to be the practitioners par excellence. It is this feature, moreover, which gave to Irish emigration, more than to most other national migrations of the nineteenth century, the character of a self-perpetuating phenomenon. For annual Irish remittances came to assume such huge proportions that the 40 percent which arrived as prepaid passage tickets alone paid for more than 75 percent of all Irish emigration in the fifty years following the famine. Contemporaries were well aware of this fact. As early as 1854 one journal noted that few emigrants traveled upon their own independent resources. Ten years later another confidently asserted that not more than 5 percent of the emigrants from County Mayo paid their own passage, while in 1883 it was observed that most of the emigrants from County Waterford traveled in the same manner. As late as 1892 a special commission appointed by the United States secretary of the treasury to study the causes of European emigration forwarded from Ireland their report that "the great and principal stimulus to emigration . . . was the constant flow of letters and money . . . from the United States . . ."[17]

Remittances stimulated emigration in still other, less tangible ways. Often when money arrived the news spread quickly through the community. Although some people tried to hide their having received a "money letter," it was more usual that they were eager to tell the neighbors of their good fortune. In many cases the amount received was even exaggerated in order to enhance the impression that the son or daughter was indeed "doing well," as the letters said they were. Among the rural Irish cash money was a scarce commodity, and the receipt of five or ten pounds made a deep impression upon younger sons and daughters. The sight of money regularly sent was assumed by them to be easily earned, an assumption made all the more attractive by the realization that they could rarely hope to earn the equivalent of one remittance if they worked two or three times as hard and long at home. The widow of a laborer remembered a sister of hers who had emigrated in the early 1880s and after four weeks sent home one pound. In Ireland, she commented, her sister would have had to work three months to earn an equal amount.[18] Such evidence of material prosperity in the United States further strengthened the resolve of young people to emigrate, and in this particular case two younger sisters followed the first within two years.

But what of the 60 percent of all remittances which came back as true "American money"? How was that utilized by the Irish at home? What uses did they make of the countless checks, money orders, and dollar bills which poured into Ireland from that land "beyond the western wave"? What effect did this vast voluntary subsidy have upon Ireland's social economy? These are questions for which answers are not as easy to find as in the case of "passage money." No thorough investigation has ever been undertaken and information has been scanty. But enough has been gathered through personal interviews and the assistance of the Irish Folklore Commission that a reasonably accurate assessment of the use of the American money is now possible.

The single most important use of the American money was to pay the rent. Irish tenant farmers probably worried more about the day on which the rent fell due (known generally as "gale day") than about any other item in their simple economy. "If you had not the rent money," recalled the wife of a small farmer, "you never lay down a night contented 'till you got it." She remembered that "many a young boy went to America just so that his people would feel safe, for he sent home the rent money every time the 'gale day' came around."[19] As late as 1893 cases were reported in the west of Ireland of "mere children" who had emigrated and were sending home half their earnings to help pay the rent, while thirty years earlier it was declared that a large portion of the money paid as rent in the four years from 1860 to 1864 came from America.[20] In 1880 a parish priest from County Kerry testified that many of the farmers in his district paid their rents with money they received from their children in America, a circumstance which still prevailed in County Mayo at the very end of the century.[21] The best generalization, applicable to the country as a whole, was probably given by an old resident of County Donegal who in speaking of his hometown remarked, "If you said that everybody in Inishowen paid the rent at one time or other with American money it would not be an exaggeration."[22]

The realization that vast sums from America were finding their way into landlords' pockets as rent infuriated some of the more passionate patriots. One such Anglophobe felt that it was nothing less than a "love-tax that landlord greed . . . filched . . . [from] the Irish exiles in America." Another insisted that the money sent by the Irish in America did the farmer no good because it was all swallowed up in rent and was thus part of a "world-wide tribute" extorted by Irish landlords. That ardent Celtophile, L. Paul-Dubois, considered rents paid in this manner as simply a "tax levied on the filial piety of child emigrants . . ." But to the Irish tenant farmers who desperately needed it, the American money often spelled the difference between holding the homestead and eviction, and in a few areas some farms even came to be called "Yankee land" because the rent on them was paid with American money. Thus their attitude toward the American money, unlike that of the professional patriots, was characterized much more by a feeling of deep gratitude to their faithful sons and daughters for sending it than by a blind hatred toward the landlords for accepting the payment. "And only for them in America," observed a retired Cork farmer, "they [his farming neighbors] would have been thrown out by the landlord."[23]

Second in importance to paying the rent was the use of the

American money to reduce local shopkeepers' bills. There was hardly a rural family in Ireland which did not find itself in debt at one time or another to the local shopkeeper. With money so scarce, the giving of goods on credit was a common practice, and very often shopkeepers extended credit solely on the strength of promised remittances. In some areas the bill was paid only once each year, usually when the Christmas check arrived. One shopkeeper in 1861 proudly declared in a letter to his local newspaper that he often made advances to poor people in his district on the strength of expected remittances from America, and that he "never lost a penny that way."[24] It is difficult to determine precisely what proportion of the rural Irish relied upon this practice, but it is clear that for a considerable number, particularly those in the poorer districts of the south and west, American money not only kept a roof over their heads but also put food on the table.

While rent and shop debts represent the two basic and most important uses of the American money, those families which did not find themselves in a state of chronic poverty were able to apply the money to needs less pressing, but equally desirable. The improvement which farmers probably longed for most was to replace the thatch on their humble cottages with slate roofs, and wherever slate roofs appeared it was generally ascribed to contributions from abroad. Less major improvements effected through the same means included the repair of floors, walls, and doors. One woman of County Donegal recalled that when her mother received fifteen pounds from an uncle in America it was promptly used to put new windows in their cottage, which had previously been without them, while another remarked that nearly all the houses in her village were improved with American money.[25]

In rare cases enough might have been sent to build a completely new house or to erect needed smaller buildings on the farm. It has been competently estimated that of 180 new houses built between 1851 and 1900 in the Kilrush Rural District of County Clare, a comparatively poor area of western Ireland, fully 50 percent were constructed with American money.[26] Perhaps the most striking single example was provided by a small farmer from County Galway who remembered that in his youth near neighbors of his lived in a smoky thatched cottage on two and a half acres of practically useless bog land. There were ten children in the family and eventually seven of them emigrated to the United States. All did well and sent money home regularly. With this money the old couple built a new house, bought more productive land, and educated a younger son for the priesthood.[27]

The loss of a farm animal, such as a cow or a horse, ranked as a major calamity among the large body of Irish peasantry. Without help from abroad such losses could not have been replaced for years. One farmer's widow recalled a case where a cow had died while calving ("one of the worst pieces of ill-luck that could happen to a poor man with a family to rear"), whereupon the parents wrote of the tragedy to a son in America. Shortly thereafter the price of a cow was sent home.[28] In another instance a woman of seventy related the following story:

> I remember well one time when I was very wee and our horse died and mind you, that was a great loss in those days. After some time I remember an American letter coming from Aunt Gracie, my father's sister . . . and I can see to this day how pleased my father was when he opened it. It was later on that we heard what pleased him. In the letter was twenty pounds . . . to buy a new horse.[29]

In this connection perhaps the most successful illustration concerns that of a farmer in County Galway who toward the end of the century was given some grazing land by the Congested Districts Board. The man had a family of eleven children, and all but three emigrated to the United States. Soon money began to arrive regularly, and with it the old farmer commenced stocking his land with hardy mountain sheep which he then sold at the local fair. After a number of years he walked into the small post office and startled the local postmistress by presenting a sum of two hundred pounds for deposit in a savings account. The money had been carefully husbanded over the years from the sale of sheep originally bought with dollars sent by his children in America. Up until that time it was thought that not all the sixty families of that small community could have together produced two hundred pounds in cash.[30]

Sometimes the American money was used to further the training of a younger member of the family. This was especially true of those families which were comparatively comfortable to begin with. In such cases the money would be employed to apprentice a son to a trade, a daughter to dressmaking or millinery, or in rare cases to provide more schooling. Occasionally the money was used to purchase a small business in the local town into which a member of the family was installed. Sometimes the money was saved to build up a dowry, or "fortune," for a younger daughter, while at times of sudden crises like death, special sums were sent to help defray the cost of a funeral and a wake. A remarkable example of what American money did for one family occurred in a district of South Clare. Eleven children were supported by a father on an income derived from forty acres and a fishing weir. While substantial in terms of Irish rural standards of the time, the income was not enough to provide for the education of all. Yet between 1880 and 1920, four sons entered professions, three daughters married professional men, and two daughters accumulated sufficiently large dowries to "marry into a good place." The money, it turned out, was all provided by an unmarried uncle in Texas.[31]

How much of the American money found its way into savings accounts is uncertain.[32] With incomplete statistics on remittances it is difficult to establish any meaningful correlation with those for savings account deposits. A glance at Figure 3 (page 118) will help make this clear. From 1848 to 1872 the only remittance statistics available are those provided by the emigration commissioners. When these are compared with savings deposits, the most obvious fact which emerges is that the onset of the famine was accompanied by a steep drop in savings and an immediately sharp rise in remittances. By 1854 more money had actually arrived as remittances than was present in all the savings accounts in the country. Doubtless the enormity of the emigrant response to the call for help sent out from Ireland served measurably to arrest the downward plunge in savings and to alter its course upward once again. But for the remainder of the 1850s and 1860s the relationship between the two is inconclusive. With the panic and depression of the 1850s in the United States, remittances fell away rapidly while savings in Ireland continued to rise until the distress of the early 1860s caused a minor slump in the curve. The rapid recovery in savings which followed was due more to improving conditions in Ireland than to the small rise in remittances.

From 1873 to 1887, if the Board of Trade remittance statistics are combined with those for American postal money orders, it would

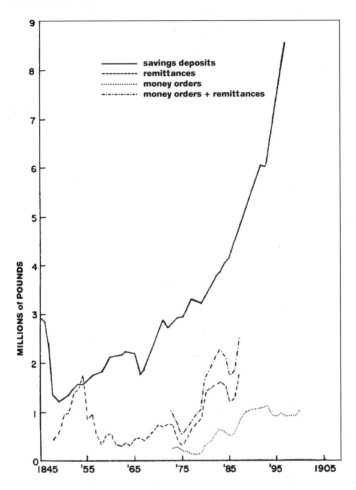

Figure 3. Irish Savings Deposits Compared with American Remittances and Money Orders (Based on sources cited in footnotes 11 and 32, Chapter VI, pp. 190 and 192, and on Appendix Tables 18 and 19)

appear that some direct relationship might have existed, since both these and savings were rising. But the increase in savings was probably more dependent upon prosperous times in Ireland, a conclusion borne out by the fact that while the American depression of the late 1870s caused a notable fall in remittances, savings in Ireland continued to mount at the same rapid pace. It is obvious, therefore, that with the possible exception of the immediate postfamine period, very little of the American money sent to Ireland during the half-century found its way into savings accounts. For the vast majority of tenant farmers and laborers who received this money there were too many immediately pressing needs, such as rent and debts, to have allowed them the luxury of salting it away for a rainy day.

There remains, then, one important question regarding the use of the American money which must be considered: was any of this money employed to buy land? By and large the answer is that very little of the total American money was used to buy land. The information gathered through personal interviews and by the Irish Folklore Commission is conclusive on this point. Individual remittances were too small to permit the purchasing of land, and in the vast majority of cases rent and debts were more urgent problems. The generalization becomes more meaningful if we look briefly at the statistics for land ownership. In 1870 only 3 percent of all farmers were owners of their own land, which in absolute terms meant some 20,000 holdings out of more than 680,000. Twenty-five years later the proportion had risen to only 12 percent. The real revolution in Irish land tenure did not begin until the advent of the Wyndham Act of 1903, which in three years more than doubled the percentage of owners to 29 percent and within fifteen years doubled it again to nearly 64 percent.[33]

Moreover, the 9 percent increase in owners which did take place in the nineteenth century was confined largely to farms of over thirty acres, by contemporary Irish standards considered comfortable, medium-sized farms. If it is remembered that American money came principally to those whose needs were the greatest, that is, the small tenant farmers and agricultural laborers, one cannot escape the conclusion that the dignity of ownership was conferred upon that small group of farmers whose basic economic position was already sound, a group which depended very little upon American money for support.

The conclusion is further strengthened if we examine the increase in ownership on a county level. The county which saw the greatest advance in land ownership between 1870 and 1896 was Londonderry, where 32.8 percent were classed as owners at the later date. Counties Cork and Clare, on the other hand, experienced extremely small increases, and by 1896 only 11.2 percent and 10.1 percent were classed as owners in those counties respectively.[34] Yet emigration from Londonderry was relatively light while that from Cork and Clare was very heavy. Since there is no reason to suppose that emigrants from Londonderry were any more generous in their remittances than the greater numbers from Cork and Clare, it is clear that it was the sounder economic status of the Ulster farmers of Londonderry which enabled them to acquire ownership of the largest number of farms.

Nevertheless there are a few exceptions and some evidence is available which indicates that land was indeed bought with American money, though not very much. A Donegal woman, for example, related that her father wished to buy a nearby farm but did not have enough money for the purchase price. An aunt was written to in the United States and soon thereafter she sent the remainder needed. The farm was bought and has remained in the family down to the present day. The widow of a small farmer recalled that in her community in County Galway only one man ever bought land with American money, and then it was simply a few small holdings of several acres. On one large estate in West Clare it has been estimated that 35 percent of all lands purchased from 1850 to 1900 was bought with American money. But the 35 percent represented only fourteen small farms bought over a period of fifty years.[35]

In some cases it was the practice to open a joint deposit account at the local bank in the names of the emigrant and his father. When money arrived from America the father deposited it in the joint account until enough had been accumulated to buy a small farm. In this way one family which owned thirteen acres of poor land was able in 1897 to buy nine additional acres for £150 — a sum saved from the small remittances sent them by their only son in the United States. In another instance around the turn of the century still another family was able to purchase twenty acres of land for £285 which had been accumulated from the remittances of their son in America.

A variation of this practice was something known as the "American out-farm." These were farms which families bought "outside" their own, that is, not adjoining their own and often some miles distant. They were usually registered in the name of whoever sent the money, and the person who looked after the "American out-farm" generally agreed to pay so much into the bank to the credit of the exiled owner, who, it was assumed, would one day return to take possession. This rarely happened, however, and the "American out-farm" was eventually settled on another member of the family. In one case in the 1880s such a person did actually return, and to a substantial farm. His descendants today are the richest people in the community.[36]

One type of American money which was not properly in the category of remittances but whose total sum must have been considerable was money which was used for the building of churches. Many rural communities were too poor to erect their own churches, and it was a common practice for the local parish priest to canvass his congregation for the names and addresses of all emigrants in America. He would then either write a personal letter to each one asking for a contribution, or, as was done in a number of instances, take a trip to the United States and seek out the emigrants himself. This latter method of soliciting funds was employed at least as early as 1851 when a priest from County Cork was deputed by the archbishop of Dublin to go to America for the purpose of collecting money, not for a church, but for an Irish Catholic University.[37] It is difficult to say how many churches were built in this fashion, but in one small area of County Galway no less than a half dozen were erected before 1900 with money solicited from Irish emigrants in America, and there are indications that Galway was not the only county so to have benefited.[38]

In perspective, what can we say about remittances and their overall impact on Ireland's social economy? Was the American money a force for good or did it also have adverse consequences? To ask such a question is not to set up a straw man, for it has been seriously maintained that because individual sums were small, they were rarely sufficient to effect any real improvement in the status of the recipient — unless the money was used for emigration. Since the bulk of it was used to pay the rent, so the argument runs, on holdings which were uneconomic (the fact that such holdings could not produce enough for their own rent proves they were uneconomic), much of this American money went to "prop up a social system in Ireland which little needed propping," and that in the case of the impoverished west the American money was "positively harmful."[39] The charge is not without substance, for there is evidence that in some instances American money came to be depended upon so habitually as a source of income that it resulted in indifference and laziness, with no attempt being made at self-improvement.[40] As late as the turn of the century one visitor to Achill Island, off the coast of County Mayo, observed that a population which was far larger than could be supported on the meager agriculture and spasmodic fishing of the area was being maintained on American money sent home by absent sons and daughters.[41]

The argument, however, fails to take into account the possible alternatives which were available. If there were no American money at all (as distinct from "passage money"), two courses of action remained, either an increase in emigration or an increase in pauperism, neither of which could be contemplated with satisfaction. In this sense it is evident that the American money actually prevented emigration from assuming even larger proportions. It may perhaps be argued that if there were no American money, conditions among the peasantry would have been so infinitely worse that the government would have been compelled to take more active and constructive steps to rectify the situation. Such optimism is unsupported by the evidence. The first of the Land Acts was not passed until 1870, and not until the Act of 1881 was any significant attempt at land reform made, and only then against great opposition. There is no reason to suppose that British policy toward Ireland would have been any less indifferent if suffering there were more acute.

As it was, the American money greatly reduced that suffering and effected substantial improvements in many areas. In 1858 the emigration commissioners were convinced that a considerable proportion of the remittances went to increase the means of small farmers and laborers and led to an improvement in the general condition of the people. Toward the end of the century it was reported to the Royal Commission on Labour that a common expression heard in the south and west of Ireland was, "We could not live without the American money." As evidence, a case was cited of a family of five in County Mayo who managed to exist with the help of £170 sent by a sister in America over a span of twenty years. In another instance an informant from County Kilkenny related that soon after her three sisters emigrated to the United States in the 1880s, they sent home five pounds regularly every three months. After that, she declared, "me famely [sic] never knew a day of poverty."[42]

At the very minimum the American money made life in Ireland tolerable for a great portion of the peasantry, a circumstance which more than counterbalanced the fact that a number of uneconomic holdings in the south and west were subsidized by these remittances. Without that subsidy many would have reverted to a condition of wretched poverty which was characteristic of the prefamine period. It may be true that some among them came to depend upon American money to such a degree that they ceased to exert themselves to improve their own circumstances. But there is no evidence to indicate that this attitude prevailed in more than a few isolated instances, while that which is available suggests that in many cases the American money acted as an incentive to self-improvement. At the very least the American money kept the wolf and the bailiff from the door, and in a number of cases raised families from poverty to comfort, if not prosperity. This was the prime importance of the golden stream, the full significance of which was pithily summarized by a retired laborer from County Clare. "I knew people," he reflected, "who would have been poor but were happy — because of American money."[43]

The second branch of the golden stream had a quite different purpose, for unlike the first, its concentration was not diverted into myriad individual rivulets to help sustain a struggling mass of tenant farmers and laborers. Rather it was directed at the maintenance of a series of organizations, political in nature, which had as their goal the reestablishment of Irish sovereignty in one form or another. The principal weapon of these groups was agitation, which was often violent, sometimes not. Although the ultimate goal of independence had to wait for the twentieth century for realization, the ground was prepared in the preceding one, while the immediate achievements of these groups were in themselves not without importance or significance. As with all political organizations, their life blood was money, and it is this aspect that is of interest to us. For without the contributions which Irish-Americans so faithfully poured into their coffers, it is doubtful that even the modest measure of success that was achieved could have been possible. We cannot here enter into a detailed analysis of the labyrinth that was nineteenth-century Irish politics, but it does behoove us to consider briefly two important points: first, the degree of financial support these organizations received from America, and second, the measure of success they were able to achieve.

By and large no other immigrant groups in nineteenth-century America developed so passionate a devotion to the land of their birth as did the sons and daughters of Erin. The Germans, the British, the Scandinavians — all retained an interest to a greater or lesser degree in the affairs of the "old country"; only among the Irish was this interest so emotionally rooted that it was transmitted to the second, third, and even fourth generations. Irish-American political history in these years is a tale of plots and counterplots, of cunning intrigue and abortive invasions. It was a savage hatred of England which animated the great body of Irish emigrants and their descendants, a hatred that Lecky ascribed to the great clearances and vast unaided emigration which followed in the wake of the famine. It was those events, as one nationalist put it, "that sowed in Irish breasts the feeling that in due time produced eager subscribers to the dynamite funds."[44]

There was also a positive side to Irish feelings that stemmed not from hatred but from the sentimental romanticism which characterized the Irish as a people. Once they had left home, however humble it may have been, their thoughts of Ireland were thereafter conditioned more by a vivid imagination of things as they ought to have been than by any reasoned remembrance of things as they were. Not without justification did Edmund Curtis, Ireland's late great historian, declare that to the millions who made a greater Ireland in America, Ireland became "either a passionate memory or an ancestral poetry."[45] This fervid romantic patriotism was perhaps best expressed in the opening stanza from "The Irish-American," a poem that appeared in the *Irish-American Almanac for 1875:*

> Columbia the free is the land of my birth
> And my paths have been all on American earth
> But my blood is as Irish as any can be,
> And my heart is with Erin afar o'er the sea.[46]

Little wonder that seven years earlier when John Francis Maguire, after an extensive tour among the Irish in America, was led to inquire whether this ocean of sentiment for Ireland and hatred for England was likely to evaporate, he could only conclude that it "may subside – so may the sea; but, like the sea, the first breath will set it again in motion, while a storm would lash it into fury."[47]

It is against this background that the contributions of the Irish in America for the support of political agitation in Ireland must be viewed. In Ireland itself the consequences implied in pushing the Celt westward were quickly recognized, and prophecies of retribution were hurled at the British almost from the very inception of heavy emigration. By 1860 even the staid London *Times* became uneasy at the thought that the relentless emigration was spreading a vengeful multitude of Irish across the American continent, and intoned the anxious warning that "We must gird our loins to encounter the Nemesis of seven centuries' misgovernment."[48] Across the Irish Sea there was no such dignity of prose, only the blunt prediction that

"They'll be coming back in ships
With vengeance on their lips!"[49]

As it was, few did come back in ships. But in 1848, a time of intense revolutionary ferment throughout all of Europe, including Ireland, the British government became sufficiently alarmed at the prospect that the American Irish might indeed return that in August of that year the order went out from the head of the Dublin constabulary to arrest, seize, and search all returned emigrants, as well as all suspicious Americans.[50] Six years later police constables in the country were reporting on the contents of private letters received from emigrants in America, while from the British minister in Washington came dispatch after dispatch to Lord Palmerston detailing the activities of a host of patriotic Irish-American clubs in Boston, New York, Chicago, and Cincinnati.[51]

All this concern was not without foundation, for the 1850s marked the beginning of a new period in Irish secret organizations, a period in which, with the flight of the leaders of Young Ireland, the center of conspiracy was transferred to the United States, and also to France. Thus, not only did money become the entering wedge of American influence, as William Forbes Adams has pointed out, but personal leadership also came to be drawn from the United States, and the nationalist movement of the next generation found "masses of eager supporters" among the incoming hordes of emigrants at a time when it had very nearly expired on the "auld sod."[52]

The first significant manifestation of this American-nurtured nationalism was Fenianism, a movement whose ultimate goal was the violent overthrow of British rule in Ireland. Launched in New York, led by the exiled hotbloods of 1848, and sustained on the contributions from thousands of Irish-Americans, Fenianism was, in Trevelyan's words, "the first reaction of the new Irish America upon the British Isles."[53] The extent of the sustenance was considerable and amounted to almost $500,000, a sum that was collected over a period of eight years from 1858 to 1866 by the Fenian Brotherhood in the United States and Canada.[54] But the small handful of ex-Civil War officers who so boldly set sail in the *Erin's Hope* in 1867 on a noble adventure of invasion were from the start doomed to dismal failure. For the fact is that Ireland in 1867 was not yet ready for that bloodshed which fifty years later brought her independence. The Irish Catholic Church opposed the Fenians as a secret society, the peasantry were apathetic, and the British were well informed. When the inspired invaders of the *Erin's Hope* finally set foot on Irish soil they were indeed greeted with open arms and open doors — British arms and British jails.[55]

Fundamentally Fenianism failed because, sprouted and nourished as it was in a hothouse of Irish-American sentiment, it was out of touch with the realities of life in Ireland. Like the Young Irelanders before them, the Fenians labored under the misapprehension that the Irish people could be aroused and united on the basis of a vague appeal to national independence. Both movements failed to recognize the true source of Irish nationality — the Irish peasant's love of the land. On that, and that alone, as John E. Pomfret has observed, could the people of Ireland be roused.[56] Still, Fenianism was not without its significance, for the outrages and violence perpetrated both in Ireland and England awakened the British from their habitual indifference to their sister isle. The agitation so stirred Gladstone that in 1869 he pushed through Parliament the bill that disestablished the Church of Ireland, in his mind a cardinal grievance of the Irish. More important, perhaps, was that the lesson of Fenianism's failure was not lost upon those of the following generation who became the prime movers of a new and more successful Irish nationalism.

If the two outstanding leaders of that newer nationalism, Michael Davitt and Charles Stewart Parnell, displayed a profounder appreciation of the land problem, they also brought to the movement an organizing genius and an incomparable leadership which became an "indispensable condition" of its success.[57] Moreover, unlike the unfortunate Fenians, these leaders were admirably suited to the times. From 1876 onward industrial depression in Great Britain, coupled with increasing overseas competition, served to drive down drastically the price of Irish agricultural produce. This steadily deteriorating position of the Irish peasantry was further compounded by a series of bad potato harvests which began in 1876 and by 1879 culminated in a near-famine. Faced with a double threat of economic annihilation, the tenant farmers of Ireland could not help but allow their rents to fall into arrears, while Irish landlords, deaf to all entreaties, stubbornly refused to lower rents and embarked upon a campaign of large-scale evictions. Resentment became rife and Ireland stood "on the brink of revolution."[58]

Into this ferment in 1879 came the Irish National Land League, founded by Michael Davitt, led by Charles Stewart Parnell, and dedicated to a program of extensive land reform. By focusing attention on the land problem the League struck upon the central issue of all Irish grievances and caught up in its support not only the vast body of peasantry, but many Irish priests as well. It used the weapons of a "rent strike," armed resistance to eviction, and social ostracism, the last of which had by 1880 added a new word to the English language — boycott. All these methods were attended with a good deal of violence, crime, and outrage, and there existed in Ireland in these years what amounted to a "land war." The speed with which these weapons were adopted by the peasantry and swept through the country was truly amazing, and for the first time Irish nationalism became not merely a restricted political movement but a social one with a broad base of popular support.

The movement spread quickly to the United States and by June of 1881 there were over twelve hundred branches of the Land League in the United States and Canada. From their eager subscribers the Irish Land League derived a good part of the means without which it could not have sustained its activities. The leading spirit in the collection of these funds was Patrick Ford, the energetic editor of the New York *Irish World* and himself an emigrant from County Galway. Fully three fourths of the sums which came to the Land League from America were credited to the exertions of Ford, and Gladstone is reported to have remarked that but for the work of the *Irish World* there would have been no agitation in Ireland. All told the amount sent to the Land League from America came to over a million dollars, a sum which was collected almost entirely in the three short years from 1880 to 1883.[59]

The organized agitation of the Land League was not fruitless, and those in America who had poured their hard-earned dollars into the struggle had just cause for self-congratulation for the achievement wrought with their gold. In 1881, thoroughly alive to the dangers in Ireland, which had been brought home to him by the Land League, Gladstone piloted through Parliament the first effective Irish Land Act of the century and thereby pointed the way to a succession of similar acts, which within two generations converted Ireland to a nation of small peasant proprietors. By his own admission this would not have been possible without the existence of the Land League.[60] The immediate results of the Land Act of 1881 were an annual reduction of rent by $20,000,000, a greater degree of security of tenure for Irish farmers, and an opportunity to seek redress of grievances in land courts. Having achieved its purpose, the Land League was formally dissolved in 1883.

For the remainder of the century the arena of nationalist struggle was shifted to the halls of Westminster, where Parnell reigned as undisputed leader of the Irish Parliamentary party until 1890. During those seven years an additional million dollars came as an expression of support from the Irish in America. But lacking the unifying drama of the land struggle and with Parnell's deposition in 1890, the next leg of the journey toward the realization of Irish independence had to await a new group of helmsmen to chart the troubled waters of the twentieth century. No longer burdened by an onerous land problem, this next generation in Ireland, and their confreres in America, could devote all their energies and resources to the settlement of the political question. The economic ground had been cleared for them, and these latter-day heirs of Fenianism and Young Ireland finally had the clear political issue on which all Irishmen could unite.

VII

Men, Manners, and Methods

THE SECOND MAJOR STREAM in the return tide from America was a human one, a stream which from a cultural interchange point of view held greater potential significance than the golden stream of American dollars. For if human beings are the most important carriers of culture, they are also its most effective transmitters, and it is in the intermingling of peoples occasioned by mass migrations that this process of interchange operates at its optimum level. Thus while the millions who flocked to America's shores in the nineteenth century enriched her society with countless contributions carried over from older, more established social orders, they also quickly adopted many of the habits, customs, values, and attitudes of the newer, more dynamic civilization in which they chose to settle. This was especially true of the Irish and the British who, unlike their German and Scandinavian contemporaries, were not faced with a formidable language barrier and for whom, as a consequence, assimilation was comparatively rapid and easy.[1]

At the same time, some of the millions of Irish who arrived as immigrants eventually decided to return to the land of their birth and carried back with them the characteristics they had acquired in America. These were the "returned Yanks," as they came to be called in Ireland. While Irish contributions to American society have been frequently discussed, most recently by Carl Wittke,[2] little is known about the "returned Yank" and the role he played in Ireland as a carrier of American influences. Information has been scanty, but with the aid of new evidence obtained partly through the help of the Irish Folklore Commission, we may now take a closer look at these "returned Yanks" and perhaps discover what impact, if any, the human return tide from America had upon life in Ireland.

The outstanding fact about this American return tide was its minuteness. Compared with the vast numbers who left Ireland it was a mere trickle. Unlike the Italian immigrants of the early twentieth century who often returned to bask in the admiration of family and community, very few Irish men or women ever voyaged eastward again after they had once crossed the Atlantic. Precise figures are unavailable, but some idea of their minute numbers can be gained from the fact that in 1871 the population of County Clare, an area of heavy emigration, was nearly 150,000. Of this number only some 100 were foreigners, the majority being Americans. While the latter figure probably represents those emigrants who had returned to stay, the number of those who returned for a visit was equally small. By the end of the century it was calculated that to each townland in Ireland no more than six Irish-Americans returned yearly either to visit or to stay.[3]

Why did any return at all? After five, ten, twenty, or more years in the United States, what compelled them to come back? The answer, it appears, is as complex and varied as that host of personal choices and desires which induced them to emigrate in the first place. The principal exception related to the women, among whom there seemed to be a fixity of purpose which was lacking among the men. It was this common feminine compulsion, moreover, which accounted for the fact that among those who came to stay, the women predominated. Quite simply the Irish girls returned in search of husbands, and they did so with an almost desperate air of intent. According to one Donegal informant, they would marry "the worst looking 'fixture' in the place just to get staying," while another revealed that in her community there was a tradition that "there is no one as easy pleased in a man as a woman who has spent a while in America."[4]

The explanation is not far to seek. Many of these women left home as young girls of seventeen or eighteen and spent the next seven or ten years of their lives working as hard as possible to save every penny they could spare to send home as remittances. They came from a land where the average age of marriage was, and still is, the oldest in the Western world, and the thought of looking for a mate did not enter their heads until they were twenty-five or older. In nineteenth-century America, where the average age at marriage for women was less than twenty, the prospects of finding a husband for a woman over twenty-five were not very promising. Some women therefore decided to return to Ireland where they hoped that advanced age would not be so great a deterrent in attracting a spouse as it seemed to be in America.

Where marriage was so late, personal beauty and physical attractiveness were less important considerations than the economics involved, and in Irish terms this meant the dowry or "fortune" that a girl possessed. The returned Yanks usually came well prepared for this. A retired cook, for example, remembered two sisters who made their "fortunes" in America and then returned to "marry into farms."[5] Sometimes women returned as much as fifteen years after they had emigrated, but with their savings as dowries they had little difficulty in finding husbands. A small farmer from County Galway recalled that in his community it was often said of such people that "she was only an old Yank but she had the money."[6] If the statement was unkind it was nonetheless true and more importantly, the marriages were usually successful.[7]

In a few cases men also came home to marry, and among these were some who were able to marry into good farms where there was no male heir, particularly if they brought back some money with them. From their point of view this was a better economic proposition than buying a new farm, for there was no necessity to expend money on buildings or stock. More often, however, the men returned because of poor health or an inability to cope with the hard pace of life and work in America. This was equally true of some women, although not all who returned for this reason found the easier life they hoped for. A few who came back were ne'er-do-wells and could get on neither in America nor in Ireland, while others returned in their old age after retiring to spend their last days in the land they knew first and loved best. Those who were thus motivated by nostalgia sometimes found readjustment difficult and embarrassing, as was the case with one literate businessman:

> There is the warmth and welcome from all. But there is
> something the heart seeks but does not get, because nothing
> can bring back old acquaintances either of scene or personal
> reminiscences. A change over the face of nature. So that the
> returned emigrant is as hazy as those who receive him. He is
> wedged in betwixt the old and the young. The old have
> altered beyond recognition. The young he has never seen.
> And it takes some time before he gets his bearings.[8]

Several returned because of the death of a father or mother, and it
was the custom that one son had to come back to take charge of the
farm and care for the surviving parent. In a few instances the eldest son
was summoned to come home and look after his aged parents after the
family had been reared and the children dispersed. Sometimes a
returned Yank simply could not decide whether he liked Ireland or
America better. The wife of a railroad engineer from County Leix
recalled how in her youth there was one woman in the community who
crossed and recrossed the Atlantic six times trying to make up her
mind and in the process came to be known locally as "the Atlantic
swimmer."[9] More pathetic was the case of a returned Yank living as a
farm laborer in County Galway who confided, "Some came home and
regretted it. I am one of these. All the money I brought with me was
soon spent."[10]

It is clear, then, that with the possible exception of the women,
there was no single reason which explained the return of the Yank. The
motives were as varied as the persons who acted upon them. The only
other exception was the Yank who returned merely to visit but did not
intend to stay. He returned largely because of a sincere desire to see his
family just once more, and also to glory in the admiration he was certain to receive in honor of the obvious evidence of his success in
America: his grand clothes, his liberal supply of money, and just as
important, the very fact that he was able to afford a return visit. He was
duly accorded the admiration he sought, and with his vanity gratified
and his funds exhausted, he once more took leave of Ireland, probably
never to return again to the land of his birth.

What sort of impression did these Yanks create when they
returned? How did the community react to them? What was its attitude toward the Yank and the land whence he returned? As far as indi-

vidual families were concerned, it was, of course, a pure joy to have a son or daughter return. Recalling perhaps the terrible finality of the American wake, a retired housekeeper could only compare such a homecoming to a resurrection, because to her "It was as if they was returnin' from the dead."[11] If it seemed less miraculous to the neighbors it was for them no less joyous an occasion, and for nights on end they came streaming to the happy home to view the Yank in all his finery, and also to inquire after the welfare of their own loved ones beyond the sea.

As is true with most people so it was with the Yanks that the initial impression they made was a visual one, and the phrase most consistently used to describe them was that America had "smartened them up." Their clothes especially were greatly admired, and as much for the quantity as for the quality. According to one farmer, "People would make a great wonder of a Yankee having two or three suits, for the ordinary man at home would have one good suit for going to Mass in and it would have to do him for years and years."[12] The women caused as great a stir, and one woman who had worked as a cook remembered the time in her youth when a girl she knew came home on a visit from America. The Yank's mother was quickly besieged by all the local females who wanted to know what Mass her daughter was planning to attend that Sunday. The reason was plain enough, for

> . . . the whole parish would be turnin' out at that Mass for to see what she'd be wearin' and they'd be talkin' about it for a week. And the next Sunday they'd all be waitin' again to see the new frock for she'd be wearin' a new frock each Sunday.[13]

These Yanks in their sartorial splendor were living advertisements for America and provided unspoken encouragement to others to emigrate. "It must be a wonderful country and the fine dacent [sic] clothes that comes from it," was a remark often heard in the west.[14]

The admiration extended beyond the Yanks' finery, for it was also noted with satisfaction that a great improvement had been effected in their manners and bearing. They were self-confident, more "self-possessed," observed a retired schoolteacher, who also noticed that "their shyness and gaucherie had left them" and that in general they were "self-determined and sometimes — men chiefly — self-opinionated."[15] In 1880 the chairman of the Civil Bill Courts in County Kerry testified to the remarkable difference between two brothers, one who had emigrated and one who had not. In every way possible — dress, manners, appearance — the Yank was vastly improved over his brother, although the question as to whether his morals were also improved was, the chairman felt, "another matter altogether."[16]

Two other traits which greatly impressed the people at home were the cleanliness and industry of the Yank, and particularly the latter characteristic. During their sojourn in the United States they had developed the habit of hard work and had imbibed a certain "go-aheadness" which, according to a retired police constable in County Mayo, was "in peculiar contrast to the lackadaisical, easy and happy-go-lucky way of living which characterized their manner of life before they left home."[17] Returned Yanks, it was observed, rose earlier in the morning and worked harder than most of their neighbors. "They were all workers," commented a local politician, while the schoolteacher reflected that a Yankee bride "worked and cleaned with a finish that far surpassed her home sisters."[18] Some Yanks did not hesitate to criticize their friends and relatives for lazy habits but all to no avail, for the force of tradition was stronger than their most vigorous protests. Perhaps the most interesting illustration of this Yankee industriousness was related by a County Kerry cobbler who recalled the story his father told of one Yank in the neighborhood who returned late in life to stay with his friends on their farm:

> He could not remain idle for a single moment, he was always busy at some kind of work on his friends' farm. When there was no work for him on the farm he would go down to the seashore and collect the wrack seaweed in heaps. One day one of his neighbors found him engaged in this work. . . . "John," he said, "what is the idea of collecting all this seaweed? Sure you have no land of your own on which to put it." "Well, I guess I . . . haven't," replied John, "but you got land and other neighbors got land, and you can all come right along and draw it home. It's a shame to see the tide taking it out to the sea again, so I thought it was better to gather it up. It will be of some use to somebody."[19]

Returning from a land fabled for its wealth, virtually all Yanks were thought to be rich, or at least reasonably comfortable.

Interestingly enough this was a reputation which many Yanks felt compelled to live up to, and liberal spending thus became another of the traits associated with them. Usually this took the form of buying drinks for friends and neighbors at the local pub where if a Yank "stood" for a few drinks during the day he was "put down as a dacent [*sic*] man."[20]

But those who spent most freely were generally the Yanks who came only to visit, not the ones who came to stay. The former could afford to be generous for they would soon be leaving again, whereas the Yank who came to stay was acutely conscious of the limited funds he brought with him. He therefore spent them with a Yankee thrift and frugality which stood in sharp contrast to the munificence of the visiting prodigal. These Yanks, moreover, had acquired a strong dislike for contracting debts and paid for everything "on the nail." They bargained with shopkeepers and saw to it that they were not overcharged. It was for these reasons that the "staying Yanks" came to earn the reputation for being "tight" or "mean" with their money, and it was not to them that the neighbors looked for their liberal libations.

If some Yanks seemed annoyingly inhibited with their money, few could be accused of restraint in speech. While clothes, manners, and money were their visible signs of identification, the American accent and a marked prolixity were their invisible though equally distinguishing insignias. The returned Yank, whether home on a visit or home to stay, was fond of talking and especially of expatiating on the wonders of America. According to one informant, they not only talked a good deal about America, but while they were at it "no one else got opening their mouths." A County Donegal woman recalled the time a neighbor ran into a particularly loquacious Yank and after finally tearing himself away, commented to her, "You know, Annie, he wasn't a blow but a constant blast."[21]

Along with their constant chatter also went a fondness for emphasizing their American accents, and many clung to the accent long after all other vestiges of their American experience had disappeared. The same was true of expressions which were considered typically American, such as "I guess," "I calculate," and "I reckon." So characteristic did these phrases become that when a railroad porter in the west of Ireland saw a group of returned Yanks alighting at the local station around the turn of the century, he hailed their arrival by announcing, "Here comes a bunch of 'I-guessers'!"[22] An illustrative incident occurred in County Antrim when a young girl, shortly after returning from the United States, wished to exhibit her new command of American speech. At a party given for her on the night of her return she kept calling, "Where is Papa?" Her father, a shy, reticent man and a Gaelic-speaker, had secreted himself in a corner of the kitchen and had not the slightest notion what it was his daughter wanted. Again she called, "Where is Papa?" Finally from his corner the old farmer answered, "I think you left it hanging behind the door."[23]

Many Yanks were also much given to boasting of their wealth, although here again it was confined largely to those home on a visit. Unless carried to extremes, however, the bragging was not greatly resented and was usually taken with a heavy grain of salt. The joy of having a Yank return, coupled with his liberal spending habits, generally led people to overlook his bluff and bluster. He was indulged his moment of glory, and his minor excesses were forgiven, for as one farmer's wife put it, "the bragging of a generous person is got over lightly."[24]

Their talk of America, however, had wider repercussions, for it tended to encourage other young people to emigrate. Their praise of the United States, reenforced as it was by the visual evidence of their own well-being, convinced many that they too would profit by journeying across the Atlantic. For some people the appearance of a well-dressed Yank was all the incentive they needed to make up their minds. Indeed the chief effect of their dress, declared one County Galway farmer, was to "reenforce the idea that America was a wonderful country to go to."[25] In 1884 the United States consul in Cork was convinced that the periodic visits of returning Yanks had a "great influence upon the minds of those with whom they . . . [came] in contact," a factor which he felt was an important cause of emigration.[26] Often returned Yanks became the targets of innumerable questions directed at them by young people who were thinking of leaving and who were anxious to learn as much as possible about wages and conditions in America. Most Yanks answered these queries soberly, if not without open encouragement.

Some Yanks actively tried to persuade others to emigrate, and a few even took back two or three people with them when they returned. In 1863 a Protestant clergyman from County Donegal related how one of his young parishioners, the only son of a small farmer, went to the United States and after a short while came back to claim his sweetheart and take her to America. When the clergyman remonstrated with the young man that he should remain in Ireland, he was met with the irresistible argument of his former parishioner that while only a laborer in Chicago, he was "as well fed as you reverence" and hoped before long to buy a farm "free of rent or taxes." The *Irish Times* regretfully noted that success stories of this type became a subject of discussion not only in the local village but at fairs, markets, and popular gatherings.[27]

The majority of Yanks, however, apparently did not try to induce others to emigrate, although according to one farmer people got the impression from the way they talked that "it was a shame to live any place else."[28] Nevertheless most Yanks were realists who had no wish to mislead those desirous of leaving. They answered all questions regarding America as best they could, and while they readily admitted the opportunities available there, they were quick to point out that nothing was gained without hard work, harder work than in Ireland. America, they made clear, was no idle paradise. For this very reason a few Yanks even went so far as to try to dissuade people from going and used the standard argument that if people worked as hard at home they would be as well off. A woman of ninety-three recalled that when her brother returned to Ireland for a visit after spending fifty successful years in the United States, he "time and again emphasized that the people who remained at home were happier . . . than those who emigrated."[29] But the evidence of success wrought through his own hard work was a far more convincing argument for those who were young, ambitious, and energetic. They were more easily impressed by the concrete results of his labors than they were by the sentimental reflections of a nostalgic old man. Happiness for them had at least some connection with material well-being.

When Yanks returned to stay, they either bought small businesses for themselves or became farmers once again. Most preferred business to farm life because of the higher social prestige attached to being a shopkeeper, and also because it was a less rigorous type of work. Since running a pub required little experience and only a small amount of capital, pubs became the favorite business sought by Yanks. In one community in County Wexford the only Yank who ever returned to stay within the memory of one informant did so to buy a pub, while as late as 1955 it was declared that every bar in Killarney was run by a Yank.[30]

Although pubs were the favorite they were not the only businesses that Yanks entered. One small farmer remembered a cousin who returned to buy a small hotel.[31] Some established little shops or country stores. In 1882 the assistant-master of Eton College, on a trip through the west of Ireland with Henry George, the American economist, noted that the country shop and house in which he found lodgings were owned and operated by returned Yanks. He also observed that the house was built with money earned in America and was bigger and cleaner than most dwellings in the area.[32] A few who returned to set up in business were unsuccessful. One such Yank was a twenty-nine-year-old engine maker who returned in the 1880s after three years in the United States. He tried to establish himself in Dublin and Cork, but when both ventures met with failure, he abandoned Ireland once again with the bitter retort that the country had no "spirit" left and was "rotten to the core."[33]

A good many returned Yanks bought farms, and if they had sufficient capital, they hired laborers to do the work for them. Some were too old for the strenuous routine of farm life and had no alternative but to hire help. The size of the farm varied with the amount of money they had been able to amass, but in the vast majority of cases they were, by Irish standards, small or medium-sized farms. In 1880 the resident agent of one 12,000-acre estate in County Wexford testified that many of the farms purchased from his estate were bought by returned Yanks, since they were the only ones who possessed the requisite capital.[34] Those who bought farms, however small, almost invariably built new houses or made extensive improvements on the existing ones. Some became fairly prosperous, and in 1867 Lord Dufferin declared that several of the most prosperous farmers on his estate were returned Yanks.[35]

A few did not succeed and one informant recalled the case of a Yank in County Mayo who, unable to get on in the United States, returned to marry and become a farmer, only to repeat his American failure in Ireland. When drunk he would trot out his only cow with the intention of selling the animal to finance his re-emigration. Always the cow was rescued and in time it came to be known locally as "the American" or "the dollar."[36] Perhaps the most successful — and ironic — story concerned the uncle of one Donegal farmer who returned with sufficient means to buy out the local landlords, a family who in their day had evicted a number of tenants and whose rent was often paid with American money.[37]

Very few Yanks were ever able to return and live solely on their savings. Those who did were generally ne'er-do-wells who spent their time drinking and in a short while squandered the limited funds they had managed to accumulate. Yanks of this type were rarely respected by the community, and in several cases they even became public charges. After the initial novelty of their return wore off the neighbors simply ignored them.

As well dressed as the Yanks were and as hard as they worked to make improvements in their houses or on their farms, they nevertheless remained objects of curiosity and admiration; rarely did they become examples to be emulated. While their clothing was much wondered at, those Yanks who paraded about in outlandish styles or colors only exposed themselves to "searbas," an Irish combination of ridicule and bitter comment. No one attempted to imitate the American styles, for while they were accepted as natural in the case of Yanks, all others were expected to conform to the habits of the community. Those who dared deviate only became the object of an even more searing "searbas," which quickly forced them back into the local mold. "People in the country," commented one Galway farmer, "do not change easily their lifelong habits or adapt themselves readily to new ways."[38]

Even those returned Yanks who tried to cling only to the new cooking techniques they had learned in America were often forced by circumstances to abandon the effort. Most "Yankee brides" married into farms and the cooking facilities available in the small cottages were of the most primitive kind. A retired schoolteacher provided the following description, which was typical of the houses in the small Galway village in which he was reared:

> There was neither grate nor range; the fire composed of peat was on the hearth, and the kettle or cooking pot was hung on a crook fastened to a bar in the chimney. The women who

saw meat roasted and fried in the States soon saw this was impossible here; everything had to be boiled. There was a large pot for the potatoes, a small one for cooking bacon and cabbage . . . a kettle for boiling water for tea, all in turn hung on this crook . . .[39]

Beyond their own homes Yanks rarely tried to introduce techniques or methods learned in America. Sometimes even attempts to make improvements in their own houses were resisted, as was the case with a sister who returned from America to live with her two old brothers. While they allowed her to have the thatch removed and replaced with a new slate roof, they objected strenuously to "rising" the house, that is, having a second story added. "By God," she was firmly told, "you're not going to make New York of Ballyfad!"[40] There were some exceptions. In one district of County Galway a returned Yank introduced a method of binding sheaves of wheat that was much more rapid than the Irish method. It became known locally as the "American belt," but there is no evidence that it spread beyond this area.[41] In County Antrim a Yank returned to establish himself as a carpenter and employed a good many techniques he had learned in America. He became fairly successful and passed on his knowledge to his apprentices.[42]

For the great majority, however, it was true that whatever techniques or methods they had acquired in America they left at the water's edge when they returned to Ireland and quickly resumed the life they had known before they had emigrated. "They were just as if they never left Ireland," reflected an informant from County Westmeath.[43] To a land agent who testified in 1880 it was "most extraordinary" that even those who returned "with all the appearance of prosperity" fell back into their old habits in a very short space of time.[44]

When it came to politics returned Yanks were no more active participants than the rest of their neighbors. Occasionally a few became members of local councils or even rose to be county councilors, but these were usually people who had shown an interest in politics even before they had emigrated. The mere fact of having lived in the United States does not appear to have whetted their political appetites or interests in Irish affairs. Sometimes a Yank of stature returned temporarily to deliver a series of political speeches as was the case with one prelate who came back in 1865 to advocate that Ireland declare herself "at once ... part and parcel of the American Republic." But such instances were rare and even the most anti-British journals did not relish the proposition.[45]

In the realm of political ideas the returned Yank seems to have made no significant impression. If he brought any back with him, he appears to have kept them to himself. In the 1880s one French observer of the Irish scene noted that at the height of the Land League agitation the peasant's hatred was directed against the landlord not because he was noble and rich, as had been the case in France, but because he was Protestant and an "invader." Even if Yanks did return with "ultra-democratic ideas," he observed, the bulk of the nation did not hold them.[46]

In conclusion it must be said that the impact of the returned Yank on Irish rural society was a negligible one. The reasons are many. For one thing he never returned in sufficiently large groups to have lent the weight of numbers to his newly acquired characteristics. It was always as an individual that he came, often because of a desire to pick up the threads of a life he knew and loved best. Moreover, as much as some might have criticized Irish habits and methods, the criticism was usually leveled by the Yankee home on a visit, a person who was much more a figure of fun and one whose remarks were generally listened to with open skepticism.

Those who returned to stay had no real wish, and in most cases were much too old, to try to introduce anything radically new or different. Furthermore none of those who returned were leaders, either of men or public opinion. They were simply ordinary people and as such could not have added the force of personal authority to any innovations they may have wished to introduce. Those who were successful in political leadership had greater opportunities for their talents in Boston, New York, or Chicago than they would have had in Ireland, and they therefore had little reason to return. Finally, it must be borne in mind that the greater proportion of returned Yanks were women, especially among those who came back to stay, and in a rural society dominated by men the activities of women were largely confined to children, cooking, and cleaning.

Perhaps fundamentally the returned Yank transferred so little of his American experience because he was not, after all, a genuine American in the eyes of the Irish. A group of strangers, if they do not represent a threat to a community, are generally respected for their differences, and over a period of years some of their customs or ideas might even infiltrate and become accepted by the society in which they have settled. But the returned Yank was at best an adapter, a hybrid whose roots were essentially in Irish soil, and he was not respected as the true bearer of new gifts. The returnee was still an Irishman and he had not been deculturated by his American experience. Thus even if he had had the inclination for innovation, which he did not, the social pressures for conformity would have presented an insuperable obstacle.

Except for the question of land, nineteenth-century Irish rural society was essentially a conservative one and well-nigh impregnable against new or exotic influences. This fact was quickly grasped by the United States consul in Cork who in 1887 observed that "the spirit of the [Irish] people leans toward contentment with things as they are than toward adoption of anything new."[47] Perhaps one of the most revealing insights into Irish society and its attitudes was penned by a contemporary of William Butler Yeats, George A. Birmingham, who wrote in 1911:

> Curiously enough, considering all they do for us, we are not fond of the Irish Americans. . . . We do not, as a rule, much like them either as settlers or visitors. . . . Their ways of life are a continual reproach to our easy going habits. We call them "Yanks" or "returned Yanks" and feel we should get on better without them. . . . They impress on us that we ought to "hustle round a bit," a thing we detest doing, and tell us that a year in America would "speed us up." We know it would, but we have not yet accepted speed as one of the ideals of life.[48]

Nevertheless there were qualities which the Yank possessed which were honestly admired, or at least wondered at, although they were rarely emulated. These were industriousness, thrift, hard work, and cleanliness; and they helped define the label "Yank," which was his badge of identification. For most, however, the label denoted only a superficial difference and did not hide the fact that fundamentally the

Yank was an Irishman who sought to return from the land of the stranger. He left no lasting influences and his only monument was his label "Yank," which was transferred to his children and grandchildren long after he had passed on. Today, in many parts of the country there are farms which are still called the "Yankee Murphy's" or the "Yankee O'Brien's," even though the present owners have never set foot on American soil. Perhaps the other thing he left behind was a legacy of tall tales about America with which he often regaled his family and friends. They may not have been believed, but along with the American letters they did much to familiarize the Irish with the "land across the herring pond," as some Yanks called America, and helped create the illusion that New York was but the next parish over from Galway.

Conclusion

The Impact of Emigration

B ETWEEN 1845 AND 1900 nearly five million men and women sailed forth from Ireland in search of new homes and brighter futures. For a country whose total population rarely exceeded eight million souls and more often numbered less than six million, this was a remarkable outpouring of human resources. In great part those who left were the young and the unmarried, those in the prime of life and health. They were people full of hope and energy — the buoyant hallmarks of youthful optimism — people who could find no adequate outlets for their vigor and ambition in the dreary pattern of Irish agriculture or the limited opportunities in Irish industry. The harsh facts of Irish economics thus became (and still remain) one of the principal underlying causes of a continuing drain on Ireland's population, the end of which is not yet in sight. Indeed for over a century the Irishman's favorite remedy for hard times has been emigration.

Of the multitudes who left, the vast majority came to the United States. Here they had friends and relatives who could smooth the way for the newcomers, and who also often provided the passage money for the Atlantic crossing. One brought out another and in this way an endless human chain stretched down through the decades of the nineteenth century. If the Irish end of that chain was anchored in the expellant economics of low wages and infrequent employment, its other end was moored in the magnetic prospect of American opportunities. The lure of America did not by itself create Irish emigration, any more than it created the stream of emigrants from Sweden, Norway, Germany, or England. The American lure, however, did condition the direction and to a lesser extent the intensity of flow of the emigrant stream. Emigrant letters, millions of them, flooded back across the Atlantic to Ireland and provided a direct, personal link between those in the land of hope and those in the land of despair. They furnished the primary source of information out of which was constructed an appealing image of America as a land of ample work, good wages, and social equality. Not all letters were uniformly favorable, but it is clear that the majority of these were sent during times of economic adversity, social distress, or personal misfortune. By far the greater proportion painted an altogether attractive picture which was not made any less alluring because of the candor and forthrightness which generally characterized their authors.

So vast and so prolonged an emigration was bound to have repercussions. The inexorable decline in population aroused an impassioned protest from the Irish press, whether Catholic or Protestant, nationalist or antinationalist. All were agreed that a shrinking populace was synonymous with domestic decay, especially when those who departed were the very "bone and sinew" of the country. Relatively few of the protests were directed against the emigrants themselves; they, after all, were the symptoms of Ireland's malady, not its cause. In any case, the clamor of journalistic dissent had not the slightest visible effect on the outflow of humanity; emigration continued unabated.

The press therefore addressed itself to an analysis of the nature of Ireland's ills and to a quest for feasible cures. Here the unanimity achieved in opposition disintegrated into a diversity of diagnoses and a host of nostrums. The great touchstone of analysis and the point of departure for most papers was the twin one of religion and politics. Catholic papers, inclined to be pronationalist in political sentiment, saw the demoralizing land system and British rule as the prime evils of Irish difficulties. Hence in their view the achievement of home rule and the reform of the land system would arrest the outward flow. Protestant papers, staunchly loyal to the Crown, regarded the lack of industry as Ireland's great bane. Nationalist agitation, they felt, merely created social unrest which frightened away investment capital and thereby served to encourage emigration.

There were elements of truth in both positions, but the real difficulty was that even with land reform there would not have been enough land to satisfy the needs of everyone. And as for investment capital, it was the lack of Irish natural resources that failed to attract it rather than nationalist agitation that repelled it. In the 1870s, moreover, Europe in general and Britain in particular were beginning a last great surge of imperialistic expansion. The handsome profits to be earned by investing in colonial enterprises — or even earlier in American railroads — were not likely to be overshadowed by the meager investment prospects in the Emerald Isle.

The Irish Catholic Church as such never took a stand on emigration; officially the clergy neither condemned nor condoned it. Official silence, however, did not mean that the Church was insensitive to the unabating flight from Erin — prelates and clergy alike, after all, were Irishmen. If it meant anything at all, the Church's silence probably reflected a sensible conviction that nothing was to be gained by mere protest. Instead, recognizing that its true mission lay in ministering to the needs of the emigrants and seeing to it that they were kept within the fold of Roman Catholicism, the Church was content to allow individual priests to take such action as they saw fit. Irish priests were practical men. Hence it comes as no surprise that the most successful guidebook for Irish emigrants to the United States was written by an Irish priest. Nor does it occasion astonishment that fully a half-dozen years before the onset of the famine a persevering priest had succeeded in establishing a seminary in Dublin for the purpose of training missionaries for service in America and other English-speaking countries favored by Irish emigrants.

Contrary to the alarmist views of most journals of the period, emigration did not have a seriously adverse effect on Ireland's economic structure. One may go further and say that emigration proved to be a useful safety valve which relieved population pressure on the land and reduced an oversupply of labor that the existing state of Irish agriculture and industry was incapable of absorbing. The departure of the emigrants thus meant more regular employment at somewhat higher wages for those who chose to remain. However, the safety valve of emigration afforded but a temporary relief, and throughout the course of the half-century there was no significant decline in the proportion of paupers in Ireland. Of greater importance was the fact that emigration made possible the consolidation of many small uneconomic land holdings and facilitated a revolutionary changeover from tillage to pasturage as the dominant form of Irish agriculture. By the turn of the century Irish agriculture rested on a far sounder economic footing than some fifty years earlier. On the other hand emigration had little to do with the retardation of Irish industry. The fact that industry remained relatively undeveloped was a cause of emigration rather than its effect, and in some measure that retardation was a reflection of the impact of British commercial policy on Ireland.

Outside the realm of economics the American emigration left a lasting impress upon Irish rural society. So widespread, so persistent, and so personally poignant a phenomenon could not fail to evoke an emotional response from the demonstrative and superstitious Irish countrymen. As a direct outgrowth of the emigration process there developed a cluster of customs, charms, and ballads which revealed the depth to which emigration had penetrated the public consciousness. The outstanding example was the American wake, an adaptation of the Irish death ceremony to commemorate the loss of the living from family and community. Since those who left were rarely expected to return, emigration meant a severance of all immediate and intimate associations — in reality, a form of death. The American wake thus provided an appropriate though tragic setting for the release of pent-up grief and had the effect of an emotional catharsis for friends, family, and emigrant alike.

The use of charms, aside from those which were supposed to ensure the safe voyage of the emigrant, betrayed the anxiety of parting lovers lest one or the other become faithless during the long separation. Ballads, on the other hand, like the American wake, sang the sorrow of emigration and reflected the distress and melancholy of those who were left behind. To some degree the sorrow was tempered by a realization that the emigrant was likely to improve himself materially in the New World, but that was small comfort to parents about to lose a son or a daughter forever. Consequently, while most ballads wished the emigrants well in their new lives abroad, they nevertheless reflected that the old lives at home were bound to be emptier and drearier.

American wakes, charms, and ballads were all direct outgrowths of the emigration phenomenon. There were indirect results as well. These were comprehended in the American return tide, the flowback from America via the emigrant channel of money and to a lesser extent of men. Over the course of the half-century the aggregate total of individual remittances reached prodigious proportions, amounting as it did to over $250,000,000. Some 40 percent of this sum came in the form of prepaid passage tickets and was sufficient to finance over three fourths of the total emigration from Ireland. In this sense Irish emigration very largely became a truly self-perpetuating phenomenon.

The remaining 60 percent was sent back as a huge voluntary subsidy, and it was this which the Irish called the "American money." Rarely returned in amounts large enough to permit the buying of land, the single greatest use of American money was to pay the rent for the multitude of small and medium-sized farms. Some was also used to pay off shopkeepers' bills, to make needed repairs on farmhouses, to replace a lost farm animal, and occasionally to finance the education of a younger member of the family. American money for many people became an important element of subsistence, and it is clear that without it the degree of misery and suffering would have been substantially greater than was actually the case. That more was not done of a constructive nature for the economy as a whole was due to the manner in which the money came back, normally in small individual sums. There was no central agency to serve as a repository for all contributions and empowered to invest large aggregate sums in enterprises deemed likely to effect significant improvements. Under the circumstances such an agency was beyond the realm of practicality. Moreover, even if one had existed it would probably have been British controlled, and this alone would have sufficed to ensure its failure. After the experiences of the famine and the bitter memories it imbedded in the Irish, it would have been a rare emigrant indeed who would willingly have sent his hard-earned remittances to a British organization.

How much more effectively American money could have been utilized by a central directing agency was illustrated by the use made of the far smaller contributions sent to various nationalist political organizations. The outstanding example was the Land League which subsisted to a large degree on the donations of the American Irish. The results achieved by the League were certainly impressive. With the benefit of hindsight, however, one wonders what it might have achieved additionally had it broadened its prospectus to include the positive function of advocating and underwriting large-scale improvements in agriculture and industry. But this perhaps was too much to ask of an essentially actionist organization whose energies were totally absorbed in a strenuous land war.

The other element which comprised the American return tide was a human one and was represented in the returned Yanks. In reality the Irish were never "birds of passage," and the number who actually made the return voyage was very small. Nevertheless enough did come back to make the returned Yank a familiar figure in almost every village and town in Ireland, although none of them made any serious attempts to introduce American techniques, methods, or ideas. Even if they had, the conservatism of rural Irish society would have militated against their acceptance. Yet there were qualities about the returned Yanks which distinguished them from their neighbors, and even if such American-acquired habits as thrift, industry, and cleanliness were not emulated, they were certainly admired. Moreover the eagerness of returned Yanks to recount the wonders of America to all who would listen added measurably to the fund of information already provided by the emigrant letters. Together they did much to familiarize the Irish with the "New Ireland" beyond the sea and helped create the illusion that New York was but the next parish over from Galway.

In retrospect, there can be no doubt that the impact of the American emigration on Ireland attained considerable proportions. The vigor of the protest from the press was evidence of the measure of alarm generated in thinking Irishmen. Yet despite this wholly natural reaction, it is plain that emigration was generally beneficial for Ireland. By the turn of the century the standard of living for the population as a whole was noticeably higher than in prefamine days, and agriculture was organized on a sounder basis. For this, emigration must claim a share of the credit. The folkloristic reaction occasioned by the American emigration is not susceptible of any evaluative judgments, and one can only note with interest and compassion how a people so strongly bound by filial ties as the Irish responded to the shattering impact of emigration.

As for the return tide, it is clear that the "American money" played a far more important role than the returned Yank. While neither contributed to the introduction of any tangible and permanent American influences, each in its own way reinforced the impression conveyed by the myriad emigrant letters of America as a land of freedom, opportunity, and equality. That impression has not yet lost its appeal for the men and women of Ireland.

Appendix

Appendix Tables

Table 1. Yearly Number of Emigrants from Ireland to the United States, 1845–1901

Year	Total Number of Overseas Emigrants from Ireland	Number Emigrating to United States	Year	Total Number of Overseas Emigrants from Ireland	Number Emigrating to United States
1845....	74,970	50,207	1873....	83,692	75,536
1846....	105,917	68,023	1874....	60,496	48,136
1847....	219,885	118,120	1875....	41,449	31,433
1848....	181,316	151,003	1876....	25,976	16,432
1849....	218,842	180,189	1877....	22,831	13,991
1850....	213,649	184,351	1878....	29,492	18,602
			1879....	41,296	30,058
1851....	254,537	219,232	1880....	93,641	83,018
1852....	224,997	195,801			
1853....	192,609	156,970	1881....	76,200	67,339
1854....	150,209	111,095	1882....	84,132	68,300
1855....	78,854	57,164	1883....	105,743	82,849
1856....	71,724	58,777	1884....	72,566	59,204
1857....	86,233	66,080	1885....	60,017	50,657
1858....	43,281	31,498	1886....	61,276	52,858
1859....	52,981	41,180	1887....	78,901	69,084
1860....	60,835	52,103	1888....	73,233	66,306
			1889....	64,923	57,897
1861....	36,322	28,209	1890....	57,484	52,110
1862....	49,680	33,521			
1863....	116,391	94,477	1891....	58,436	53,438
1864....	115,428	94,368	1892....	52,902	48,966
1865....	100,676	82,085	1893....	52,132	49,122
1866....	98,890	86,594	1894....	42,008	39,597
1867....	88,622	79,571	1895....	54,349	52,047
1868....	64,965	57,662	1896....	42,222	39,952
1869....	73,325	66,467	1897....	35,678	32,822
1870....	74,283	67,891	1898....	34,395	30,878
			1899....	42,890	38,631
1871....	71,067	65,591	1900....	45,905	41,848
1872....	72,763	66,752	1901....	39,210	35,535

Source: *Commission on Emigration and Other Population Problems 1948–1954: Majority Report* (in mimeograph) (Ministry for Social Welfare [Eire], 1954), pp. 309–311.

Table 2. Population of Ireland and Its Provinces, 1841–1901

Year	Ireland	Leinster	Munster	Ulster	Connaught
1841	8,196,597	1,982,169	2,404,460	2,389,263	1,420,705
1851	6,574,278	1,682,320	1,865,600	2,013,879	1,012,479
1861	5,888,564	1,547,635	1,513,558	1,914,236	913,135
1871	5,412,377	1,339,451	1,393,485	1,833,228	846,213
1881	5,174,836	1,278,989	1,331,115	1,743,075	821,657
1891	4,704,750	1,191,782	1,173,643	1,619,814	719,511
1901	4,456,546	1,150,485	1,075,075	1,581,351	649,635

Table 3. Rate of Population Decrease in Ireland and Its Provinces, 1841–1901

Decade	Ireland	Leinster	Munster	Ulster	Connaught
1841–51	19.85%	15.25%	22.47%	15.69%	28.81%
1851–61	11.50	12.86	18.53	4.85	9.59
1861–71	6.67	8.11	7.93	4.23	7.33
1871–81	4.39	4.51	4.48	4.92	2.90
1881–91	9.08	7.13	11.92	7.07	11.79
1891–1901	5.23	3.26	8.29	2.28	10.08

Source: *Census of Ireland, 1901. Part II. General Report*, pp. 4 and 169 [Cd. 1190], H.C. 1902, cxxix.

Table 4. Overseas Emigration from Ireland by Destination, 1851–1900

Period	Total Overseas Emigration	U.S.A. No.	U.S.A. %	Canada No.	Canada %	Australia–New Zealand No.	Australia–New Zealand %	Other Overseas Countries No.	Other Overseas Countries %
1851–60	1,216,265	989,880	81.4	118,118	9.7	101,541	8.3	6,726	0.6
1861–70	818,582	690,845	84.4	40,079	4.9	82,917	10.1	4,741	0.6
1871–80	542,703	449,549	82.8	25,783	4.8	61,946	11.4	5,425	1.0
1881–90	734,475	626,604	85.3	44,505	6.1	55,476	7.5	7,890	1.1
1891–1900	460,917	427,301	92.7	10,648	2.3	11,448	2.5	11,520	2.5
Total and Average	3,772,942	3,184,179	85.3	239,133	5.6	313,328	7.9	36,302	1.2

Source: Commission on Emigration and . . . Population Problems . . . p. 119.

Table 5. Number and Percentage of Immigrants to the United States, 1821–1900

Period	Total of All Immigrants	Irish No.	Irish % of Total	British No.	British % of Total	German No.	German % of Total	Scandinavian No.	Scandinavian % of Total
1821–50	2,455,815	1,038,824	42.3	367,933	15.0	593,841	24.2	16,966	0.7
1851–60	2,598,214	914,119	35.2	423,974	16.3	951,667	36.6	24,680	0.9
1861–70	2,314,824	435,778	18.8	606,896	26.2	787,468	34.0	126,392	5.4
1871–80	2,812,191	436,871	15.5	548,043	19.5	718,182	25.6	243,016	8.6
1881–90	5,246,613	655,482	12.5	807,357	15.4	1,452,970	27.7	656,494	12.5
1891–1900	3,687,564	390,179*	10.6	270,019*	7.3	505,152	13.7	371,512	10.1
Total and Average	19,115,221	3,871,253	22.5	3,024,222	16.6	5,009,280	26.9	1,439,060	6.4

Source: Twelfth Census of the United States, 1900. Population. Part I, Vol. I, p. cii.
*Estimated for the year ending June 30, 1899.

Table 6. Irish- and Foreign-Born Population of Continental United States, 1850–1900

Year	Total U.S. Population	Total Foreign-Born	Total Irish-Born	% of Irish-Born In Foreign-Born Population	% of Irish-Born In U.S. Population
1850	23,191,876	2,244,602	961,719	42.8	4.15
1860	31,443,321	4,138,697	1,611,304	38.9	5.12
1870	38,558,371	5,567,229	1,855,827	33.3	4.81
1880	50,155,783	6,679,943	1,854,571	27.8	3.70
1890	62,622,250	9,249,547	1,871,509	20.2	2.80
1900	75,568,686	10,341,276	1,615,459	15.6	2.13

Sources: *Twelfth Census of the United States*, Vol. I, p. xix. "Statistical Review of Immigration, 1819–1910. Distribution of Immigrants, 1850–1900," *Senate Doc. No. 756, 61st Cong., 3rd sess.*, p. 416.

Table 7. Distribution of Irish-Born in United States by Six Selected Occupations, 1870–90

Occupations	1870	1880	1890
Laborers (not specified)			
Number	229,199	225,122	203,639
Percentage of work force	24.1	22.9	19.9
Servants			
Number	145,956	122,194	168,969
Percentage of work force	15.4	12.5	15.8
Farmers			
Number	88,923	107,708	100,095
Percentage of work force	9.4	11.0	9.4
Agricultural laborers			
Number	43,398	24,236	25,140
Percentage of work force	4.6	2.5	2.3
Cotton mill operatives			
Number	36,112	38,663	37,245
Percentage of work force	3.8	3.9	3.5
Railroad employees			
Number	37,822	32,931	33,263
Percentage of work force	4.0	3.3	3.1
Total work force in all occupations	947,234	978,854	1,066,162
Total in six selected occupations	581,410	550,854	568,351
Percentage of total work force in six selected occupations	61.3	56.2	53.3

Source: *U.S. Census Reports, 1870–1890.*

Table 8. Seven States with Highest Number of Irish-Born Population, 1850–1900

Year	Total Irish-Born in U.S.	Irish in 7 States		Number of Irish-Born						
		Total No. Irish-Born	% of Total Irish-Born	Mass.	Conn.	N.Y.	N.J.	Penn.	Ohio	Ill.
1850	961,719	747,880	77.7	115,917	26,689	343,111	31,092	151,723	51,562	27,786
1860	1,611,304	1,167,295	72.4	185,434	55,445	498,072	62,006	201,939	76,826	87,573
1870	1,855,827	1,340,974	72.2	216,120	70,630	528,806	86,784	235,798	82,674	120,162
1880	1,854,571	1,322,637	71.3	226,700	70,638	499,445	93,079	236,505	78,927	117,343
1890	1,871,509	1,360,677	72.7	259,902	77,880	483,375	101,059	243,836	70,127	124,498
1900	1,615,459	1,216,797	75.1	249,916	70,994	425,553	94,844	205,909	55,018	114,563

Source: *U.S. Census Reports, 1850–1900.*

Table 9. Percentage of Illiteracy among Irish Population, 1851–1901

Area	1851	1861	1871	1881	1891	1901
Ireland						
Population over age 5.....	46.8	38.7	33.4	25.2	18.4	13.7
Age group 12–40.........	37.2*	29.1*	23.8†	15.8	9.5	6.3‡
Leinster						
Population over age 5.....	39.0	31.1	27.0	20.3	15.4	11.3
Age group 12–40.........	29.5*	21.6*	17.5†	11.2	7.3	4.7‡
Munster						
Population over age 5.....	55.5	46.1	39.2	28.5	19.9	14.0
Age group 12–40.........	45.1*	35.7*	28.8†	15.2	7.9	4.7‡
Ulster						
Population over age 5.....	35.3	30.0	26.4	20.3	15.4	12.5
Age group 12–40.........	27.0*	21.7*	18.1†	12.9	8.8	6.3‡
Connaught						
Population over age 5.....	66.3	57.1	49.3	37.9	27.4	20.7
Age group 12–40.........	54.0*	44.8*	37.0†	24.1	14.0	9.3‡

Source: *Census of Ireland. General Reports, 1851–1901.*
* Computed.
† Age group 15–40.
‡ Age group 14–40.

Table 10. Letters Sent from United States to United Kingdom, 1854–75

Year	No. of Letters	Year	No. of Letters
1854	2,137,611	1865	1,895,377
1855	1,937,572	1866	2,270,365
1856	1,997,571	1867	2,348,571
1857	1,917,934	1868	2,484,931
1858	1,603,609	1869	2,767,216
1859	1,534,189	1870	3,716,031
1860	1,658,950	1871	4,539,718
1861	1,591,644	1872	5,569,033
1862	1,391,386	1873	6,114,566
1863	1,521,243	1874	6,303,834
1864	1,780,443	1875	5,323,937

Source: *Annual Reports of the Postmaster General of the United States, 1854–1875.*

Table 11. Number and Percentage of Holdings above One Acre in Ireland, 1841–1901

Year	Total Holdings*	1–5 Acres		5–15 Acres		15–30 Acres		Over 30 Acres	
		No. of Holdings	%	No. of Holdings	%	No. of Holdings	%	No. of Holdings	%
1841	691,114†	310,436	44.9	252,799	36.6	79,342	11.5	48,625	7.0
1851	608,066	88,083	15.5	191,854	33.6	141,311	24.8	149,090	26.1
1861	610,045	85,469	15.0	183,931	32.4	141,251	24.8	157,833	27.8
1871	592,590	74,809	13.7	171,383	31.5	138,647	25.5	159,303	29.3
1881	577,739	67,071	12.7	164,045	31.1	135,793	25.8	159,834	30.4
1891	572,640	63,464	12.3	156,661	30.3	133,947	25.9	162,940	31.5
1901	590,175	62,855	12.2	154,418	29.9	134,091	26.0	164,483	31.9

Source: *Agricultural Statistics of Ireland, with detailed report for the year 1901*, p. 15 [Cd. 1170], H.C. 1902, cxvi–Part I.
* Includes holdings of less than one acre.
† Does not include holdings of less than one acre.

Table 12. Decline in Tillage and Rural Population in Ireland's Poor Law Unions, 1851–81

Grouping of Poor Law Unions (by % Decrease of Ploughed Land)	No. of Unions with Decrease within % Range	Acres Ploughed		Rural Population*		% of Decrease, 1851–81	
		1851	1881	1851	1881	Area Ploughed	Rural Population
I (0%–20%)	24	448,956	411,888	647,475	559,310	8.3	13.6
II (20%–30%)	17	496,177	366,854	551,795	404,029	26.1	26.8
III (30%–40%)	32	940,498	604,451	1,085,686	782,063	35.7	28.0
IV (40%–50%)	26	793,301	437,668	886,182	614,354	44.8	30.7
V (50% or over)......	18	452,965	190,792	525,385	343,599	57.9	34.6

Source: Saorstat Eireann, *Agricultural Statistics, 1847–1926* (Dublin, 1928), p. lxi.
* Population outside towns of 1500 inhabitants or more.

Table 13. Decline in Tillage and Rural Population in Ireland's Poor Law Unions, 1881–1911

Grouping of Poor Law Unions (by % Decrease of Ploughed Land)	No. of Unions with Decrease within % Range	Acres Ploughed		Rural Population*		% of Decrease, 1881–1911	
		1881	1911	1881	1911	Area Ploughed	Rural Population
I (0%–10%)	14	263,206	250,679	353,834	270,907	4.8	23.4
II (10%–20%)	19	429,306	365,931	427,820	322,719	14.8	24.6
III (20%–30%)	30	460,085	348,303	608,564	450,602	24.3	26.0
IV (30%–40%)	24	380,010	247,058	568,483	415,733	35.0	26.9
V (40% or over)	24	394,389	222,524	620,024	451,106	43.6	27.2

Source: *Ibid.*
* Population outside towns of 1500 inhabitants or more.

Table 14. Average Weekly Wages of Agricultural Laborers in Ireland and Its Provinces, 1833–95

Year	Ireland	Munster	Leinster	Ulster	Connaught
1833–40	4s. 6d.	3s. 11d.	4s. 6d.	5s. 4d.	3s. 8d.
1845	4 8	4 0	4 10	5 3	3 11
1850	4 10	4 9	4 11	5 1	4 1
1862	7 2	6 10	7 2	7 5	7 0
1870	7 10	8 1	7 5	8 3	7 10
1880	9 0	9 6	9 0	10 0	7 0
1881	9 0	9 6	9 0	10 0	7 0
1886	9 4	9 5	9 5	9 10	8 4
1893	9 5	10 0	9 5	9 10	8 2
1894	10 0	10 0	10 6	10 6	8 6
1895	9 6	9 3	10 0	10 0	8 6

Source: A. L. Bowley, *Wages in the United Kingdom in the Nineteenth Century* (Cambridge, 1900), p. 50. See also his "The Statistics of Wages in the United Kingdom during the last Hundred Years. (Part III) Agricultural Wages—Ireland," *Journal of the Royal Statistical Society*, Vol. LXII (June 1899), pp. 400–403.

Table 15. Number of Paupers and Percentage of Total Population in Ireland, 1852–95

Year	No. in Workhouses	Percentage of Population	Year	No. in Workhouses	Percentage of Population
1852	166,821	2.60	1874	46,981	0.88
1853	129,401	2.06	1875	45,945	0.87
1854	95,190	1.54	1876	43,652	0.82
1855	79,211	1.30	1877	43,594	0.82
1856	63,235	1.04	1878	47,022	0.88
1857	50,665	0.84	1879	49,996	0.93
1858	45,790	0.76			
1859	40,380	0.67	1880	54,246	1.02
			1881	52,789	1.03
1860	41,271	0.69	1882	50,563	0.99
1861	45,136	0.78	1883	50,315	1.00
1862	53,668	0.93	1884	47,625	0.96
1863	57,910	1.01	1885	46,468	0.94
1864	56,525	0.99	1886	46,104	0.94
1865	53,917	0.95	1887	45,488	0.94
1866	50,280	0.90	1888	45,218	0.94
1867	52,154	0.94	1889	43,838	0.93
1868	53,690	0.97			
1869	52,247	0.94	1890	42,517	0.91
			1891	40,914	0.87
1870	49,186	0.89	1892	40,437	0.87
1871	46,005	0.85	1893	41,160	0.89
1872	45,753	0.85	1894	41,254	0.89
1873	46,711	0.87	1895	40,578	0.89

Source: *Annual Report of the Local Government Board for Ireland*, p. 8 [c. 4051], H.C. 1884, xxxviii. *Annual Report of the Local Government Board for Ireland*, p. 10 [c. 8153], H.C. 1896, xxxviii.

Table 16. Number of Inhabited Houses and Rate of Decrease in Ireland and Its Provinces, 1841–1901

Year	Ireland		Leinster		Munster		Ulster		Connaught	
	No.	% of Decrease	No.	% of Decrease	No.	% of Decrease	No.	% of Decrease	No.	% of Decrease
1841	1,328,839		306,459		364,637		414,551		243,192	
1851	1,046,223	21.27	258,012	15.81	267,073	26.76	351,855	15.12	169,253	30.40
1861	995,156	4.88	236,614	8.29	243,267	8.91	351,655	.06	163,620	3.33
1871	961,380	3.39	227,462	3.87	234,757	3.50	345,464	1.76	153,697	6.06
1881	914,108	4.92	216,225	4.94	219,631	6.44	332,832	3.66	145,420	5.39
1891	870,578	4.76	208,189	3.98	202,668	7.84	326,547	1.89	133,174	7.85
1901	858,503	1.43	205,867	1.20	193,663	4.36	332,106	+1.80	126,867	5.21

Source: *Census of Ireland for 1901. Part II. General Report*, pp. 7 and 170 [Cd. 1190], H.C. 1902, cxxix.

Table 17. Classification and Distribution of House Accommodation
in Ireland, 1841–91

Year	Total No. of Families	No. of Families with Given Class of Accommodation			
		1st	2nd	3rd	4th
1841	1,472,739	31,333	241,664	574,386	625,356
1851	1,204,319	39,370	292,280	588,440	284,229
1861	1,128,300	44,302	333,440	553,496	197,062
1871	1,067,598	49,693	357,752	432,774	227,379
1881	995,074	57,673	403,862	443,247	90,292
1891	932,113	62,613	454,870	359,308	55,322

Source: T. W. Grimshaw, *Facts and Figures About Ireland* (Dublin,
1893), p. 18.

Table 18. Remittances Sent from North America to the United Kingdom,
1848–87

Year	Amount in Pounds	Amount in Dollars*	Year	Amount in Pounds	Amount in Dollars*
1848.... £	460,000	$2,300,000	1869.... £	639,335	$3,196,675
1849....	540,000	2,700,000	1870....	727,408	3,637,040
1850....	957,000	4,785,000	1871....	702,488	3,512,440
1851....	990,000	4,950,000	1872....	749,664	3,748,320
1852....	1,404,000	7,020,000	1873....	724,040	3,620,200
1853....	1,439,000	7,195,000	1874....	485,566	2,427,830
1854....	1,730,000	8,650,000	1875....	354,356	1,771,780
1855....	873,000	4,365,000	1876....	449,641	2,248,205
1856....	951,000	4,755,000	1877....	667,564	3,337,820
1857....	593,165	2,965,825	1878....	784,067	3,920,335
1858....	472,610	2,363,050	1879....	855,631	4,278,155
1859....	520,019	2,600,095	1880....	1,403,341	7,016,705
1860....	534,476	2,672,380	1881....	1,505,794	7,528,970
1861....	374,061	1,870,305	1882....	1,573,552	7,867,760
1862....	360,578	1,802,890	1883....	1,611,201	8,056,005
1863....	383,286	1,916,430	1884....	1,575,756	7,878,780
1864....	332,172	1,660,860	1885....	1,239,280	6,196,400
1865....	481,580	2,407,900	1886....	1,272,959	6,364,795
1866....	498,028	2,490,140	1887....	1,751,353	8,756,765
1867....	543,029	2,715,145			
1868....	530,000	2,652,820	Total £34,040,000		$170,200,000

Source: *Thirty-Third General Report of the [Colonial Land and] Emi-
gration Commissioners, 1872,* p. 78 [c. 768], H.C. 1873, xviii. *Statistical
Tables relating to Emigration and Immigration, from and into the United
Kingdom in the year 1887, and Report to the Board of Trade thereon,* p. 18,
H.C. 1888 (2), cvii.

*Computed on ratio of £1 = $5.

167

Table 19. Money Orders Sent from the United States to the
United Kingdom, 1872–1900

Year	Amount in Dollars	Amount in Pounds *	Year	Amount in Dollars	Amount in Pounds *
1872†...$	747,426	£149,485	1887....	$3,818,940	£763,788
1873....	1,364,476	272,495	1888....	4,826,558	965,311
1874....	1,491,320	298,244	1889....	5,117,169	1,023,434
1875....	1,149,382	229,876	1890....	5,211,262	1,042,252
1876....	1,018,355	203,671	1891....	5,438,926	1,087,785
1877....	805,339	161,067	1892....	5,459,315	1,091,863
1878....	807,183	161,436	1893....	5,740,593	1,148,118
1879....	894,859	178,972	1894....	4,889,130	977,826
1880....	1,625,943	323,188	1895....	4,671,676	934,335
1881....	2,001,990	400,398	1896....	4,962,508	992,501
1882....	2,740,362	548,072	1897....	4,689,838	937,968
1883....	3,194,127	638,825	1898....	4,637,306	937,461
1884....	3,024,700	604,940	1899....	4,666,156	933,231
1885....	2,661,248	532,249	1900....	5,166,259	1,033,252
1886....	2,897,722	579,544			
			Total	$95,720,068	£19,144,014

Source: *Annual Reports of the Postmaster General of the United States,
1872–1900.*

* Computed on ratio of £1 = $5.

† Represents the first nine months of operation of Postal Money Order
Convention between the United States and the United Kingdom.

Notes and
Bibliography
Index

Notes and Bibliography

NOTE: Official British publications are referred to by title, command number, date, and volume number. The following abbreviations have been used.* *ICD: Irish Catholic Directory*, Dublin. *IER: Irish Ecclesiastical Record. IFC: Irish Folklore Commission*, Dublin. *NA: National Archives*, Washington, D.C. *NLI: National Library of Ireland*, Dublin. *PRO: Public Record Office. RIA: Royal Irish Academy*, Dublin. *SSIJ: Journal of the Statistical and Social Inquiry Society of Ireland*.

NOTES
Chapter I. Causes and Characteristics

[1] Even before the famine the rate of emigration had been increasing rapidly, and it has been estimated that as many as 400,000 of the 780,000 who came to the United States in the 1850s probably would have come anyway. Gerald Shaughnessy, *Has the Immigrant Kept the Faith? A Study of Immigration and Catholic Growth in the United States, 1790-1920* (New York, 1925), p. 79.

[2] *Census of Ireland, 1901. Part II. General Report*, p. 109 [Cd. 1190], H.C. 1902, cxxix. It has been pointed out, however, that although one of the most important, emigration was not the only factor which caused this dramatic reduction in Irish population; declining fertility also played a part. The Irish birth rate began declining as early as 1850 and was not due to a decline in specific legitimate fertility (that is, number of children per family), but to three other factors: (1) a decline in the percentage of women of child-bearing age; (2) a rise in the average age at marriage for women; and (3) most important of all, a decline in the amount of marriage. Emigration was doubtless an important causal element in the first, but its influence on the other two is less clear. Abstention from marriage appeared as a custom among the Irish before the advent of the famine and its concomitant large-scale emigration, although the precise date of its appearance is uncertain. But while emigration did not directly cause or introduce late marriage, the continuance of emigration after the famine strongly reenforced the custom. G. R. C. Keep, "The Irish Migration to North America in the Second Half of the Nineteenth Century," unpublished Ph.D. dissertation (Trinity College, Dublin, 1951), pp. 17-19.

Perhaps one of the shrewdest observations on Ireland's declining population was made in 1861 by the *Northern Whig* (July 17, 1861), which enunciated a sociological principle widely accepted in the twentieth century: "When men are conscious of bettering circumstances, they exercise prudence, they obtain a relish for the comforts of existence, they will not marry until they are tolerably certain not only of securing them, but of being able to transmit them to their children. To the fact that the Irish population is gradually acquiring these feelings and desires [that is, a higher 'ideal of comfort'], quite as much as to the vast exodus of the people . . . we attribute this decline of population . . ."

3 Julius Isaac, *Economics of Migration* (London, 1947), p. 143.

4 N. H. Carrier and J. R. Jeffery, *External Migration: a Study of the Available Statistics 1815-1920* (London, 1953), p. 50.

5 In a century of emigration dating from the famine almost every rural area lost at least 50 percent of its population, and some lost as much as 70 percent. The long-run effect of emigration on the male-female ratio of Ireland's population was negligible. In 1841 the male proportion of the population was 49.2 percent; in 1901 it stood at 49.3 percent. *Ibid.*, pp. 50, 104.

6 T. W. Freeman, *Ireland: Its Physical, Historical, Social and Economic Geography* (London, 1950), p. 133. In 1841 less than 20 percent of the population lived in towns, but by 1936 over 40 percent were doing so.

7 In an effort to throw some light on the regional origins of the emigration, G. R. C. Keep, the most recent student of the problem, took great pains to analyze a scale of emigration intensities (that is, intensity of emigration per hundred average population) devised by the emigration commissioners for each county in the period 1851-1901, in the hope that it might reveal some general principle by which to explain the areas of high emigration. Although he found that five of the six counties of highest emigration intensity coincided with five of the six counties of highest absolute emigration, no principle was thereby revealed. Neither modern farm size nor land use, he found, could uniformly explain the whole area of high emigration intensity. And as for wealthy versus poor counties, there appeared to be no significant correlation with emigration. Poor counties as well as rich ones suffered high emigration intensities. Keep was finally reduced to postulate what he declared to be an "exceedingly obvious consideration." He noted that no county of higher than average intensity of emigration stood in isolation from any similar county and that all such counties were contiguous. On this basis he advanced the theory of a "contagion" of emigration which had the strongest hold in the southwestern counties of Clare, Kerry, and Cork and spread northeastward to the outskirts of Ulster. Unfortunately, he did not clearly explain the process by which this "contagion" was transmitted. Keep, *op. cit.*, pp. 39-44.

8 *Census of Ireland, 1901*, p. 150. Between 1861 and 1901 the proportion of Protestants had risen only from 12 to 13 percent. Interestingly enough it was Ulster, the stronghold of Protestantism, which saw the sharpest decline in Roman Catholics and even there it was a decline of merely 6 percent over a period of forty years.

9 *Population of the United States in 1860; compiled from the original returns of the Eighth Census* (Washington, D.C., 1864), p. xxxii.

10 John O'Grady, "Irish Colonization in the United States," *Studies*, Vol. XIX (September 1930), pp. 393-394. A correspondent of *United Ireland* wrote from the United States (February 7, 1885) that while Germans came equipped as immigrants, the Irish

did not. He was "astonished" at the number of young Irishmen who could not plough. Moreover no Irishman seemed to know how to milk cows; in Ireland that was woman's work: "Did you ever see a man milking cows in Ireland?"

[11] *Royal Commission on Labour. The Agricultural Labourer. Vol. IV. Ireland. Part IV.*, p. 89 [c. 6894-XXX], H.C. 1893-94, xxxvii-Part I.

[12] *Twenty-ninth General Report of the Colonial Land and Emigration Commissioners, 1869*, p. 2 [4159], H.C. 1868-69, xvii. T. W. Grimshaw, *Facts and Figures About Ireland* (Dublin, 1893), p. 16. *Minutes of Evidence . . . taken before Her Majesty's Commissioners appointed to inquire into the financial relations between Great Britain and Ireland . . .* p. 114 [c. 7720-I], H.C. 1895, xxxvi. Oscar Handlin, *Boston's Immigrants 1790-1865* (Cambridge, Mass., 1941), p. 52.

[13] Randall W. MacDonnell, "Statistics of Irish Prosperity," SSIJ, Vol. III, Part XXII (December 1862), p. 274. C. H. Oldham, "The Incidence of Emigration on Town and Country Life in Ireland," *SSIJ*, Vol. XIII, Part XCIV (November 1913-June 1914), p. 213. R. C. Geary, "The Future Population of Saorstat Eireann and Some Observations on Population Statistics," *SSIJ*, Vol. XV (1935-36), p. 23.

[14] September 7, 1863.

[15] *Limerick Reporter,* November 17, 1857; see also Dublin *Weekly Telegraph*, August 1, 1857; *Roscommon Journal*, November 21, 1857.

[16] Max Farrand, *The Development of the United States*, p. 233, as quoted in W. A. Carrothers, *Emigration from the British Isles* (London, 1929), p. 222. With the revelations of the Grant administration scandals coming in the midst of the depression, Irishmen were warned that not only were "thousands idling and starving their lives away" in America, but that this was also "a country of swindling from the President down." *Clare Journal*, June 5, 1876.

[17] Harry Jerome, *Migration and the Business Cycle* (New York, 1926), Ch. IV; Brinley Thomas, *Migration and Economic Growth* (Cambridge, Eng., 1954), pp. 83-122.

[18] *The Atlantic Migration, 1607-1860. A History of the Continuing Settlement of the United States* (Cambridge, Mass., 1940), p. 16.

[19] E. Strauss, *Irish Nationalism and British Democracy* (London, 1951), p. vi. Report from Robert Murray, manager of the Provincial Bank of Ireland, to Lord Clarendon, lord lieutenant of Ireland, January 1, 1850, *Larcom Papers*, NLI MS 7600. L. Paul-Dubois, *Contemporary Ireland* (Dublin, 1908), p. 227. Stephen Gwynn, *Irish Books and Irish People* (Dublin, 1919), p. 9.

[20] *Agricultural Statistics of Ireland for the year 1870*, p. v [c. 463], H.C. 1872, lxiii.

[21] "The monotony of the potato diet was depressing enough, but the ease of its preparation . . . could scarcely fail to reduce the art of living to its lowest functional value. The fact that the potato demanded no other help to its ingestion than some salt, nor to its service but bare fingers, was not inducive of refinement, personal or otherwise. What pride could be taken in the home, or what call was there for ceremony however elementary, to welcome a meal that was about to be shared with the pigs and the poultry, and from the same cauldron?" Redcliffe N. Salaman, *The History and Social Influence of the Potato* (Cambridge, 1949), p. 338.

[22] Alice E. Murray, *A History of the Commercial and Financial Relations Between England and Ireland from the Period of the Restoration*, new ed. (London, 1907), p. 358.

[23] John E. Pomfret, *The Struggle for Land in Ireland, 1800-1923* (Princeton, 1930), p. 23.

24 E. P. Brooks to John Hay, July 1, 1880, *Cons. Desp.*, Cork, Vol. 7 (RG 59), NA.

25 Personal interview with Mr. Daniel Regan, age 85, July 22, 1955, County Home, Clonakilty, Co. Cork.

26 MS notebook of Michael MacEnri, IFC.

27 Lawrence to Webster, December 2, 1851, *Diplomatic Desp.*, Great Britain, Vol. 63 (RG 59), NA.

28 Adams to William H. Seward, September 22, 1865, *Papers Relating to Foreign Affairs, Accompanying the Annual Message of the President to the First Session Thirty-ninth Congress, Part I* (Washington, D.C., 1866), pp. 561-563. *Cork Examiner*, May 24, 1862.

29 *The Atlantic Civilization: Eighteenth Century Origins* (Ithaca, 1949), p. 309

30 C. M. Arensberg and S. T. Kimball, *Family and Community in Ireland* (Cambridge, Mass., 1940), pp. 155-156.

31 Paul-Dubois, *Contemporary Ireland*, p. 359. D. A. Chart, "Two Centuries of Irish Agriculture. A Statistical Retrospect, 1672-1905," *SSIJ*, Vol. XII, Part LXXXVIII (November 1907-June 1908), p. 171. R. C. Geary, "Some Reflections on Irish Population Questions," *Studies*, Vol. XLIII, No. 170 (Summer 1954), p. 172. *Freeman's Journal*, May 10, 1873. *Report from the Select Committee on Law of Rating (Ireland)*, p. 321, H.C. 1871 (423), x. *Tuam Herald*, May 18, 1901. *Newry Examiner*, March 10, 1853. *Cork Examiner*, April 9, 1873. William Forbes Adams, *Ireland and Irish Emigration to the New World from 1815 to the Famine* (New Haven, 1932), p. 392.

32 *Fourteenth General Report of the Colonial Land and Emigration Commissioners, 1854*, p. 10 [1833], H.C. 1854, xxviii. See Ch. VI for a more detailed analysis of remittances and their uses.

33 *Cork Examiner*, June 22, 1871.

34 Carrothers, *Emigration from the British Isles*, p. 293. *Tenth General Report of the Colonial Land and Emigration Commissioners, 1850*, p. 1 [1204], H.C. 1850, xxiii. *Twelfth General Report of the Colonial Land and Emigration Commissioners, 1852*, p. 14 [1499], H.C. 1852, xviii. Hansen, *Atlantic Migration*, p. 181.

Chapter II. The Lure of America

1 London *Daily News*, September 9, 1864, in *Larcom Papers*, NLI MS 7607.

2 *Report from the Select Committee on Outrages (Ireland)* . . . p. 355, H.C. 1852 (438), xiv.

3 *Cork Examiner*, June 6, 1860.

4 *Nation*, May 3, 1851. *Dublin Evening Post*, June 14, 1864, in *Larcom Papers*, NLI MS 7608. *Limerick Reporter*, August 29, 1873. *Londonderry Standard*, April 21, 1853.

5 *Galway Vindicator*, April 7, 1869. *Londonderry Standard*, June 5, 1863. Adams, *Ireland and Irish Emigration*, p. 340.

6 *Northern Whig*, May 9, 1863. *Report from the Select Committee on Tenure and Improvement of Land (Ireland) Act*, p. 152, H.C. 1865 (402), xi. *Report from the Select Committee on Law of Rating (Ireland)*, pp. 253-254. *Irish Times*, August 15, 1868, in *Larcom Papers*, NLI MS 7613. Madame de Bovet, *Three Months in Ireland* (London, 1891), p. 280.

7 *Galway Vindicator*, April 24, 1869.

8 Table 9 in the Appendix.

9 Table 10 in the Appendix.

[10] Unfortunately most of these letters have been lost or destroyed. The greater proportion of them were received by poor tenant farmers or struggling agricultural laborers, people who were not inclined to save such documents. In many cases where letters actually were preserved, the dynamics of Irish rural society militated against their continued preservation. For when a farmer's son finally did marry and brought his bride into the house as the new mistress, one of her first acts in asserting her new position of authority was to root out and destroy all evidence of the preceding imperium, that of her mother-in-law. Countless letters thus found their destiny in the flames of a blazing turf fire.

Nevertheless, by appealing directly to those people in Ireland who might still be in possession of American letters it has been possible to assemble a modest collection. Although the collection is small in comparison with the millions of letters which were written and received, those assembled may provide as representative a sampling as is now possible to obtain. They were written by people in all walks of life — humble laborers, domestic servants, farmers, and professional men — and in all the major religious denominations, Roman Catholic, Protestant (that is, Church of Ireland), and Presbyterian. They came from the crowded cities of the eastern seaboard and the prairie farms of the great Midwest, as well as from the frontier towns and ranches along the Pacific shore. And they were destined for all classes in all areas of Ireland. The small tenant farmers and agricultural laborers of the south and west, the more substantial farmers of Ulster, the city workers of Dublin and Belfast – were the happy recipients of these letters.

For a fuller quantitative and chronological description of the letters collected, see bibliography.

[11] The usual opening sentence ran something as follows: "Dear Father and Mother, I take this favorable opportunity to write these few lines hoping the arrival of this letter finds you in good health as it leaves me at present, thanks be to God for his kind mercies to us all . . ." This type of salutation was as characteristic of Protestants (that is, Church of Ireland) and Presbyterians, as it was of Roman Catholics.

[12] *The Irish Emigrant's Guide for the United States* (Boston, 1851), p. 12.

[13] Margaret McCarthy to her mother, father, brothers, and sisters, September 22, 1850, *Correspondence relating to Kingwilliamstown,* Quitrent Office Collection, PRO, Dublin. (Unless otherwise indicated, all letters cited are in writer's possession as originals or photostatic copies of the originals.)

[14] Bartholomew Colgan to his friend, December 20, 1854, Elmwood, Illinois. William H. Francis, M.D., to his nephew, October 10, 1879, Cascade, Iowa. Samuel Buchanan to his mother, February 16, 1870, Cincinnati, *Buchanan Papers,* Box PC 431, NLI.

[15] J. F. Costello to his father, mother, sister, and brothers, January 11, 1883, White River Valley, Washington Territory.

[16] Andrew Pauley to his uncle, August 21, 1854, Philadelphia.

[17] P. J. Finnerty to his brother, April 25, 1869, Waterloo, Iowa. Mrs. Keenan to her brother, November 24, 1888, Boston. Private report of Tom Gallagher, in writer's possession.

[18] Patrick McKeown to his sisters, June 24, 1905, Philadelphia.

[19] Thomas Bernard Delany to his uncle, August 29, 1853, Washington, D.C. Delany also delivered himself of some equally pungent observations on the slavery system then in vogue in the nation's capital: "There are as you know 31 states in the American Union, which are divided into free states and slave states. I am in a slave district, and all

the states south of me are slave states. Any white man can go into the market here, and buy a black man, or black woman or boy or black girl the same way that he can buy a horse or an ox or a hog. And the laws here allow the white man to treat his black fellow man as he would treat his ox or his horse. The black man has to work for his white master all his life as a slave – without any wages. If he refuse he's tied up & whipped. I have seen men – gentlemen if you please – tie up their black women slaves, strip them & whip them for something or other. I must cut this short. The slave states are not good for a white labouring man. For all the work on great plantations & farms is done by these slaves. 'Tis most usual for a wealthy farmer or planter to own 100, 200, 400, & even 500 of these niggers. If he should want ready cash at any time he may sell some of them. If he marries his daughter he gives her so many niggers as a fortune [that is, dowry], and if he dies, he wills his niggers away as he wills his money or sheep."

20 James Chamberlain to his mother and brothers, January 27, 1889, Boston.

21 *Connaught Telegraph*, April 30, 1887. Annie Heggarty to her friend, July 19, 1884, Ottumwa, Iowa. Patrick McKeown to his sisters, December 21, 1889, Philadelphia.

22 Thomas Bernard Delany to his uncle, *op. cit.* James Chamberlain to his mother and brothers, March 18 (1890?), Boston. *Ibid.*, January 27, 1889, Boston. Mary D'Arcy to her uncle, March 14, 1884, Denver, *Lalor Family Papers*, Box B 30, NLI.

23 George Dillon to his cousin, January 31, 1868, Tomales, California, *ibid.*

Something of the energy which was characteristic of mid-nineteenth-century Americans, particularly in the far west, was well portrayed in a letter written in 1851 by a prosperous liquor dealer and commission merchant in San Francisco to his brother in Belfast: "You can form no idea of the fine city this now is and the fine substantial fire-proof brick buildings that abound in many parts of it, which would not disgrace even the great metropolis London. But the most astonishing part of the business is that these fine buildings, the grading and planking of the streets, also the building of so many fine wharfs, and more still in progress, is but the work of a few months. The Americans are certainly a very go ahead sort of people. We have now in this mushroom city, which comparatively speaking is but the growth of a night, all the comforts and luxuries to be obtained in the old cities of the Mother Country." Thomas Vogan to his brother, February 1, 1851, San Francisco, D.O.D. 268/7, PRO, Belfast.

24 Samuel Buchanan to his sister, June 30, 1894, Silver, South Carolina, *Buchanan Papers*, Box PC 431, NLI.

25 Thomas Bernard Delany to his uncle, *op. cit.*

26 Ellen Rowntree to her brother, August 26, 1851. Philadelphia. *Nation*, June 14, 1851. Patrick McKeown to his sisters, September 3, 1883, Philadelphia. McKeown doubtless must also have impressed his sisters with the observation that in Philadelphia "almost every family has a house to themselves let it be large or small and a great many working people own the houses the[y] live in."

27 Daniel Guiny to his mother and brothers, August 9, 1850, Buffalo, *Correspondence relating to Kingwilliamstown, op. cit.*

28 Anastasia Dowling to Mrs. Dunny, January 20, 1870, Buffalo. Patrick McKeown to his sisters, April 22, 1894, Philadelphia.

29 Not all were agreed that high wages were so important or attractive. Some pointed out that the high cost of living and the hard work left them with little more than they had had in Ireland, and they therefore warned their friends in Ireland that comfort and

America were not necessarily synonymous terms. The wife of a laborer in Taunton, Massachusetts, tried to drive this point home to her nephew in Dublin in a letter she wrote him in 1890: "Michael you spoke about America. One Pound in Ireland is just as good as Two Pound in America. You would do Better in Ireland than you would here. Michael this living is high here, it takes all a man can make to live here and work hard for it the People that come out here are very sorry that they ever came. Michael if half the People saved there Money in Ireland and work as hard as they do here they could take Comfort in Ireland." Margaret Kenney to her nephew, March 9, 1890, Taunton, Mass.

Much more succinct was the statement of an Irishman living in New York City who wrote to an Ulster journal in 1901: "Men get better wages here, true: they earner it harder; it goes quicker." Reprinted in *Kilkenny Journal*, September 25, 1901.

[30] J. F. Costello to his father, mother, sister, and brothers, *op. cit.* In that part of the country there were other attractions as well: "When Sunday comes, takes rifle or shotgun, go out hunting. Wild animals of all descriptions abound here, and as for wild ducks they are as thick as the cows to home. Also pheasants & grouse & you can take your gun, or four if you want to, and nobody will ask where is your license. All you want is enough to buy a gun. To sum all up this is a free country."

[31] Patrick Dunny to his father, brothers, and sisters, December 30, 1856, Philadelphia.

[32] Owen Growney to his father and mother, January 26, 1899, San Francisco. Reprinted in *Limerick Reporter*, August 2, 1867.

[33] Daniel Rowntree to his brother, March 20, 1852, Washington, D.C.

[34] *Kilkenny Journal*, June 22 1859.

[35] Michael Corr to his sisters, December 9, 1855, Philadelphia.

[36] James Dixon to his sister, September 4, 1855, Philadelphia.

[37] M. M. McFadden to his uncle, January 30, 1892, Mapleton, Iowa. James MacFadden to his uncle, October 17, 1897, Battle Creek, Iowa.

Mingling with various nationalities had quite another effect in California, still pretty much of a frontier region in 1868, as evidenced by the following account from a dairy farmer in Tomales: ". . . this is a wild contry to what You are used to. We represent all Nations of People in California and they live rough talk and act the same. The old proverb is doe as they doe in Rome. So we are verrey rough for I have forgotten what little manners and politeness that I have . . ." George Dillon to his cousin, June 7, 1868, Tomales, California, *Lalor Family Papers*, Box B 30, NLI.

[38] James Chamberlain to his mother and brothers, 1890, Boston.

[39] Patrick McKeown to his nephew, September 11, 1904, Philadelphia. Competition did not come solely from the non-English-speaking immigrants; sometimes it was to be found among the Irish from different counties. The Dublin-born foreman of a concern in Brooklyn wrote to his brother in 1889 that he was having a hard time keeping his position, "owing to Corkonian opposition which you know is very strong here." Daniel Rowntree to his brother, August 9, 1889, Brooklyn, New York.

[40] Francis Wolsey to his brother, June 8, 1877, Greenpoint, Long Island.

[41] Clare *Independent*, July 31, 1880.

[42] Some emigrants were lured less by the blandishments of recruiting agents than by a cold calculation of the dollars they would receive as a bounty for enlisting of their own

volition. One Irishman writing to his parents from Boston in 1864 was a model of candor: "... dear parents this is a *free country*, there is no one here forced to [en]list if they don't like, and so by us — except we were citizens but by 'Gor' the bounty was very tempting, and I enlisted the first day I came here: I have sent you in this letter $360: I expect it will amount of £50 of our money. ... The bounty I enlisted for is $700 I have got only $400 in hand; the remainder I will get at so much every 6 months along with my pay ..." Copy of letter enclosed in dispatch of William B. West, U.S. consul, Dublin, to William H. Seward, secretary of state, April 20, 1864, *Cons. Desp.*, Dublin, Vol. 4 (RG 59), NA.

43 For example, on October 18, 1862 the *Kilkenny Journal* printed a letter from an Irish farmer in Prairie Springs, Iowa, who strongly advised against emigrating at that time and who himself had good cause to fear that one or both of his sons would be drafted. Nor was the tragedy of Irishmen slaughtering each other merely an empty threat. On October 22, 1861, three months after the first battle of Bull Run, an Irishman in Philadelphia wrote to his family in County Carlow a vivid account of the meeting of two Irish regiments on the field of battle, one northern and the other southern. All day long the two regiments opposed each other in a furious struggle over the great object of contention – the green flag of Erin. Four times that "poor green flag" changed hands and in the end it was the northern regiment, the 69th of New York, that bore it from the field in triumph. But the cost in human slaughter was truly "grivious to every irishman" for "there was more lives lost over that flag than anny other one object was on the field ..." Patrick Dunny to his father, brothers, and sister, October 22, 1861, Philadelphia.

44 Maurice Sexton to his brothers and sisters, November 24, 1861, Boston.

45 Stewart Bates to his uncle, July 1, 1863, Chicago.

46 Copy of letter enclosed in dispatch of William B. West, U.S. consul, Dublin, to William H. Seward, secretary of state, April 20, 1864, *op. cit.*

47 *Cork Examiner*, August 10, 1860. Five years later one journal remarked, "Why, all the world knows that the Yankee hates Paddy." *Newry Commercial Telegraph*, September 5, 1865.

48 B. Colgan to his friend, June 13, 1862, Carson City, Nevada Territory. J. F. Costello to his father, mother, sister, and brothers, *op. cit.*

49 Reprinted in *Londonderry Standard*, December 29, 1866. Printed in *Kilkenny Journal*, February 23, 1870. B. Colgan to his friend, *op. cit.*

50 Nathaniel Carrothers to William Carrothers, December 5, 1853, Westminster, Ontario, *Irish Emigrants' Letters from Canada 1839-1870* (in mimeograph) (Belfast, 1951), pp. 15- 16.

51 John Ard to his brother, April 8, 1871, Westfield, New York.

52 Julia Lough to her sister, January 18, 1891, Winsted, Conn.

53 Printed in *Leinster Express*, April 15, 1854.

54 James Dixon to his sister, March 7, 1868, Fort Ross, Calif.

55 Seumas MacManus, "A Revolution in Ireland," *Catholic World*, Vol. LXIX, No. 412 (July 1899), p. 528.

56 H. Dorian, "Donegal 60 Years Ago," unpublished MS (Londonderry, 1896), pp. 60-66. Photostatic copy in IFC.

In one case in County Kilkenny the "Scholar" was absent when an American letter arrived. The recipients, eager to learn who wrote the letter, decided to try to decipher the contents themselves, and neatly spread out the pages on a table. On one of the sheets they noticed a very long word.

"Ah!" exclaimed one of the party, "that must be from Peter Jackman." Peter, it seems, had recently emigrated and was an exceptionally tall man! MS notebook of Martin Walsh, IFC.

In another instance an equally remarkable demonstration of Irish ingenuity was used to discover the identity of a letter writer. A woman in County Wexford had three sons, all of whom emigrated to America in the 1880s. She could not read or write so she used to ask a neighbor, Jim, to read the letters for her when they arrived. Jim could not read either, but he used to pretend that he could. He would make up the letter as he went along, telling of the weather and conditions in America. Once, when in the process of this delicate maneuver, the old mother became impatient.

"Which one of them is it from, Jim?" she asked. Jim, of course, did not know and tried to evade the question by saying that he had not reached the end of the letter yet. By this time his inspiration was failing him and he began to stammer. "Ah!" said the old woman when she heard him stammering. "I know which one of them wrote it. It's from Terry; he always had a stoppage in his speech." MS notebook of J. G. Delaney, IFC.

[57] There was another use to which American letters were put in order to obtain money. A young Oxford undergraduate on holiday with a friend in the west of Ireland in 1858 left the following account of an experience they had in County Galway: "A few professional beggars came round. . . . One old lady had evidently the last new thing in begging, a letter to her 'poor darlint boy as was gone to Merrikey, and would ye bestow a thrifle, good gintlemen, to pay the bit o' postage, God bless yer bewtifle young faces.' Of course, we would, every mother's son of us. What an affectionate exemplary parent! When we returned, a few days afterwards, she was again in correspondence with her beloved son, far away from her yearning tenderness, beyond the broad Atlantic, and, indeed, I have reason to believe from information which I gathered from the driver and our fellow-passengers, that this disconsolate mother writes to her exiled child every day, except Sundays." S. R. Hole, *A Little Tour in Ireland* (London, 1859), pp. 56-57.

[58] *Nation*, March 1, 1851.

Chapter III. The Futile Protest: Press and Pulpit

[1] A cynic might be strongly tempted to view all such protestations as bordering on hypocrisy. There was hardly a newspaper, whether Protestant or Catholic, tory or nationalist, that did not carry advertisements by sailing and steamship companies on rates and accommodations for emigrants, all prominently displayed on the front page. The *Newry Examiner*, for example, though strongly opposed to emigration, carried three such advertisements in 1852 (February 25) and by 1857 (March 7) was carrying four. The *Clare Journal* lamented (September 11, 1854) that the passion for emigration would shortly leave Ireland without an Irishman, and yet it probably helped stimulate the "passion" with a large advertisement on page 1 by an American shipping firm on emigrant fares from Liverpool to the United States. The *Kilkenny Journal* piously declared that it did not wish to encourage emigration (April 18, 1883) and therefore refused to publish gratis any information designed as helpful hints to intending emigrants. Yet on the front page of the very same issue were prominently displayed no less than five advertisements by

steamship companies for the emigrants' edification. Doubtless the newspapers, many of which were small, could ill afford to forego so lucrative a source of income. But the divorcing of principles from pocketbook nevertheless added an air of insincerity to the former.

2 In 1863 the Catholic clergy were warned that "unless they aid in checking the exodus [they too] will have to emigrate, or they will be like shepherds without flocks." *Tipperary Advocate*, May 9, 1863.

3 After earnestly advising young Irish men and women to stay at home and help reconstruct the nation on "solid foundations," the *Tuam Herald* (April 6, 1889) sadly admitted that "It is hard to instill that lesson of personal and patriotic prudence into their hearts, so fever-mad are they now on going." The *Leinster Express* (October 15, 1864) was more blunt: ". . . it is idle to expect that people will stay at home and starve, or patriotically pine under pecuniary disadvantages."

4 One notable exception was the *Londonderry Standard*, a Protestant, anti-tory, anti-nationalist journal and vigorous exponent of the rights of small farmers and laborers.

5 *Clare Journal*, May 6, 1872.

6 *Cork Examiner*, June 4, 1891.

7 *Belfast News-Letter*, May 22, 1901.

8 *Dundalk Democrat*, July 20, 1861. *Nation*, June 24, 1871. *Freeman's Journal*, July 8, 1851; May 21, 1901. The often quoted statement from Mill was " 'When the inhabitants of a country quit that country *en masse*, because its Government will not make it a fit place to live in, the Government is judged and condemned.' " *Nation*, November 28, 1863. Among those who were convinced that the British were deliberately intent upon depopulating the country was the Clare *Independent* which angrily declared that "It suits our rulers to make the country 'a desert and call it peace.' " March 17, 1883.

9 *Connaught Telegraph*, April 3, 1880. *Drogheda Argus*, October 21, 1863. *Limerick Reporter*, July 19, 1861. *Newry Examiner*, November 4, 1854. *Tipperary Advocate*, May 3, 1873. *Roscommon Journal*, April 26, 1862. *Galway Vindicator*, March 28, 1883. *Cork Examiner*, June 4, 1891. *Tuam Herald*, June 1, 1901.

10 *Cork Examiner*, May 22, 1901. *Galway Vindicator*, February 25, 1860. *Nation*, November 28, 1863. *Limerick Reporter*, September 22, 1865. *Kilkenny Journal*, April 21, 1883. *Sligo Champion*, May 16, 1885.

11 *Cork Daily Reporter*, May 5, 1863. *Clare Journal*, May 11, 1899. *Dublin Evening Post*, June 22, 1871.

12 *Dublin Evening Mail*, April 1, 1857; May 21, 1860. *Newry Commercial Telegraph*, July 20, 1861. *Carlow Sentinel*, June 7, 1851. *King's County Chronicle*, October 26, 1853. *Mayo Constitution*, October 30, 1860; March 27, 1866. *Cork Constitution*, June 3, 1891. *Dublin Daily Express*, May 21, 1901. *Irish Times*, May 22, 1901. *Saunder's News Letter*, July 11, 1851. *Leinster Express*, December 12, 1863. *Belfast News-Letter*, October 4, 1854; June 20, 1881; May 22, 1901.

13 *Londonderry Standard*, October 3, 1866; December 15, 1866; May 12, 1880; May 22 and May 24, 1901. *Northern Whig*, June 22, 1871; June 24, 1881. *Waterford Daily Mail*, June 23, 1871.

14 *Kilkenny Journal*, April 18, 1883. *Nation*, June 13, 1863. *Dundalk Democrat*, July 13, 1861. *Clare Independent*, March 17, 1883. *Tipperary Advocate*, July 20, 1861; June 5, 1880.

15 *Tuam Herald*, May 18, 1901.

[16] *Roscommon Journal*, April 27, 1872. This same paper also noted that "Those who are on the move are full of hope and excitement, and in some cases . . . full also of whiskey."

[17] *Cork Daily Reporter*, May 2, 1863; see also *Dublin Evening Post*, June 3, 1861.

[18] *Clare Journal*, May 6, 1872; June 15, 1891.

[19] *Dublin Morning Post*, August 5, 1857, in *Larcom Papers* NLI MS 7600. *Cork Southern Reporter*, as quoted in *Dublin Evening Mail*, June 21, 1864.

[20] Not until a hundred years later, when the Irish had obtained their independence and passions had cooled considerably, did this view come to be generally accepted: ". . . it is no immediate economic loss to be deprived of productive power which is not being utilised and which can be retained only at expense to the community at large." *Commission on Emigration and Other Population Problems 1948-1954; Majority Report* (in mimeograph) (Dublin, Ministry for Social Welfare, 1954), p. 137. However, the commission went on to state that in the long run emigration probably represented a serious loss of "economic potential" since in their view the country's resources were not yet fully developed.

[21] *Leinster Express*, July 9 and September 17, 1853; May 12, 1860; October 10, 1863. Dublin *Daily Express*, May 6, 1857; January 16, 1864. *Cork Constitution*, July 19, 1861. *Newry Commercial Telegraph*, June 27, 1871. *Dublin Evening Mail*, June 24, 1891. *Newry Commercial Telegraph*, June 30, 1881.

[22] *Belfast News-Letter*, October 4, 1854; June 20, 1881. *Mayo Constitution*, March 14, 1865; April 14, 1863. *Irish Times*, May 14, 1880; June 22, 1881.

[23] *Londonderry Standard*, April 7, 1869; March 31 and May 3, 1881. *Northern Whig*, May 27, 1863; June 22, 1871; June 2, 1891; May 22, 1901.

[24] *Dundalk Democrat*, November 22, 1862. *Sligo Champion*, May 16, 1885. *Nation*, March 13, 1880. *Cork Examiner*, June 4, 1891; May 22, 1901. *Limerick Reporter*, September 26, 1873. *Freeman's Journal*, June 4, 1891. *Tuam Herald*, April 23, 1887.

[25] *Kilkenny Journal*, June 17, 1861; May 2, 1863. *Galway Vindicator*, February 4, 1860; October 4, 1862; April 8 and May 2, 1863; January 13, 1883; September 3, 1887; June 6, 1891; November 2, 1895. *Roscommon Journal*, April 13, 1850; April 27, 1872; May 14, 1881. *Nation*, June 21, 1851; October 10, 1863. *Newry Examiner*, March 31, 1852; March 19, 1853.

[26] *Dundalk Democrat*, July 13, 1861; April 9, 1864; May 25, 1901. *Freeman's Journal*, April 25, 1885; May 21, 1901. *Clare Independent*, August 5, 1882. *Tuam Herald*, May 19, 1888; June 8 and June 15, 1901. *Drogheda Argus*, May 25, 1901.

[27] *Clare Journal*, May 6, 1872; April 27, 1899. *Cork Daily Reporter*, April 4 and April 20, 1860. *Dublin Evening Post*, June 22, 1871.

[28] *Leinster Express*, May 3, 1873. On November 15, 1859, the *Mayo Constitution* urged that "if men would exert the same energy at home which they are forced to use abroad, there is bread to be earned in the old country still." This view was heartily endorsed by the *Irish Times* the following year (April 11, 1860): "If the Irish peasant could be induced to devote a tithe of the energy to the improvement of his position here, which he must exert to live in the States, he would not think of emigration." See also *Carlow Sentinel*, June 7, 1851.

[29] *Irish Times*, January 20, 1864, in *Larcom Papers*, NLI MS 7607.

[30] *Irish Times*, April 15, 1865, in *Larcom Papers*, NLI MS 7610. See also: *Belfast News-*

Letter, June 22, 1871; May 12, 1883; May 22, 1901. *Leinster Express*, November 12, 1859; April 23, 1864. *Irish Times*, December 27, 1866; June 22, 1881.

31 *Northern Whig*, May 22, 1901. *Londonderry Standard*, April 21, 1853; May 12, 1880; May 24, 1901. Many Protestant newspapers would have been interested and doubtless irritated by an exchange that took place during the American Civil War between Charles Francis Adams, American minister to Great Britain, and William H. Seward, secretary of state. Wrote Adams: "Amidst the many speculations which appear in the public journals concerning the causes of great emigration to America, I do not recollect to have seen any reference to the fact that the Irish Catholic is scarcely regarded as having any rights which his English brother is not tempted to violate on the smallest provocation." To this Seward replied with firm conviction that "Nothing . . . can [arrest Irish emigration] but an adoption [by the British government] of our own great principle of an absolute divorce between the church and the state." Adams to Seward, August 25, 1864, Seward to Adams, September 16, 1864, *Papers Relating to Foreign Affairs, Accompanying the Annual Message of the President to the Second Session Thirty-eighth Congress, Part II* (Washington, 1865), pp. 282, 299-300.

32 *Irish People*, October 8, 1864; June 1 and June 15, 1901. *Flag of Ireland*, June 17, 1871; October 25, 1873. *United Ireland*, January 13, 1883.

Apparently the Irish people themselves were not entirely blameless. At the peak of the emigration during the early 1880s, a period of severe crop failures and intense Land League agitation, the *Flag of Ireland* (May 29, 1880) was furious at the thought that farmers were emigrating with the unpaid rent money they were advised to withhold by the Land League. If this was true, it cried, then the nation was the loser by the land agitation because "What the landlords have not lost, the tenants have not gained if they are paying their rents to English shipowners."

33 *Irish People*, February 11, 1865. *United Ireland*, February 7, 1885. R. C. Geary, "Irish Economic Development Since the Treaty," *Studies*, Vol. XL, No. 160 (December 1951), p. 400.

It may be observed that the Irish have had self-government for over a generation, and yet emigration still remains one of their most pressing problems. Today the political uses of the emigration outcry are at an end and although it is still condemned in principle, social and economic remedies to stem its flow are no longer so profusely proposed. The twentieth-century Irish have come to accept emigration as a "gigantic fact" which is neither "good" nor "bad." "The only thing we can do about a fact of this kind," one of them recently advised, "is to make the best of it." R. C. Geary, "Some Reflections on Irish Population Questions," *Studies*, Vol. XLIII, No. 170 (Summer 1954), p. 173.

34 Oliver MacDonagh, "The Irish Catholic Clergy and Emigration during the Great Famine," *Irish Historical Studies*, Vol. V, No. 20 (September 1947), pp. 287-302, *passim*. In 1852 a priest from County Armagh admitted that he actually encouraged some members of his parish to emigrate when he thought there was no chance for their improvement in Ireland. See *Report from the Select Committee on Outrages (Ireland)* . . ., p. 354.

35 *Kilkenny Journal*, May 2, 1863. *Roscommon Journal*, May 2, 1868. *Belfast News-Letter*, March 25, 1853. *Minutes of Evidence taken before Her Majesty's Commissioners on Agriculture. Part I*, p. 96 [c. 2778-I], H.C. 1881, xv.

36 A. I. Shand, *Letters from the West of Ireland 1884* (London, 1885), p. 115. *Second Report from the Select Committee of the House of Lords on Land Law (Ireland)*, p. 270, H.C.

1882 (379), xi. W. H. Hurlbert, *Ireland Under Coercion: The Diary of an American* (Boston, 1888), pp. 95-96. *Minutes of Evidence . . . on Agriculture. Part I*, p. 1048.

[37] "Pastoral Address of the Catholic Archbishops and Bishops, to the Catholic clergy and people of Ireland, August 5, 1859," *ICD* (Dublin, 1860), p. 244. It was not until almost a century later that the Irish Catholic hierarchy issued a pastoral devoted exclusively to the question of emigration. Here again they did not concern themselves with the effect of emigration on Ireland nor did they urge the clergy to use their influence to dissuade people from emigrating. As in the nineteenth century, this was a matter for individual priests and bishops. Instead the pastoral dealt with the problem of whether the emigrants abroad retained their faith, particularly in Great Britain which in the post-World War II period became the principal country of attraction for the Irish unemployed. *Irish Times*, June 22, 1955.

[38] *Dublin Evening Mail*, June 4, 1860. *Freeman's Journal*, June 4, 1860. "Pastoral from the Most Reverend Dr. Cullen, Archbishop of Dublin, October 30, 1863," *ICD* (Dublin, 1864), pp. 287-288. In addition to those published in newspapers and the *ICD*, the only other printed collection of pastoral letters extant for this period are those of Archbishop Cullen. In the entire collection not one pastoral was devoted to the problem of emigration. See Right Rev. Patrick F. Moran, ed., *The Pastoral Letters and Other Writings of Cardinal Cullen, Archbishop of Dublin, 1850-1878* (Dublin, 1882), 3 vols.

[39] *Catholic Telegraph*, April 25 and November 21, 1863; January 30, 1864.

[40] *Minutes of Evidence . . . on Agriculture, Part I*, p. 500. P. A. Sheehan, "The Effect of Emigration on the Irish Church," *IER*, 3rd series, Vol. III, No. 10 (October 1882), p. 613.

[41] James Cardinal Gibbons, "Irish Immigration to the United States," *IER*, 4th series, Vol. I (February 1897), pp. 97-109. The cardinal concluded that he would not discourage Irish immigration to the United States because there were at stake "the interests of the Catholic religion, which in this land and in this age are largely bound up with the interests of the Irish people."

[42] *Londonderry Standard*, September 13, 1855. *Tuam Herald*, October 19, 1901.

[43] *Weekly Telegraph*, January 1, 1853. On June 21, 1856, this paper was succeeded by the *Catholic Telegraph and Irish Sun*, which ran until 1866 when it too ceased publication. For a generation no paper claimed to speak for the Church until in 1889 the *Irish Catholic* made its appearance, and it has remained the Church's spokesman down to the present day.

[44] *Weekly Telegraph*, March 11, 1854; April 11, 1857. *Catholic Telegraph*, June 12, 1858; April 7, 1860; April 18, 1863; May 21, 1864. *Irish Catholic*, May 25, 1901.

[45] April 4, 1853. The *News-Letter*, however, was motivated by deeper —and cleverer — motives than mere taunting. Pointing out that as a result of the emigration Irish priests were likely to face penury at home, it suggested that they accept an endowment from the State. If the priests accepted, the journal doubtless saw their proposal as an entering wedge to dissociate the Irish Catholic Church from Rome, perhaps with the ultimate aim in mind of converting the entire clergy to the Church of Ireland.

[46] "Pioneer Priests," *All Hallows Annual 1953-1954*, p. 131. In this connection it is interesting to note that unlike the Germans who often emigrated in well-organized groups which included ministers, the Irish, like the British, emigrated primarily as individuals; established priests rarely accompanied them – that was a job for missionaries with specialized training. Only when the rapid growth of Irish overseas communities

created a demand for priests did the Irish Catholic Church respond by establishing missionary-training institutions.

Requests to All Hallows for priests came from all over the United States. See, for example, the following letters: Rev. Eugene O'Connell, San Francisco, June 15, 1853; Bishop J. N. Boyle, Newark, December 15, 1853; Bishop O'Regan, Chicago, September 18, 1854, Rev. Patrick McCabe, Dubuque, August 9, 1856; Rev. William J. Hamilton, Jacksonville, October 14, 1856; Rev. Thomas Lynch, Burlington, September 9, 1859; Bishop William H. Elder, Houston, Miss., October 25, 1859. *All Hallows Annual 1953-1954*, pp. 131-154.

Appeals were also made to the Irish at home for the support of All Hallows. See *Weekly Telegraph*, September 17, 1853; January 28, 1854.

[47] Alexander J. Peyton, *The Emigrant's Friend; or Hints on Emigration to the United States of America, Addressed to the People of Ireland* (Cork, 1853), p. 47, in *Haliday Collection*, Vol. 2139, No. 13, RIA. The real reason for Peyton's trip to America was to collect funds for an Irish Catholic University, for which purpose he was personally chosen by Archbishop Cullen of Dublin. There is no evidence that the Archbishop ever objected to the priest's letters or their contents.

To anyone reading Peyton's guide the advice to remain "quiet and contented" at home must have sounded strangely ironical, or at worst insincere, coming as it did at the end of a pamphlet which began by extolling the virtues of America in the most rapturous terms: "To say that America is not a great country, would be stating what is not true; to say it is a wonderful country is simply stating a fact. . . . An ample field is open to all, without favour or affection, and the only passport to wealth is good conduct and industry. Such in a few words, is the state of America." *Ibid.*, p. 2.

[48] Edward J. Maguire, "John O'Hanlon's Irish Emigrant's Guide for the United States: A Critical Evaluation," unpublished Ph.D. dissertation (St. Louis University, St. Louis, 1951), pp. i-xv. The title of this work is misleading. It is really more of a critical edition than a critical evaluation of the guide. Unfortunately Maguire never indicates how many editions the guide went through nor does he assess such important points as how widely it circulated, how effective it was, and what its stature was in relation to other guides of the time.

Chapter IV. The Visible Result: Land and Labor

[1] Table 11 in the Appendix.

[2] J. E. Cairnes, *Political Essays* (London, 1874), pp. 179-181.

[3] *Agricultural Statistics of Ireland . . .1901*, pp. 10-14 [Cd. 1170], H.C. 1902, xcvi-Part I.

The long-range, indirect effects of emigration on Irish landholding were considerable and important. Even before Ireland had gained its independence the government had launched a program of subdividing the large estates and creating many small farms. Without the heavy emigration of the previous century, thought T. W. Freeman, it was doubtful whether this "agricultural revolution" could have been possible: ". . . if Eire had to support three times as many people as it does now on the same area of land a return to subsistence farming would be inevitable over a large part of the country." *Emigration and Rural Ireland* (Dublin, 1945), pp. 6-7.

[4] C. H. Oldham, "Economic Development in Ireland," *SSIJ*, Vol. X, Part LXXX (November 1899-June 1900), pp. 558-559. *Agricultural Statistics . . . 1901*, p. viii. Thomas Kennedy, "Fifty Years of Irish Agriculture," SSIJ, Vol. X, Part LXXXIX (November 1898-June 1899), pp. 403-404. Grimshaw, *Facts and Figures About Ireland*, p. 21. Geary, "Future Population of Saorstat Eireann . . ." pp. 29-30.

[5] Grimshaw, *op. cit.*, p. 21.

[6] Geary, *op. cit.*, p. 29.

[7] Freeman, *Emigration* . . . p. 2. Saorstat Eireann, *Agricultural Statistics, 1847-1926* (Dublin, 1928), pp. xliv-xlv. Table 12 in the Appendix.

[8] *Agricultural Statistics . . . 1901*, p. vii. Table 12 in the Appendix. Hans Staehle, "Statistical Notes on the Economic History of Irish Agriculture, 1847-1913," *SSIJ*, Vol. XVIII (1950-51), p. 446.

[9] Staehle, "Statistical Notes . . ." p. 454.

[10] Saorstat Eireann, *Agricultural Statistics*, pp. xlii-xlv.

[11] *Seventh Annual Report of the Commissioners for Administering the Laws for Relief of the Poor in Ireland* (hereafter referred to as *Annual Report of the Poor Law Commissioners*), pp. 33-36 [1785], H.C. 1854, xxix. *Newry Examiner*, April 9, 1853. It seems that some farmers even tried using the threat of emigration as a means by which to have their rents lowered. One such farmer, encountered on a rent-reducing pilgrimage to his landlord, confessed to an English doctor that if the reduction were denied him he was ready to give up the farm and emigrate to America — with the help of his unpaid rent. See John Forbes, *Memorandums Made in Ireland in the Autumn of 1852*, Vol. II (London, 1853), pp. 263-265. *Report from the Select Committee of the House of Lords on the Tenure (Ireland) Bill*, p. 203, H.C. 1867 (518), xiv. Oldham, "Economic Development . . ." p. 562.

[12] John Locke, *Ireland's Recovery, or, Excessive Emigration and its Reparative Agencies in Ireland* (London, 1853), p. 10, in *Haliday Collection*, Vol. 2138, No. 9, RIA. Lord St. Germans to Lord Aberdeen, January 1854, *Larcom Papers*, NLI MS 7600. *Sixteenth General Report of the Emigration Commissioners, 1856*, pp. 10-11. *Ninth Annual Report of the Poor Law Commissioners*, pp. 10-11 [2105], H.C. 1856, xxviii. Rev. Thomas Jordan, "Effects of Emigration: can it be made a means of relieving Distress?" *SSIJ*, Vol. I (July 1856), p. 381. William Donnelly to Sir Thomas Larcom, January 29, 1857, *Larcom Papers*, NLI MS 7600. MacDonnell, "Statistics of Irish Prosperity," p. 276. Lord Dufferin, *Irish Emigration and the Tenure of Land in Ireland* (London, 1867), pp. 25-26. *Irish Times*, June 22, 1871.

[13] John K. Ingram, *Considerations on the State of Ireland* (Dublin, 1863), pp. 9-10. A. L. Bowley, "The Statistics of Wages in the United Kingdom during the last Hundred Years. (Part III) Agricultural Wages — Ireland," *Journal of the Royal Statistical Society*, Vol. LXII (June 1899), p. 398.

[14] *Newry Examiner*, May 26, 1852; April 8, 1854. *Dublin Evening Post*, May 10, 1851. J. N. Murphy, *Ireland: Industrial, Political and Social (London, 1870)*, pp. 204-206. *Minutes of Evidence . . on Agriculture, Part I*, p. 371.

[15] *Eighth Annual Report of the Poor Law Commissioners*, p. 13 [1945], H.C. 1854-55, xxiv. The complaint to Senior was made by a Poor Law inspector who despaired that "The higher the wages the quicker I lose them: they go as soon as they have saved the passage-money. I had a cook and housekeeper, a very respectable woman. She is gone off with the stable-boy. I remonstrated against her making so bad a match. 'Och,' she said, 'he'll do

in America.' " Nassau W. Senior, *Journals, Conversations and Essays relating to Ireland*, Vol. II (London, 1868), pp. 53-54. Shand, *Letters from the West of Ireland*, p. 58. *Tuam Herald*, April 6, 1889.

16 Robert Murray to Lord Clarendon, January 1, 1850, *Larcom Papers*, NLI MS 7600. *Thirteenth General Report of the Colonial Land and Emigration Commissioners, 1853*, pp. 11-12 [1647], H.C. 1852-53, xl. *Eighth Annual Report of the Poor Law Commissioners*, p. 15. John McKane, "What Are the Economic Results of the Continuous Emigration from Ireland?" *Transactions of the National Association for the Promotion of Social Science* (n.p., 1867), pp. 577-584, as quoted in Edith Abbott, *Historical Aspects of the Immigration Problem: Select Documents* (Chicago, 1926), pp. 361-367. Bowley, "Statistics of Wages . . ." *op. cit.*

17 *Sixth Annual Report of the Poor Law Commissioners*, p. 8 [1645], H.C. 1852-53, 1. *Seventh Annual Report of the Poor Law Commissioners*, p. 35. *Tenth Annual Report of the Poor Law Commissioners*, p. 14 [2235], H.C. 1864, xxv. *Seventeenth Annual Report of the Poor Law Commissioners*, p. 7 [3338], H.C. 1857-sess. 2, xxii.

18 Paul-Dubois, *Contemporary Ireland*, pp. 361-362.

19 Table 16 and Table 2 in the Appendix.

20 Grimshaw, *Facts and Figures*, pp. 16-18. Fourth-class houses he defined as all single-gle-room houses made of mud or perishable material, third-class houses were somewhat better with two to four rooms and windows; second class included a good farmhouse in the country or a small town house having five to seven rooms and windows; first-class were all houses of a better description.

Fourth-class accommodation he defined as all individual families living in fourth-class houses, or two families sharing third-class houses, three families or more sharing second-class houses, or five or more families in first-class houses. Third-class accommodation meant single families occupying third-class houses, or four or five families in first-class houses. Second-class accommodation designated single families in second-class houses, or two to three families in first-class houses. First-class accommodation specified single families in first-class houses.

21 Table 17 in the Appendix.

22 Murray, *History of . . . Financial Relations . . .* pp. 386-388.

23 Oldham, "Economic Development . . . " pp. 549-552.

24 *Limerick Reporter*, April 23, 1889. Shand, *Letters from . . . Ireland*, pp. 146-147. D. A. Chart, *An Economic History of Ireland* (Dublin, 1920), p. 149.

25 E. J. Riordan contended in his *Modern Irish Trade and Industry* (London, 1920), p. 261, that the decrease in population was probably the most important single factor accounting for the dearth of Irish industry. But he never elaborated his contention and chose instead to dwell on the injurious effects of English action — and inaction — vis-à-vis Irish industry. He finally concluded (p. 290) that Ireland's industrial decline in the seventy years following the famine was due primarily to Britain's restrictive policies.

The latter position is supported by George O'Brien, the leading economic historian of Ireland. Discussing the period prior to the famine he declared that it was England's manipulation of protective duties and bounties which served to impede the development of Irish manufactures. As a result, when England finally embraced free trade in the 1840s, the few infant Irish industries that did exist received the final *coup de grâce* by being exposed to the "full pressure of British competition" before they were "sufficiently developed to withstand it." The one exception was the linen industry in Ulster which continued to flourish, a fact to be attributed to the superior land system there. The existence of the "Ulster custom," O'Brien argued, allowed capital to accumulate for investment purposes by guaranteeing compensation to the farmer for any, improvements which he effected and thereby encouraged saving. The absence of any comparable benefits in the south discouraged saving and prevented the amassing of investment capital. *The Economic History of Ireland from the Union to the Famine* (London, 1921), pp. 446-447, 578.

[26] *Spectator*, October 18, 1851, p. 997, as quoted in Abbott, *op. cit.*, pp. 127-128.

Chapter V. The Invisible Result: Cant and Custom

[1] What is surprising is that so little has been written about this aspect of the Irish scene. Neither the literature nor the newspapers of the period contain much information, although Padraic Colum in his *The Road Round Ireland* (New York, 1926), pp. 172-178, gives a brief description of an American wake he had attended in the west of Ireland in the early 1920s. Data have been obtained primarily from answers to a questionnaire constructed by the writer and circulated by the Irish Folklore Commission through its network of professional interviewers during the early months of 1955, and also from personal interviews conducted by the writer during the summer months of that same year. For a detailed description of the geographical distribution of the questionnaire see the Bibliography. A copy of the questionnaire itself may be found in the author's doctoral dissertation which is on file at Deering Library, Northwestern University, Evanston, Illinois.

The great majority of people interviewed were well advanced in years, generally in their seventies and eighties, since such people were the ones most likely to have had first-hand experiences of the phenomena under consideration. In each case the mental clarity and dependability of the informant was ascertained by a professional IFC interviewer, and in view of the fact that the questions dealt with general social phenomena and the personal experiences of the informants rather than with a recollection of specific dates or events, there seems little reason to doubt the accuracy of the data gathered. Moreover a good deal of confirmatory evidence from interviewers all over Ireland, as well as evidence obtained by the writer in personally conducted interviews, has generally corroborated the information collected in any given area. It is of course possible that there are certain inaccuracies or exaggerations, but insofar as it has been possible to do so, such data have been excluded. Much of the material was gathered on tape recorders and then transcribed verbatim into IFC notebooks, so that in many cases the writer was as close to the prime sources of information as was possible under the circumstances.

[2] The best and most recent work on Irish wakes is Hans Hartmann, *Der Totenkult in Irland-Ein Beitrag zur Religion der Indogermanen* (Heidelberg, 1952), especially pp. 112-117 and 151-172. Clerical opposition to Irish wakes dates back to at least the early seventeenth century. In 1618 they were denounced as "abuses" which gave "pain to pious and religious souls." John Brady, "Funeral Customs of the Past," *IER*, 5th series, Vol. LXXVIII (November 1952), p. 334. Carleton's description of an Irish wake is quoted in S. F. Milligan and A. Milligan, *Glimpses of Erin* (London, 1888), pp. 203-205.

[3] Michael MacDonagh, *Irish Life and Character* (London, 1898), p. 374.

[4] MS notebook of Conall O'Byrne, No. III, IFC.

[5] Robert Lynd, *Home Life in Ireland* (London, 1909), p. 120. *Irish People*, June 15, 1901. *Tuam Herald*, June 22, 1901.

[6] MS notebooks of Conall O'Byrne, Nos. I, II, III; Seamus Mulcahy; J. G. Delaney; M. J. Murphy; Ciaran Bairead; Michael Corduff, IFC. Personal interviews with Mrs. Teresa Dunne, age 86, July 2, 1955, Dublin; Mr. Cathal O'Shannon, age 70, July 1, 1955, Dublin.

[7] MS notebook of Michael Corduff, IFC.

[8] Personal interview with Mr. Francis McManus, age 45, January 8, 1955, Dublin.

[9] MS notebooks of Conall O'Byrne, Nos. I, II, III; Joseph Wade, IFC.

[10] MS notebook of Conall O'Byrne, No. III, IFC.

[11] Harriet Martineau, *Letters from Ireland* (London, 1852), p. 140.

[12] MS notebook of Conall O'Byrne, No. I, IFC.

[13] MS notebooks of P. J. Gaynor; M. J. Murphy; Conall O'Byrne, No. II; Tadgh Murphy, IFC.

[14] A. M. Sullivan, *New Ireland*, 6th ed. (New York, 1878), p. 165.

[15] Milligan and Milligan, *op. cit.*, p. 205.

[16] MS notebooks of P. J. Gaynor; Ciaran Bairead, No. I, IFC.

[17] MS notebooks of M. J. Murphy; Ciaran Bairead, No. II; Conall O'Byrne, No. III, IFC. Personal interviews with Mr. Jerry O'Leary, age 65, July 23, 1955, Killarney, Co. Kerry; Mr. Pat Shannon, age 71, July 9, 1955, County Home, Ennis, Co. Clare; Mr. Thomas Brosnan, age 69, July 9, 1955, County Home, Ennis, Co. Clare; Mr. Jim Kennedy, age 74, July 23, 1955, County Home, Killarney, Co. Kerry; Mr. Padraig Donovan, age 87, July 23, 1955, County Home, Killarney, Co. Kerry. Private reports of Mr. Sean MacGrath and Mr. Tom Gallagher, in writer's possession.

[18] There is some evidence that local parish priests opposed the American wakes and sometimes denounced them from the pulpit. In at least one case in County Galway the objection stemmed from a belief that too much money was spent on the wake, money which people could ill afford. It was also felt that excessive drinking was indulged in. On the whole, however, clerical opposition was probably less important a factor in the near-disappearance of the American wake than was the progress made in the means of transportation, as well as the outbreak of World War I and the American immigration restrictions that followed it. MS notebook of Ciaran Bairead, No. II, IFC.

Nevertheless, there is one type of American wake that is still practiced in parts of Ireland, especially in County Donegal, and is much grimmer in nature. This kind of wake is occasioned by the death of a member of a family who was living in America as an emigrant. Whenever such a death occurs a wake is held for that person in Ireland at the house of his parents. MS notebook of Conall O'Byrne, No. I, IFC.

[19] Conrad M. Arensberg, *The Irish Countryman* (Cambridge, Mass., 1938), Ch. VI.

[20] MS notebook of M. J. Murphy, IFC.

[21] MS notebook of P. J. Gaynor, IFC.

[22] MS notebook of M. J. Murphy, IFC.

[23] Private report of Mr. Sean MacGrath.

[24] MS notebook of Sean O'Dubhda, IFC.

[25] Private report of Mr. Sean MacGrath. MS notebook of Conall O'Byrne, No. II, IFC.

Personal interview with Rev. Canon N. D. Emerson, January 29, 1955, Dublin.

[26] MS notebook of Michael Corduff, IFC.

[27] MS notebook of Sean O'Dubhda, IFC.

[28] MS notebook of Sean O'Keefe, IFC.

[29] Broadsheet Collection of Irish Street Ballads, No. 139, NLI.

[30] *Ibid.*, No. 225. In all these ballads the Irish pronunciation of America is as if the word were spelled "Amerikey" or "Amerikay."

[31] MS notebook of Sean O'Keefe, IFC.

[32] MS notebook of Mary O'Neill, IFC.

[33] MS notebook of Ciaran Bairead, No. I, IFC.

[34] MS notebook of Conall O'Byrne, No. III, IFC.

[35] Broadsheet Collection of Irish Street Ballads, No. 131, NLI.

[36] MS notebook of Ciaran Bairead, No. I, IFC.

[37] *Ibid.*

[38] Broadsheet Collection of Irish Street Ballads, No. 198, NLI.

[39] MS notebook of J. J. O'Donnell, IFC. Three years after he emigrated the poet was killed in an accident in an iron foundry.

[40] *Walton's 132 Best Irish Songs and Ballads* (Dublin, 1955), p. 107.

[41] Broadsheet Collection of Irish Street Ballads, No. 67, NLI.

[42] MS notebook of Sean O'Keefe, IFC.

Chapter VI. Alms and Agitation

[1] C.O. 384/83, PRO, London.

[2] The seven Liverpool firms were Harnden and Co.; McMurray and Co.; Grimshaw and Co.; Tapscott and Co.; Byrne and Co.; Mr. Toole, Roche and Co.; Brown, Shipley and Co. *Ibid. Twenty-eighth General Report of the Emigration Commissioners, 1868*, p. 3 [4024], H.C. 1867-68, xvii.

[3] *Twentieth General Report of the Emigration Commissioners, 1860*, p. 14 [2696], H.C. 1860, xxix. *Thirty-third General Report of the Emigration Commissioners, 1873*, p. 10 [c. 768], H.C. 1873, xviii. *Statistical Tables relating to Emigration and Immigration . . . in the year 1887, and Report to the Board of Trade thereon*, p. 18, H.C. 1888 (2), cvii.

[4] Table 18 in the Appendix.

[5] W. Neilson Hancock, "On the Remittances from North America . . ." p. 283. As early as 1853 one journal was led to comment that these huge aggregate remittances formed a "vast colonial fund" from which not only the recipients, but the whole country benefited – "just the same as if [the remittances] were lodged in the national exchequer." *Carlow Sentinel*, July 23, 1853.

[6] *Twenty-third General Report of the Emigration Commissioners, 1863*, p. 12 [3199], H.C. 1863, xv. John O'Rourke, *The History of the Great Famine of 1847, with Notices of Earlier Irish Famines* (Dublin, 1875), p. 504. Peter Condon, "The Irish in Countries other than Ireland – I. In the United States," *Catholic Encyclopedia*, Vol. VIII (New York, 1910), p. 144.

By 1950 annual remittances from Irish emigrants amounted to $37,800,000 and represented Ireland's greatest source of overseas revenue, exceeding the next greatest overseas revenue, that from the export of cattle, by $1,400,000. As in earlier years, the bulk of these remittances came from the United States. *St. Louis Globe-Democrat*, July 12, 1950.

A decade earlier Professor George O'Brien commented: "From the point of view of the balance of payments . . . remittances play a part identical with . . . income from investments abroad. It is the existence of these and other similar payments from abroad that makes Ireland such a strong creditor country and, therefore, so financially independent [!] and so capable . . . of undertaking extensive schemes of internal development without recourse to foreign lenders." "New Light on Irish Emigration," *Studies*, Vol. XXX (March 1941), pp. 30-31.

[7] *Dublin Evening Post*, March 11, 1852. John Locke, *Ireland's Recovery . . .* p. 2. *Freeman's Journal*, September 28, 1865, in *Larcom Papers*, NLI MS 7610.

[8] *King's County Chronicle*, July 20, 1853. Mary A. Frawley, *Patrick Donohoe* (Washington, D.C., 1946), p. 149. Carl Wittke, *We Who Built America. The Saga of the Immigrant* (New York, 1939), p. 125.

[9] Edward Blacker, cashier of the Bank of Ireland, to William Donnelly, registrar-general, July 30, 1862, *Larcom Papers*, NLI MS 7605. *Catholic Telegraph*, March 16, 1861. Table 18 in the Appendix.

[10] Henry B. Hammond to William H. Seward, April 17, 1862, *Cons. Desp.*, Dublin, Vol. 3 (RG 59), NA. *Annual Report of the Postmaster General, 1871* (Washington, D.C., 1872) p. xxx.

[11] See Table 19 in the Appendix. In the first nine months of operation of the postal money-order convention signed with the German Empire in 1872, German settlers in the United States sent back a little over $420,000, or slightly more than one half the Irish total. But in the same period the German immigrants received nearly as much as they sent ($310,000) while money-orders sent from the whole United Kingdom were less than one fifth the amount sent from the United States. *Annual Report of the Postmaster General, 1872*, pp. 251-252; *Annual Report . . .* 1873, pp. 213-214.

Although money orders were issued in a total of forty-six states and territories, the six states of Illinois, Massachusetts, New Jersey, New York, Ohio, and Pennsylvania together accounted for more than half the total sum. For the remainder of the century these six states, with comparatively little variation, continued to account for well over 50 percent of the total money orders sent to the United Kingdom. When it is remembered that during the entire half-century these six states also contained over 70 percent of the total Irish-born population in the United States, there can be little doubt that the great majority of money orders sent to the United Kingdom were ultimately destined for Ireland.

[12] Hancock, "On the Remittances . . ." p. 282. See also Table 19 in the Appendix.

[13] *Catholic Telegraph*, March 16, 1861. John Francis Maguire, *The Irish in America* (London, 1868), pp. 321-322.

[14] *Report from the Select Committee on Outrages (Ireland) . . .* p. 452, H.C. 1852 (438), xiv. Personal interview with Mr. Martin Kissane, age 87, July 23, 1955, County Home, Killarney, Co. Kerry. MS notebook of J. J. O'Donnell, IFC.

[15] Maguire, *Irish in America*, p. 318.

[16] C.O. 384/83, PRO, London. *Twenty-eighth General Report of the Emigration*

Commissioners, 1868, op. cit. Thirty-second General Report of the Emigration Commissioners, 1872, p. 4 [c. 562], H.C. 1872, xvi. *Twenty-second General Report of the Emigration Commissioners, 1862*, p. 12 [3010], H.C. 1862, xxii. Carrothers, *Emigration from the British Isles*, p. 206.

[17] *King's County Chronicle*, November 1, 1854. *Mayo Constitution*, March 15, 1864. *Waterford Daily Mail*, April 20, 1883. "Letter from the Secretary of the Treasury, transmitting a Report of the Commissioners of Immigration upon the causes which incite immigration to the United States. Vol. I. Reports of Commissioners, 1892," *Ex. Doc.* No. 235, Part I, 52nd Cong., 1st sess., pp. 208-209.

[18] Personal interview with Mrs. Teresa Dunne, age 86, July 2, 1955, Dublin.

[19] MS notebook of Conall O'Byrne, No. I, IFC.

[20] *Royal Commission on Labour . . . Ireland. Part IV*, p. 16. *Sligo Champion*, as quoted in *Dublin Evening Post*, March 8, 1864, in *Larcom Papers*, NLI MS 7607.

[21] *Report of Her Majesty's Commissioners of Inquiry into the Working of the Landlord and Tenant (Ireland) Act, 1870 . . . Vol. III. Minutes of Evidence. Part II*, p. 759 [c. 2779-II], H.C. 1881, xix. *Royal Commission of Inquiry into the Procedure and the Methods of Valuation . . . Vol. II. Minutes of Evidence*, p. 866 [c. 8859], H.C. 1898, xxxv.

[22] MS notebook of Conall O'Byrne, No. II, IFC.

[23] Thomas F. Meehan, "English Taxation in America," *North American Review*, Vol. CXLV, No. 372 (November 1887), pp. 565-566. Thomas Power O'Connor, *The Parnell Movement* (London, 1886), p. 293. Paul–Dubois, *Contemporary Ireland*, p. 305. Personal interview with Mr. Padraig Donovan, age 87, July 23, 1955, County Home, Killarney, Co. Kerry. Personal interview with Mr. Dan Regan, age 85, July 22, 1955, County Home , Clonakilty, Co. Cork.

[24] *Kilkenny Journal*, August 21, 1861. See also MS notebooks of Ciaran Bairead, No. I; Tadgh Murphy; Thomas Moran; Dermot O'Sullivan, IFC.

[25] MS notebooks of Conall O'Byrne, Nos. II and III, IFC.

[26] Private report of Mr. Sean MacGrath, in writer's possession.

[27] MS notebook of Ciaran Bairead, No. II, IFC.

[28] *Ibid.*, No. I.

[29] MS notebook of Conall O'Byrne, No. II, IFC.

[30] Private report of Mr. Tom Gallagher, in writer's possession.

[31] Private report of Mr. Sean MacGrath.

[32] Statistics on savings accounts have been gathered from the following sources: W. Neilson Hancock, *Report on Deposits . . . in Ireland, 1840-1869* (Dublin, 1870), p. 5; also his *Report on Statistics of Savings Invested in Ireland . . . 1860-1872* (Dublin, 1873), p. 4. *Report on Certain Statistics of Banking in Ireland . . . 1876-1885*, p. 7 [c. 4681], H.C. 1886, lxxi. *Banking, Railway, and Shipping Statistics, Ireland . . . 1901*, p. 7 [Cd. 806], H.C. 1902, cxvi–Part I.

[33] Hooker, *Readjustments of Agricultural Tenure*, p. 222.

[34] Computed from *Agricultural Statistics of Ireland for 1901*, pp. 52-67, and *Report of Irish Land Commissioners for . . . 1923* (Dublin, 1928), pp. 62-63.

[35] MS notebooks of Conall O'Byrne, No. II; Ciaran Bairead, No. I, IFC. Private report of Mr. Sean MacGrath.

[36] Private report of Mr. Sean MacGrath. MS notebook of Ciaran Bairead, No. I, IFC.

191

[37] Alexander J. Peyton, *The Emigrant's Friend* . . . (Cork, 1853), p. v, in *Haliday Collection*, Vol. 2139, No. 13, RIA.

[38] MS notebooks of Ciaran Bairead, Nos. I and II; M. J. Murphy, IFC. Sometimes money came without the asking, but not always for churches. One Irish emigrant living in New York was so enthusiastic about the field sports of his hometown in County Kilkenny that he was moved to send two pounds for the support of a local race track. So noble a gesture could not go unnoticed and was seized upon by the local paper for an appeal to its readers: ". . . surely those who will participate in the enjoyment ought to come forward with much greater generosity." *Kilkenny Journal*, August 14, 1861

[39] Keep, "The Irish Migration to North America . . ." pp. 151-152.

[40] MS notebook of Conall O'Byrne, No. I, IFC.

[41] Robert Lloyd Praeger, *The Way That I Went: An Irishman in Ireland*, 2nd ed. (Dublin, 1939), p. 192.

[42] *Eighteenth General Report of the Emigration Commissioners, 1858*, p. 13 [2395], H.C. 1857-58, xxiv. *Royal Commission on Labour*, pp. 16, 75. Personal interview with Mrs. Teresa Dunne, age 86, July 2, 1955, Dublin.

[43] Personal interview with Mr. Pat Shannon, age 71, July 9, 1955, County Home, Ennis, Co. Clare.

[44] W. E. H. Lecky, *Leaders of Public Opinion in Ireland*, new ed., Vol. II (London, 1903), p. 183. O'Connor, *Parnell Movement*, p. 117.

[45] Edmund Curtis, *A History of Ireland*, 3rd ed. (London, 1937), p. 370.

[46] As quoted in Abbott, *Historical Aspects of the Immigration Problem*, p. 530.

[47] Maguire, *Irish in America*, p. 610.

[48] As quoted in Dublin *Daily Express*, May 4, 1860, in *Larcom Papers*, NLI MS 7602.

[49] *Connaught Telegraph*, March 30, 1901.

[50] F.O. 5/498, PRO, London.

[51] H.O. 45/OS 6039, PRO, London. See also dispatches of John Crampton to Lord Palmerston, February 4 and 12, 1856, F.O. 5/640, PRO, London.

[52] H. B. C. Pollard, *The Secret Societies of Ireland* (London, 1922), p. 46. Adams, *Ireland and Irish Emigration*, p. 398. Strauss, *Irish Nationalism and British Democracy*, p. 106.

[53] George Macaulay Trevelyan, *British History in the Nineteenth Century and After (1782-1919)*, 2nd ed. (London, 1937), p. 350.

[54] John O'Leary, *Recollections of Fenians and Fenianism*, Vol. I (London, 1896), pp. 135-36.

[55] Although the "invasion" and attempted uprising was a complete fiasco, the British took no unnecessary risks and clamped upon the country a series of oppressive coercion acts which amounted to a state of martial law. Arrests were frequent and were made on the slightest suspicion of Fenian activity. The zealousness with which arrests were made unhappily created an additional burden for the already overworked American consul in Dublin, William B. West. In the twelve months between September 1865 and September 1866 at least eighty-eight American citizens were arrested and charged with complicity in the Fenian conspiracy. Each appealed to West for help and within that year the consul wrote no less than four hundred letters and dispatches on their behalf. West's problem was complicated by the fact that many of those arrested were naturalized American citizens, an official transfer of national allegiance which the British did not yet recognize. As a result the American consul could intercede only where documentary evidence was produced to prove that the persons involved were native-born Americans. In these

cases he was able to secure their freedom but only on condition that they leave Ireland on the first available ship. For those naturalized Americans who might have been innocent visitors to the land of their birth he could do nothing. Eventually most of them were released by the courts for lack of evidence but not before enduring some indignities and humiliations. *Cons. Desp.*, Dublin, Vol. 6 (RG 59), NA.

⁵⁶ Pomfret, *Struggle for Land in Ireland*, p. 105.

⁵⁷ T. W. Moody, "The New Departure in Irish Politics, 1878-9," in H. A. Cronne, T. W. Moody, and D. B. Quinn, eds., *Essays in British and Irish History in Honour of James Eadie Todd* (London, 1949), p. 331.

⁵⁸ Strauss, *Irish Nationalism* . . . pp. 162-163.

⁵⁹ Pomfret, *Struggle for Land* . . . pp. 128-129. *Belfast News-Letter*, June 18, 1881. *Dictionary of American Biography*, Vol. VI (New York, 1931), p. 518. James J. Green, "American Catholics and the Irish Land League, 1879-1882," *Catholic Historical Review*, Vol. XXV, No. 1 (April 1949), pp. 40-41.

⁶⁰ Pomfret, *op. cit.*

Chapter VII. Men, Manners, and Methods

¹ Americans of the 1850s and 1860s thought it would take three generations for the Irish to become thoroughly Americanized, although some things, they regretfully admitted, the Irish picked up much too quickly. One of these was a rapid absorption of the spirit of equality, a fact which led one English observer to note that while the Irish might consent to do the most menial tasks for the Americans, they did them "haughtily and with a fierce independence." It was "terror" of the Irish servant, he felt, that drove Americans into living in hotels, a terror born of the dread of Irish revenge whenever the hypersensitive Celts felt themselves slighted. In evidence he offered the following story which, he claimed, was typical of the times: ". . . a lady, lately come out from England, in calling on a friend in New York, enquired of an Irish servant whether 'his mistress was at home.' Of course, no American dares speak of the 'master' or 'mistress' of a household: such terms were abolished with slavery. No wonder the Irishman was indignant; but he speedily saw his way to revenge. 'No ma'am,' he replied, very courteously, 'the fact is, *I don't keep one at present.*' " John White, *Sketches from America* (London, 1870), p. 371.

² Carl Wittke, *The Irish in America* (Baton Rouge, 1956).

³ *Clare Journal*, September 25, 1873. Seumus MacManus, "A Revolution in Ireland," *Catholic World*, Vol. LXIX, No. 412 (July 1899), pp. 525-526.

⁴ MS notebooks of Conall O'Byrne, Nos. II and III, IFC.

⁵ Personal interview with Miss Margaret Corry, age 67, July 9, 1955, County Home, Ennis, Co. Clare.

⁶ MS notebook of Ciaran Bairead, No. II, IFC.

⁷ Some women, however, resorted to a bit of deception to achieve their ends, as is illustrated in the following incident related by an informant from County Donegal: "I know one case where there was a farm of land for sale, and this lady who was a returned Yankee went to the auction. There was another young man for the same farm and he went to the auction too. She bid on the farm, and the auctioneer kept askin' for an advance after such a bid. She and the boy got at it, and in the long reach the boy bought

the farm. But what happened then? In a year or so, be gobs, says this boy to himself, she must have plenty of money when she bid so strongly against me to get the farm, and the next thing he met her and he made friends with her, and after some time they both got married. And it was owing to her biddin' on the farm that he was allowin' she had the money. But it turned out afterwards she had the price of no farm, but she wanted people to believe that she had money so that she would have a chance of gettin' a man, and it worked in her case." MS notebook of Sean O'Heochaidh, IFC.

More fortunate were the individuals involved in the following tale from a County Galway informant in his late seventies: "A girl from this village went to America many years before 1900 and did well. . . . After some years she came home. As soon as a man in Carnmore [the local village] — Hughie O'Hanley — her own name was Peggy Duggan — heard she had come home with some money he asked her in marriage and the marriage was arranged. It was the custom in those times that a party, called 'an Cleamhnas,' was held in the bride's home some days previous to the marriage. Some time during the night . . . the girl's dowry was handed over to her future husband. It was customary for him to make a present of some of the money to some member of the girl's family, her mother or a younger sister, if such there were. On this occasion he gave a pound note, or what he thought was such, to her mother. They were all illiterate. Next day the mother gave the 'pound' to a son of hers who also lived with them, to buy some groceries in Galway [city]. When he went into the shop he was told it was a ten-pound note! He bought the groceries and gave his mother the change that remained from one pound. He kept the other nine and shortly after . . . went to America, paying his passage with them. . . . He never returned." MS notebook of Ciaran Bairead, No. I, IFC.

8 MS notebook of Sean O'Keefe, IFC.

9 Personal interview with Mrs. Kate Tynan, age 60, September 25, 1955, Meelick, Portlaoise, Co. Leix.

10 MS notebook of Ciaran Bairead, No. I, IFC.

11 Personal interview with Mrs. Teresa Dunne, age 86, July 2, 1955, Dublin.

12 MS notebook of Conall O'Byrne, No. II, IFC.

13 Personal interview with Mrs. Teresa Dunne, op. cit.

14 MS notebook of Tadgh Murphy, IFC.

15 Private report of Mr. Tom Gallagher, in the writer's possession.

16 *Minutes of Evidence . . . on Agriculture.* Part I, p. 1013.

17 MS notebook of Michael Corduff, IFC.

18 MS notebook of Matthew O'Reilly, IFC. Private report of Mr. Tom Gallagher.

19 MS notebook of Tadgh Murphy, IFC. The question may properly be asked whether it is correct to attribute the change in returned Yanks to their American experience. After all, might these people not have been the more active and industrious type even before they went to America? It is doubtless true that emigration is a selective process and that generally speaking it is the more adventurous and energetic members of a society who emigrate. Nevertheless in the case of the Irish it would appear that such qualities as industriousness and "go-aheadness" which came to be specifically associated with returned Yanks were merely latent or dormant in Ireland and there seemed to be few or no incentives in the Irish scene to urge them to the surface. As early as 1853, for example, one priest from County Cork spoke of "that sluggish inertness, that drowsy listlessness," which seemed to characterize the Irish at home. (See Alex. J. Peyton, *The*

Emigrant's Friend . . . p. vi.) A decade later the *Northern Whig* asserted (April 29, 1863) that only in America were the Irish able to "redeem" their national character because, "Without motives to industry at home, they were censured as incurably idle; without the means of saving, they were blamed as thriftless; with nothing to live for in the future, they were denounced for living wholly in the present; without the means of culture, their tendency to low and sensual pleasures was pharisaically deplored. . . . The Irish do not cease to be Keltic or Romanists by crossing the Atlantic. They do, however, cease to be indolent or improvident."

[20] MS notebook of Thomas Moran, IFC.

[21] MS notebooks of Conall O'Byrne, Nos. I and III, IFC.

[22] Personal interview with Mr. John Kirby, age 75, July 23, 1955, County Home, Killarney, Co. Kerry.

[23] MS notebook of M. J. Murphy, IFC.

[24] MS notebook of Conall O'Byrne, No. I, IFC.

[25] MS notebook of Ciaran Bairead, No. I, IFC.

[26] John G. Piatt to John Davis, assistant secretary of state, July 30, 1885, *Cons. Desp.*, Cork, Vol. 9 (RG 59), NA.

[27] *Irish Times*, November 28, 1863, in *Larcom Papers*, NLI MS 7607.

[28] MS notebook of Conall O'Byrne, No. I, IFC.

[29] MS notebook of Michael MacEnri, IFC.

[30] MS notebook of J. G. Delaney, IFC. Personal interview with Mr. Jerry O'Leary, age 65, July 23, 1955, Killarney, Co. Kerry.

[31] MS notebook of Ciaran Bairead, No. I, IFC.

[32] J L. Joynes, *The Adventures of a Tourist in Ireland* (London, 1882), p. 54.

[33] Phillipe Daryl, *Ireland's Disease: Notes and Impressions* (London, 1888), p. 195.

[34] *Minutes of Evidence . . . on Agriculture*, pp. 852-853.

[35] Lord Dufferin, *Irish Emigration . . .* pp. 195-196.

[36] MS notebook of Michael Corduff, IFC.

[37] MS notebook of Conall O'Byrne, No. III, IFC.

[38] MS notebook of Ciaran Bairead, No. II, IFC. An interesting exception to the generalization was the observation of an American Catholic bishop of mixed Negro-Irish descent who traveled through Ireland in 1878. When he arrived in the city of Limerick he made the following entry in his diary under the heading of June 20: "The people were not as poor in appearance as I had been led to expect. . . . the poor young women here seem better clad and less care-worn than the young women of the same class in Galway. One sees . . . a bearing superior to their condition in a very great number — and in the towns many are dressed in the fashions. I consider that this in part comes from the American return-tide." "MS diary of Bishop J. A. Healy," Holy Cross University Library, Worcester, Mass.

[39] Private report of Mr. Tom Gallagher. An American folklorist who traveled through Ireland in the early 1890s found lodgings one night in a small village in County Donegal. He noted that his landlady, who had kept house for twenty years and had reared a family of four children, possessed one iron kettle as her only cooking utensil and added that she "baked, boiled and brewed in it." J. Schafer, ed., *Memoirs of Jeremiah Curtin* (Madison, 1940), pp. 458-459.

[40] MS notebook of M. J. Murphy, IFC.

[41] MS notebook of Ciaran Bairead, No. I, IFC.

[42] Personal interview with Mr. Cathal O'Shannon, age 70, July 1, 1955, Dublin.

[43] MS notebook of Joseph Wade, IFC.

[44] *Minutes of Evidence . . . on Agriculture*, p. 950.

[45] *Dundalk Democrat*, April 29, 1865.

[46] Baron E. de Mandat-Grancey, *Paddy at Home*, 2nd ed. (London, 1887), p. 77.

[47] Louis Richmond to F. W. Seward, assistant secretary of state, December 15, 1887, *Cons. Desp.*, Cork, Vol. 7 (RG 59), NA.

[48] George A. Birmingham, *The Lighter Side of Irish Life* (London, 1911), p. 211.

BIBLIOGRAPHY
I. SOURCE MATERIALS

A. Emigrant Letters

As was stated in Chapter II, all letters are in the writer's possession as originals or photostatic copies of originals, except where otherwise indicated in individual footnotes. The total number of letters collected was 222 and of this number, 189 were original manuscripts; eighteen letters were in mimeographed form and fifteen were culled from provincial Irish newspapers. Sixty-six letters fell in the period 1787-1848 and the remaining 156 were distributed as follows: 32 in 1850-59; 32 in 1860-69; 24 in 1870-79; 29 in 1880-89; 24 in 1890-99; 11 in 1900-07.

B. Irish Folklore Commission

At the time of writing, the material returned by IFC interviewers was not yet bound. Consequently all notebooks are referred to by name of interviewer and county of location. In all, a total of twenty-one interviewers located in sixteen different counties returned twenty-six 100-page notebooks more or less completely filled. During 1955 questionnaires were distributed in and notebooks received from all counties of above-average emigration intensity, with the exception of Limerick, as well as from representative counties in each of the four provinces. The following notebooks were received and used:

Province of Leinster	County	Province of Ulster	County
Patrick O'Connor	Kildare	Michael J. Murphy	Antrim
Martin Walsh	Kilkenny	P. J. Gaynor	Cavan
James G. Delaney	Longford	Sean O'Heochaidh	Donegal
Matthew O'Reilly	Meath	Conall O'Byrne (3)	Donegal
Joseph Wade	Westmeath		
James G. Delaney	Wexford	Province of Connaught	County
		Ciaran Bairead (2)	Galway
		Frank Burke	Galway
Province of Munster	County	Mary O'Neill	Galway
Dermot O'Sullivan	Kerry	Lliam O'Briain	Leitrim
Sean O'Dubhda	Kerry	Thomas Moran	Mayo
Tadgh Murphy	Kerry	Michael Corduff	Mayo
Seamus Mulcahy	Tipperary	Michael MacEnri	Mayo
Sean O'Keefe	Waterford	James J. O'Donnell	Roscommon

C. Personal Interviews

During the summer months of 1955 personal interviews were conducted by the writer with people from six different counties, five of which were areas not covered by interviewers of the Irish Folklore Commission. The six counties were Clare, Cork, Kerry, Leix, Tyrone, and Londonderry. The information collected supplemented and also corroborated the data submitted by the IFC interviewers.

D. Government Documents

1. MANUSCRIPT

A. Irish

Correspondence relating to Kingwilliamstown, Quitrent Office Collection, PRO, Dublin. D.O.D. Class 556, PRO, Belfast. D.O.D. Class 268, PRO, Belfast. D.O.D. Class 682, PRO, Belfast.

B. American

The following are all part of Record Group 59 in the National Archives, Washington, D.C.: *Consular Despatches,* Belfast, 11 vols., 1796-1906. *Consular Despatches,* Cork, 12 vols., 1800-1906. *Consular Despatches,* Dublin, 11 vols., 1790-1906. *Consular Despatches,* Galway, 1 vol., 1834-63. *Consular Despatches,* Londonderry, 3 vols., 1835-78. *Despatches to Consuls,* Vols. 9 and 25. *Diplomatic Despatches,* Great Britain, 1850-60.

C. British

The following are all located in the Public Record Office, London: C.O. 384, Emigration, Original Correspondence, Secretary of State. F.O. 5, General Correspondence, United States of America. H.O. 45, Ireland.

2. PRINTED

A. Irish

Commission on Emigration and Other Population Problems 1948-1954: Majority Report (in mimeograph) (Ministry for Social Welfare, 1954).

Department of Industry and Commerce, *Agricultral Statistics 1847-1926. Report and Tables* (Dublin, 1928).

Irish Land Commission, *Report of the Irish Land Commission for the period from 1st April, 1923, to 31st March, 1928* . . . (Dublin, 1928).

B. American

Annual Reports of the Postmaster General of the United States, 1846-1900, 54 vols. A complete set of these reports is available at the Library of the Post Office Department, Washington, D.C.

Diplomatic Correspondence and Foreign Relations of the United States, 1861-1899 (Washington, 1902).

"Letter from the Secretary of the Treasury, transmitting a Report of the Commissioners of Immigration upon the causes which incite immigration to the United States. Vol. I. Reports of Commissioners, 1892," *Ex. Doc.* No. 235, Part I, 52nd Cong., 1st sess.

Papers Relating to Foreign Affairs, Accompanying the Annual Message of the President to the Second Session Thirty-eighth Congress, Part II (Washington, 1865).

Papers Relating to Foreign Affairs, Accompanying the Annual Message of the President to the First Session Thirty-ninth Congress, Part I (Washington, 1866).

"Statistical Review of Immigration. 1819-1910. Distribution of Immigrants, 1850-

1900," *Senate Doc.* No. 756, 61st Cong., 3rd sess.

Census Reports of the United States: Seventh Census, 1850. Eighth Census, 1860. Ninth Census, 1870, Vol. I. Tenth Census, 1880, Vol. I. Eleventh Census, 1890, Parts II and III. Twelfth Census, 1900, Vol. I.

C. British

(1) Census of Ireland. General Reports: 1851 Part VI [2134], H.C. 1856, xxxi. 1861 Part V [3204-IV], H.C. 1863, lxi. 1871 Part III [c. 1377], H.C. 1876, lxxxi. 1881 Part II [c. 3365], H.C. 1882, lxxvi. 1891 Part II [c. 6780], H.C. 1892, xc. 1901 Part II [Cd. 1190], H.C. 1902, cxxix.

(2) General Reports of the (Colonial Land and) Emigration Commissioners: 10th 1850 [1204], H.C. 1850, xxiii. 11th 1851 [1383], H.C. 1851, xxii. 12th 1852 [1499], H.C. 1852, xviii. 13th 1853 [1647], H.C. 1852-53, xl. 14th 1854 [1833], H.C. 1854, xxviii. 15th 1855 [1953], H.C. 1854-55, xvii. 16th 1856 [2089], H.C. 1856, xxiv. 17th 1857 [2249], H.C. 1857-Sess. 2, xvi. 18th 1858 [2395], H.C. 1857-58, xxiv. 19th 1859 [2555], H.C. 1859-Sess. 2, xiv. 20th 1860 [2696], H.C. 1860, xxix. 21st 1861 [2842], H.C. 1861, xxii. 22nd 1862 [3010], H.C. 1862, xxii. 23rd 1863 [3199], H.C. 1863, xv. 24th 1864 [3341], H.C. 1864, xvi. 25th 1865 [3526], H.C. 1865, xviii. 26th 1866 [3679], H.C. 1866, xvii. 27th 1867 [3855], H.C. 1867, xix. 28th 1868 [4024], H.C. 1867-68, xvii. 29th 1869 [4159], H.C. 1868-69, xvii. 30th 1870 [c. 196], H.C. 1870, xvii. 31st 1871 [c. 369], H.C. 1871, xx. 32nd 1872 [c. 562], H.C. 1872, xvi. 33rd 1873 [c. 768], H.C. 1873, xviii.

(3) Annual Reports of the Poor Law Commissioners: 6th [1645], H.C. 1852-53, 1. 7th [1785], H.C. 1854, xxix. 8th [1945], H.C. 1854-55, xxiv. 9th [2105], H.C. 1856, xxviii. 10th [2235], H.C. 1857-Sess. 2, xxii. 17th [3338], H.C. 1864, xxv.

(4) Agricultural Statistics of Ireland: 1861 [3156], H.C. 1863, lxix. 1870 [c. 463], H.C. 1872, lxiii. 1881 [c. 3332], H.C. 1882, lxxiv. 1891 [c. 6777] H.C. 1892,lxxxviii. 1901 [Cd. 1170], H.C. 1902, cxvi-Part I.

(5) Reports of Royal Commissions:

(a) Devon Commission, *Digest of Evidence taken before Her Majesty's Commissioners of Inquiry into the state of the Law and Practice in respect to the Occupation of Land in Ireland. Part I* (Dublin, 1847).

(b) Richmond Commission, *Preliminary Report from Her Majesty's Commissioners on Agriculture* [c. 2778], H.C. 1881, xv.

(c) Richmond Commission, *Minutes of Evidence taken before Her Majesty's Commissioners on Agriculture. Part I* [c. 2778-I], H.C. 1881, xv.

(d) Richmond Commission, *Digest and Appendix to Part I of the Evidence taken before the Royal Commission on Agriculture; with Reports of the Assistant Commissioners* [c. 2778-II], H.C. 1881, xvi.

(e) Bessborough Commission, *Report of Her Majesty's Commissioners of Inquiry into the Working of the Landlord and Tenant (Ireland) Act, 1870, and the Acts amending the same. Vol. III. Minutes of Evidence. Part II* [c. 2779-II], H.C. 1881, xix.

(f) Royal Commission on Labour, *Royal Commission on Labour. The Agricultural Labourer. Vol. IV. Ireland. Part IV* [c. 6894-XXI], H.C. 1893-94, xxxvii-Part I.

(g) Financial Relations Commission, *Minutes of Evidence up to the 28th March 1895, taken before Her Majesty's Commissioners appointed to inquire into the financial relations between Great Britain and Ireland, with appendices* [c. 7720-I], H.C. 1895, xxxvi.

(h) Fry Commission, *Royal Commission of Inquiry into the procedure and practice and the methods of valuation followed by the Land Commission, the Land Judge's Court, and the Civil Bill Courts in Ireland under the Land Acts and the Land Purchase Acts. Vol. II. Minutes of Evidence* [c. 8859], H.C. 1898, xxxv.

(6) Parliamentary Reports:

(a) *Annual Report of the Local Government Board for Ireland, being the Twelfth Report under "The Local Government Board (Ireland) Act,"* 35 & 36 Vic., c. 69 [c. 4051], H.C. 1884, xxxviii.

(b) *Annual Report of the Local Government Board for Ireland, being the Twenty-fourth Report under "The Local Government Board (Ireland) Act,"* 35 & 36 Vic., c. 69 [c. 8153], H.C. 1896, xxxviii.

(c) *Emigration Statistics of Ireland for 1901* [Cd. 976], H.C. 1902, cxvi Part II.

(d) *Report from the Select Committee of the House of Lords on the Tenure (Ireland) Bill [H.L.],* H.C. 1867 (518), xiv.

(e) *Report from the Select Committee on Law of Rating (Ireland),* H.C. 1871 (423), x.

(f) *Report from the Select Committee on Outrages (Ireland); with Proceedings of the Committee, Minutes of Evidence, Appendix and Index,* H.C. 1852 (438), xiv.

(g) *Report from the Select Committee on Tenure and Improvement of Land (Ireland) Act,* H.C. 1865 (402), xi.

(h) *Report on Certain Statistics of Banking in Ireland and Investments in Government and India Stocks . . . 1876-85* [c. 4681], H.C. 1886, lxxi.

(i) *Report on the Banking, Railway, and Shipping Statistics of Ireland, for the half-year ending 30th June 1901* [Cd. 806], H.C. 1902, cxvi-Part I.

(j) *Second Report from the Select Committee of the House of Lords on Land Law (Ireland); with the Proceedings of the Committee, Minutes of Evidence, Appendix, and Index,* H.C. 1882 (379), xi.

(k) *Statistical Tables relating to Emigration and Immigration, from and into the United Kingdom in the year 1887, and Report to the Board of Trade thereon,* H.C. 1888 (2), cvii.

E. Non-Governmental Documents
1. MANUSCRIPT
A. National Library of Ireland

Buchanan Papers.

Lalor Family Papers.

Larcom Papers, MSS 7600-7616.

Letters from Missionaries in America (microfilm).

Letters of Myles Walter Keogh.

William Smith O'Brien Papers.

B. Irish Folklore Commission

Hugh Dorian, "Donegal 60 Years Ago. A True Historical Narrative," unpublished MS (Londonderry, 1896) (photostatic copy).

C. Holy Cross College Library, Worcester, Massachusetts

"Diary of Bishop James A. Healy."

D. In Writer's Possession

Private report of Mr. Tom Gallagher, March 1955. Private report of Mr. Sean MacGrath, June 1955.

2. Printed

Broadsheet Collection of Irish Street Ballads, 8 vols., NLI.

Patrick F. Moran, ed., *The Pastoral Letters and Other Writings of Cardinal Cullen, Archbishop of Dublin, 1850-78*, 3 vols. (Dublin, 1882).

F. Newspapers

Ballinrobe Chronicle, and Mayo Advertiser. 1866-1901.

Belfast News-Letter. 1853-55; 1858-1901.

Carlow Sentinel, and Leinster Agricultural, Commercial and Literary Advertiser. 1850-53; 1874-81; 1883-84; 1885-1901.

Catholic Telegraph and *Irish Sun.* 1857-66.

Clare *Independent, and Tipperary Catholic Times.* 1876-84.

Clare Journal, and Ennis Advertiser. 1854-76; 1888-1901.

Connaught Telegraph. 1879-1901.

Constitution; or, Cork Advertiser. 1856-1901.

Cork Examiner. 1859-1901.

Drogheda Argus, and Leinster Journal. 1859-1901.

Dublin *Daily Express.* 1851-1901.

Dublin Evening Mail. 1851-1901.

Dublin Evening Post. 1851-75.

Dundalk Democrat and People's Journal. 1859-1901.

Flag of Ireland. 1868-81.

Freeman's Journal and Daily Commercial Advertiser. 1850-1901.

Galway Vindicator, and Connaught Advertiser. 1859-98.

Irish Catholic. 1889-1901.

Irish People. 1863-65; 1899-1901.

Irish Times, and Daily Advertiser. 1860-1901.

Kilkenny Journal, and Leinster Commercial and Literary Advertiser. 1850-51; 1859-1901.

King's County Chronicle and General Provincial Intelligencer. 1853-55; 1885-1901.

Leinster Express; Kildare, Queen's and King's Counties, Meath, Wicklow, Dublin, and Midland Mercantile and Agricultural Advertiser. 1853-1901

Limerick Chronicle. 1852-55; 1859-1901.

Limerick Reporter and Tipperary Vindicator. 1857-95.

Londonderry Standard. 1853-1901.

Mayo Constitution. 1853-71.

Nation. 1851-91.

Newry Commercial Telegraph. 1858-1901.

Newry Examiner & Louth Advertiser. 1852-57

Northern Whig. 1850; 1856-1901.

Roscommon Journal, and Western Reporter. 1850-55; 1857; 1859-60; 1862-66; 1868-73; 1875; 1879-88; 1890-92; 1895; 1898; 1899.

Saunder's News-Letter and Daily Advertiser. 1850-79.

Sligo Champion. 1883-1901.

Southern Reporter, and Cork Daily Commercial Courier. 1856-71.

Tipperary Advocate. 1860-85.

Tuam Herald. 1879; 1886-1901.

United Ireland. 1881-98.

Waterford Daily Mail, and Daily Telegraph Sheet. 1869-1901.

Weekly Telegraph. 1853-56.

II. SECONDARY MATERIALS

A. Unpublished Dissertations

Keep, G. R. C., "The Irish Migration to North America in the Second Half of the Nineteenth Century" (Trinity College, Dublin, 1951).

MacDonagh, Oliver, "Irish Emigration During the Great Famine 1845-52" (M.A. thesis, University College, Dublin, 1946).

Maguire, Edward J., "John O'Hanlon's Irish Emigrant Guide for the United States: A Critical Evaluation" (St. Louis University, St. Louis, 1951).

B. Reference Works

Carrier, N. H., and J. R. Jeffrey, *External Migration: a Study of the Available Statistics 1815-1950* (London, 1953).

Crone, John S., *A Concise Dictionary of Irish Biography* (New York, 1928).

Grimshaw, T. W., *Facts and Figures About Ireland* (Dublin, 1893).

Irish Catholic Directory, annual volumes, 1850-1901.

MacDowall, Alexander B., *Facts About Ireland. A Curve-History of Recent Years* (London, 1888).

Thom's Directory, annual volumes, 1850-1901.

C. Pamphlets

Barry, Michael Joseph, *Irish Emigration Considered* (Cork, 1863).

Freeman, T. W., *Emigration and Rural Ireland* (Dublin, 1945).

Hancock, W. Neilson, *Report on Deposits and Cash Balances in Joint Stock Banks in Ireland, 1840-1869* (Dublin, 1870).

------, *Report on Statistics of Savings Invested in Ireland in Joint Stock Banks and in Savings Banks, and in Government Funds; and on Statistics of Bank Note Circulation in Ireland, 1860-1872* (Dublin, 1873).

Ingram, John K., *Considerations on the State of Ireland . . .* (Dublin, 1863).

Locke, John, *Ireland's Recovery, or, Excessive Emigration and its Reparative Agencies in Ireland* (London, 1853).

Peyton, Alexander J., *The Emigrant's Friend; or Hints on Emigration to the United States of America, Addressed to the People of Ireland* (Cork, 1853)

D. Articles

Bowley, A. L., "The Statistics of Wages in the United Kingdom during the last Hundred Years. (Part III.) Agricultural Wages – Ireland," *Journal of the Royal Statistical Society,* Vol. LXII (June 1899), pp. 395-404.

Brady, John, "Funeral Customs of the Past," *IER,* 5th series, Vol. LXXVIII

(November 1952), pp. 330-339.

Chart, D. A., "Two Centuries of Irish Agriculture. A Statistical Retrospect, 1672-1905," *SSIJ*, Vol. XII, Part LXXXVIII (November 1907-June 1908), pp. 162-174.

Condon, Peter, "The Irish in Countries other than Ireland – I. In the United States," *Catholic Encyclopedia*, Vol. VIII (New York, 1910), pp. 132-145.

Connell, K. H., "Land and Population in Ireland, 1780-1845," *Economic History Review*, 2nd series, Vol. II, No. 3 (1950), pp. 278-289.

"Father Hand," *All Hallows Annual 1953-1954*, pp. 16-32.

Geary, R. C., "The Future Population of Saorstat Eireann and some Observations on Population," *SSIJ*, Vol. XV (1935-36), pp. 15-35.

------, "Irish Economic Development Since the Treaty," *Studies*, Vol. XL, No. 160 (December 1951), pp. 399-418.

------, "Some Reflections on Irish Population Questions," *Studies*, Vol. XLIII, No. 170 (Summer 1954), pp. 168-177.

Gibbons, James Cardinal, "Irish Immigration to the United States," *IER*, 4th series, Vol. I (February 1897), pp. 97-109.

Green, James J., "American Catholics and the Irish Land League, 1879-1882," *Catholic Historical Review*, Vol. XXXV, No. I (April 1949), pp. 19-42.

Grimshaw, T. W., "A Statistical Survey of Ireland, from 1840 to 1888," *SSIJ*, Vol. IX, Part LXVIII (December 1888), pp. 321-361.

Hancock, W. Neilson, "On the Remittances from North America by Irish Emigrants, considered as an indication of character of the Irish race, and with reference to some branches of the Irish Labourers' Question," *SSIJ*, Vol. VI, Part XLIV (April-November 1873), pp. 280-290.

Harkness, D. A. E., "Irish Emigration," in Walter F. Willcox, ed., *International Migrations*, Vol. II (New York, 1931), pp. 261-282.

Jordan, Thomas, "Effects of Emigration: can it be made a means of relieving Distress?" *SSIJ*, Vol. I (July 1856), pp. 378-384.

Keep, G. R. C., "Official Opinion on Irish Emigration in the Later 19th Century," *IER*, 5th series, Vol. LXXXI, No. 6 (June 1954), pp. 412-421.

Kennedy, Thomas, "Fifty Years of Irish Agriculture," *SSIJ*, Vol. X, Part LXXIX (November 1898-June 1899), pp. 398-404.

MacDonagh, Oliver, "The Irish Catholic Clergy and Emigration during the Great Famine," *Irish Historical Studies*, Vol. V, No. 20 (September 1947), pp. 287-302.

MacDonnell, Randall W., "Statistics of Irish Prosperity," *SSIJ*, Vol. III, Part XXII (December 1862), pp. 268-278.

MacManus, Seumas, "A Revolution in Ireland," *Catholic World*, Vol. LXIX, No. 412 (July 1899), pp. 522-532.

Meehan, Thomas F., "English Taxation in America," *North American Review*, Vol. CXLV, No. 372 (November 1887), pp. 563-567.

Moody, T. W., "The New Departure in Irish Politics, 1878-9," in H. A. Cronne, T. W. Moody, and D. B. Quinn, eds., *Essays in British and Irish History in honour of James Eadie Todd* (London, 1949), pp. 303-333.

O'Brien, George, "New Light on Irish Emigration," *Studies*, Vol. XXX (March 1941), pp. 17-31.

O'Grady, John, "Irish Colonization in the United States," *Studies*, Vol. XIX (September 1930), pp. 387-407.

Oldham, C. H., "Economic Development in Ireland," *SSIJ*, Vol. X, Part LXXX (November 1899-June 1900), pp. 548-567.

, "The Incidence of Emigration on Town and Country Life in Ireland," *SSIJ*, Vol. XIII, Part XCIV (November 1913-June 1914), pp. 207-218.

"Pioneer Priests," *All Hallows Annual, 1953-54*, pp. 131-172.

Scanlan, Michael, "The American Letter," *Shamrock*, Vol. XI, No. 391 (April 1874), p. 462.

Sheehan, P. A., "The Effect of Emigration on the Irish Church," *IER*, 3rd series, Vol. III, No. 10 (October 1882), pp. 602-615.

Smith, Goldwin, "Why Send More Irish to America?" *Nineteenth Century*, Vol. XIII, No. 76 (June 1883), pp. 913-919.

Staehle, Hans, "Statistical Notes on the Economic History of Irish Agriculture, 1847-1913," *SSIJ*, Vol. XVIII (1950-51), pp. 444-462.

Sullivan, A. M., "Why Send More Irish Out of Ireland?" *Nineteenth Century*, Vol. XIV, No. 77 (July 1883), pp. 131-144.

E. Books

Abbott, Edith, *Historical Aspects of the Immigration Problem: Select Documents* (Chicago, 1926).

Adams, William Forbes, *Ireland and Irish Emigration to the New World from 1815 to the Famine* (New Haven, 1932).

Arensberg, Conrad M., *The Irish Countryman* (Cambridge, Mass., 1938).

Arensberg, Conrad M., and Solon T. Kimball, *Family and Community in Ireland* (Cambridge, Mass., 1940).

Bagenal, Philip H., *The American Irish and Their Influence on Irish Politics* (London, 1882).

Birmingham, George A., *The Lighter Side of Irish Life* (London, 1911).

Bovet, Madame de, *Three Months' Tour in Ireland* (London, 1891).

Bowley, Arthur L., *Wages in the United Kingdom in the Nineteenth Century* (Cambridge, 1900).

Brown, Stephen J., *The Press in Ireland. A Survey and a Guide* (Dublin, 1937).

Cairnes, J. E., *Political Essays* (London, 1874).

Carrothers, W. A., *Emigration from the British Isles; with Special Reference to the Development of the Overseas Dominions* (London, 1929).

Chart, D. A., *An Economic History of Ireland* (Dublin, 1920).

Colum, Padraic, *The Road Round Ireland* (New York, 1926).

Connell, K. H., *The Population of Ireland, 1750-1845* (Oxford, 1950).

Curtis, Edmund, *A History of Ireland*, 3rd ed. (London, 1937).

Daryl, Philippe, *Ireland's Disease: Notes and Impressions* (London, 1888).

Dufferin, Lord, *Irish Emigration and the Tenure of Land in Ireland* (London, 1867).

Eversley, Lord, *Gladstone and Ireland, the Irish Policy of Parliament from 1850-1894* (London, 1912).

Ferenczi, Imre, ed., *International Migrations*, Vol. I (New York, 1929).

Forbes, John, *Memorandums Made in Ireland in the Autumn of 1852*, Vol. II (London, 1853).

Frawley, Mary A., *Patrick Donahoe* (Washington, D.C., 1946).

Freeman, T. W., *Ireland: Its Physical, Historical, Social and Economic Geography* (London, 1950).

Gwynn, Stephen, *Irish Books and Irish People* (Dublin, 1919).

Hale, Edward Everett, *Letters on Irish Emigration* (Boston, 1852).

Hammond, J. L., *Gladstone and the Irish Nations* (London, 1938).

Handlin, Oscar, *Boston's Immigrants 1790-1865* (Cambridge, Mass., 1941).

Hansen, Marcus L., *The Atlantic Migration 1607-1860. A History of the Continuing Settlement of the United States* (Cambridge, Mass., 1940).

Hartmann, Hans, *Der Totenkult in Irland-Ein Beitrag zur Religion der Indogermanen* (Heidelberg, 1952).

Hole, S. R., *A Little Tour in Ireland* (London, 1859).

Hooker, Elizabeth R., *Readjustments of Agricultural Tenure in Ireland* (Chapel Hill, 1938).

Hurlbert, W. H., *Ireland Under Coercion: The Diary of an American* (Boston, 1888).

Isaac, Julius, *Economics of Migration* (London, 1947).

Jerome, Harry, *Migration and Business Cycles* (New York, 1926).

Johnson, Stanley C., *A History of Emigration from the United Kingdom to North America, 1763-1912* (London, 1913).

Joynes, J. L., *The Adventures of a Tourist in Ireland* (London, 1882).

Kraus, Michael, *The Atlantic Civilization: Eighteenth-Century Origins* (Ithaca, 1949).

Lampson, G. Locker, *A Consideration of the State of Ireland in the Nineteenth Century* (London, 1907).

Lecky, W. E. H., *Leaders of Public Opinion in Ireland*, 2 vols., new ed. (London, 1903).

Lynd, Robert, *Home Life in Ireland* (London. 1909).

MacDonagh, Michael, *Irish Life and Character* (London, 1898).

Maguire, John Francis, *The Irish in America* (London, 1868).

Mandat-Grancey, Baron E. de, *Paddy At Home ("Chez Paddy")*, 2nd ed. (London, 1887).

Martineau, Harriet, *Letters from Ireland* (London, 1852).

Milligan, S. F., and A. L. Milligan, *Glimpses of Erin* (London, 1888).

Mooney, Thomas, *Nine Years in America*, 2nd ed. (Dublin, 1850).

Murphy, J. N., Ireland: *Industrial, Political and Social* (London, 1870).

Murray, Alice E., *A History of the Commercial and Financial Relations between England and Ireland from the Period of the Restoration*, new ed. (London, 1907).

O'Brien, George, *The Economic History of Ireland from the Union to the Famine* (London, 1921).

O'Connor, Sir James, *History of Ireland, 1798-1924*, 2 vols. (New York, 1925).

O'Connor, Thomas Power, *The Parnell Movement* (London, 1886).

O'Hanlon, John, *The Irish Emigrant's Guide for the United States* (Boston, 1851).

O'Leary, John, *Recollections of Fenians and Fenianism*, 2 vols. (London, 1896).

O'Rourke, John, *The History of the Great Irish Famine of 1847, with Notices of Earlier Irish Famines* (Dublin, 1875).

Palmer, Norman Dunbar, *The Irish Land League Crisis* (New Haven, 1940).

Paul-Dubois, L., *Contemporary Ireland* (Dublin, 1908).

Pollard, H. B. C., *The Secret Societies of Ireland* (London, 1922).

Pomfret, John E., *The Struggle for Land in Ireland 1800-1923* (Princeton, 1930).

Praeger, Robert Lloyd, *The Way That I Went: An Irishman in Ireland*, 2nd ed. (Dublin, 1939).

Riordan, E. J., *Modern Irish Trade and Industry* (London, 1920).

Salaman, Redcliffe N., *The History and Social Influence of the Potato* (Cambridge, 1949).

Schafer, Joseph, ed., *Memoirs of Jeremiah Curtin* (Màdison, 1940).

Senior, Nassau W., *Journals, Conversations and Essays Relating to Ireland*, 2 vols. (London, 1868).

Shand, A. I., *Letters from the West of Ireland 1884* (London, 1885).

Shaughnessy, Gerald, *Has the Immigrant Kept the Faith? A Study of Immigration and Catholic Growth in the United States 1790-1920* (New York, 1925).

Strauss, E., *Irish Nationalism and British Democracy* (London, 1951).

Sullivan, A. M., *New Ireland*, 6th ed. (New York, 1878).

Thomas, Brinley, *Migration and Economic Growth* (Cambridge, 1954).

Trevelyan, George Macaulay, *British History in the Nineteenth Century and After (1782-1919)*, 2nd ed. (London, 1937).

Walshaw, R. S., *Migration to and from the British Isles. Problems and Policies* (London, 1941).

Walton's 132 Best Irish Songs and Ballads (Dublin, 1955).

White, John, *Sketches from America* (London, 1870).

Wittke, Carl, *The Irish in America* (Baton Rouge, 1956).

------, *We Who Built America. The Saga of the Immigrant* (New York, 1939).

F. A Brief Update on Bibliographical Sources

The following is a select bibliography of articles and books for this paperback edition published since 1958 relating to Ireland and the American emigration.

Doyle, David N., and Owen D. Edwards, eds. *America and Ireland, 1776-1976*. New York: Greenwood Press, 1980.

Fitzpatrick, David, " 'A Share of the Honeycomb': Education, Emigration, and Irishwomen," in Mary Daly and David Dickson, eds. *The Origins of Popular Literacy in Ireland: Language Change and Educational Development, 1700-1920*. Dublin: Trinity College Department of Modern History, 1990.

Fitzpatrick, David, *Irish Emigration, 1801-1921*. Dublin: Economic & Social History Society of Ireland, 1984.

Fitzpatrick, David, "Irish Emigration in the Later Nineteenth Century," *Irish Historical Studies*, 22 (September 1980).

Hatton, Timothy J., and Jeffrey G. Williamson, "After the Famine: Emigration from Ireland, 1850-1913," *Journal of Economic History*, 53 (Sept. 1993), 575-600.

Holland, Dennis. *The American Connection: U.S. Guns, Money, and Influence in Northern Ireland*. New York: Penguin, 1988.

Kennedy, Robert E. *The Irish: Emigration, Marriage, and Fertility*. Berkeley: U. of

California Press, 1975.

Mageean, Deirdre M., "Emigration from Irish Ports," *Journal of American Ethnic History*, 13, no. 1 (Fall 1993), 6-30.

Miller, Kerby A., *Emigrants and Exiles: Ireland and the Irish Exodus to North America*. New York: Oxford University Press, 1985.

Miller, Kerby A., "For Love and for Liberty: Irishwomen, Emigration, and Domesticity in Ireland and America, 1815-1920," in Patrick O'Sullivan, ed., *The Irish World Wide: History. Heritage Identity, Volume Four: Irish Women and Irish Migration.* London: Leicester U. Press, 1994.

Neville, Grace, " 'She never then after that forgot him': Irishwomen and Emigration to the United States in Irish Folklore," *Mid-America*, 74 (Oct. 1992), 253-70.

Nolan, Janet. *Ourselves Alone: Women's Emigration from Ireland, 1885-1920.* Lexington: U. Press of Kentucky, 1989.

Potter, George. *To the Golden Door: The Story of the Irish in Ireland and America.* Boston: Little, Brown & Co., 1960.

Smyth, William J., "Irish Emigration, 1700-1920," in P. C. Emmer and M. Morner, eds. *European Expansion and Migration: Essays on the Intercontinental Migration from Africa, Asia and Europe.* New York: Berg [dist. by St. Martin's], 1992.

't Hart, Marjolein, "Irish Return Migration in the Nineteenth Century," *Journal of Economic and Social Geography*, 76, no. 3 (1985), 223-31.

Ward, Alan. *Ireland and Anglo-American Relations, 1890-1922.* Toronto: U. of Toronto Press, 1969.

Index

Aberdeen, Lord, 76
Adams, Charles Francis, 14
Adams, William Forbes, 15, 19, 125
Agriculture: land system, 10-12; subdivision of land, 14, tenure of land, 71-72, 185n3; use of land, 72-76; tillage, 73-74, changes in, 74-76; pasturage, 73-76; labor, 76-79, 83-85; and American money, 119-120. *See also* Economy
Akron, Ohio, letter from, 34
All Hallows seminary, trains missionaries, 67
America: business crises in, 8-10; as goal of Irish, 15-17, image of 18-21; attractions of, 20-21, 28-31; difficulties in, 20, 31-36; lure of, 148. *See also* United States
"American fever," 19
American money: distinguished from passage money, 111-112; social uses of, 113-121, and Irish economy, 121-123; political uses of, 123-128, 151-152
"American out-farm," described, 120-121
American wake: origin of, 87-89; significance of, 88, described, 87-93; avoided by emigrants, 93; importance of, 93; waning of, 93
"Amerikay letther," ritual of, 43-44
Arensberg, C. M., 14

Ballads: reflect emigration theme, 96-102, melancholy of, 96-97, on causes of emigration, 97-98; reflect hope of prosperity, 100; reflect loneliness and wish to return, 101-102
Ballinrobe Chronicle, 51
Bank of Ireland, 109
Baring Brothers, 106
Battle Creek, Iowa, letter from, 33
Belfast News-Letter, 54; on emigration, 55, 60; on need for industries, 62; on emigration and Irish clergy, 63-64, 67
Belfast *Northern Whig*, 51, 53
Birmingham, George A. (*pseud.*), on returned Yanks, 142
Board of Trade, 107
Boston, letters from, 26, 27, 33, 35

Boston *Pilot*, 108
Bowley, A. L.: on emigration and labor, 77, and employment, 79
Britain, 13, 50
Buffalo, N. Y., letter from, 29-30

Cahill, Daniel W.: letters from America, 68; on remittances, 109; on women as remitters, 110
Canada, and Irish emigration, 16
Cant, Irish use of, 86n
Carleton, William, 87
Carson City, Nevada Territory, letter from, 36
Catholic Church, *see* Irish Catholic Church
Catholic Telegraph, 68
Cattle, increase in, 75. *See also* Agriculture
Caul, as emigrant charm 94
Charms, used in emigration, 94
Chicago, letter from, 35
Church building, and American money, 121
Cincinnati, letters from, 24, 36
Civil War, and emigration, 8, 34-35
Clare Journal, on emigration, 53-54
"Come With Me O'er Ohio," poem, 45-46
Condon, Peter, 107
"Convoy," at American wakes, 92
Cork *Constitution*, 51
Cork Examiner, 35, 55, 67; on unemployment, 14, on emigration, 15, 54; on "American fever," 19
Cork *Southern Reporter*, 51
Curtis, Edmund, on Irish-Americans, 124
Customs, social, 150

Davitt, Michael, 126-127
Debts, and American money, 114-115
Denver, letter from, 27
Domestic servants, and emigration, 78
Donahoe, Patrick, 108
Donnelly, William, 76-77
Drogheda Argus, 51
Drunkenness, warnings against, 21
Dublin, Archbishop of, on emigration, 64